FIREFIGHTER

Other Mountain Movers Books

BodyChange™
(by Montel Williams and Wini Linguvic)

A Dozen Ways to Sunday
(by Montel Williams, with Daniel Paisner)

Life Lessons and Reflections
(by Montel Williams)

Practical Parenting
(by Montel Williams and Jeffrey Gardère, Ph.D.)

FIREFIGHTER

Herman Williams, Jr.

with
James Hall

MOUNTAIN
MOVERS
PRESS

an imprint of
Hay House, Inc.
Carlsbad, California • Sydney, Australia
Canada • Hong Kong • United Kingdom

Published and distributed in the United States by:
Mountain Movers Press, an imprint of Hay House, Inc., P.O. Box 5100, Carlsbad, CA 92018-5100 • (800) 654- 5126 • (800) 650-5115 (fax) • www.hayhouse.com / Hay House Australia Pty Ltd, P.O. Box 515, Brighton-Le-Sands, NSW 2216 • *phone:* 1800 023 516 *e-mail:* info@hayhouse.com.au

Editorial supervision: Angela Lee, Jill Kramer
Design: Julie Davison • *Interior photos:* Courtesy of the author, unless otherwise noted

Library of Congress Cataloging-in-Publication Data

Williams, Herman, 1931-
    Firefighter / Herman Williams, Jr. ; with James Hall.
        p. cm.
    ISBN 1-58825-006-7 (hc. : alk. paper)
    1. Williams, Herman, Jr 2. African American fire fighters—Biography. 3. United States—Race relations. I. Hall, James.
II. Title.

TH9118.W55 A3 2002
363.37'092—dc21
    [B]

                                                    2001056266

ISBN 1-58825-006-7

05 04 03 02   4 3 2 1
1st printing, February 2002

Printed in the United States of America

To Marjie, my wife,
I dedicate this book . . .
and to our children.

❧ CONTENTS ❧

❧ PREFACE ☙

I'd been thinking a lot about the life of a firefighter for this book, because the danger and heroism people on the outside see in our work we pretty much take for granted, and I needed to look at our job with fresh eyes in order to explain it well.

The worst memories had to do with the loss of life of both civilians and firefighters who risked their lives to save people but found that the odds went against them.

But at least the days of multiple firefighter deaths seemed to be over. A record number of deaths had occurred in 1947, when 27 firefighters died in Texas putting out a ship fire. Firefighting technology and communications had been updated, new standards of safety were introduced, and building codes were improved. But this only had the effect of making the rarer deaths of firefighters harder to take. In telling my story, I recalled the pain that resulted from the death of a single firefighter in the Clipper Mills tragedy. But every firefighter's death caused pain for everyone in the department. The black bunting was draped over the fire station door, but it didn't do justice to the gloom we felt.

At least the days when scores of firefighters would die in a single blaze were over. Times had changed.

They changed again on September 11, 2001.

I was one of the many Americans who couldn't sleep that night. Each of us handled the shock, disbelief, and pain in our own way. There was so much to absorb—350 firefighters missing or dead. It took a day or so to get a full count.

New York's fire chief was a good man. I knew him.

The enormous amount of destruction and loss of life was hard to take. It took courage just to look at the images on television.

But like a counterbalance to the crime, people found their heroes. They were the firefighters, the rescue workers, and the police. If anyone had forgotten how selfless and risky the job of fire fighting was, the valiant men and women who put in 36-hour shifts to dig through shaky rubble was a reminder. It was an inspiration.

The year I retired from the fire department, 2001, was a time that I'll never forget—one that has caused me more heartbreak and devastation than I've ever known. But I've also never been more proud to have been part of a profession that is truly noble and worthy.

— Herman Williams, Jr.
October 11, 2001

ACKNOWLEDGMENTS

I'd like to acknowledge all of the friends, family members, and co-workers who have helped me along the way. Without their involvement in my life, I would not have been "the Chief."

And to James Hall, whose ability to unearth my story and help me commit it to the page has me overwhelmed.

❦ CHAPTER ONE ❦

Harlem to Baltimore

If you live a life, you spend a good part of it putting out fires. Family crises. Problems at work. Emergencies challenging your ability to respond.

Like everyone, I've faced my share of conflagrations, and a lot of these were the lethal kind, the ones that physically burn.

I am a firefighter by profession.

I am an American. By race, God made me a black man.

My name is Williams; I carry on the name of my father, Herman Williams, Sr.

I watched him the night he faced the eruption of Harlem. There were no flames that time, but it was an inferno of another kind, the first time I would witness an African-American community tear itself apart. In our multiethnic tenement, where I learned tolerance, people didn't know what to do as our section of New York City was rocked by rioting. What would my father do? I was scared, and I looked to him. How he would respond would leave an impression, and add to the knowledge

I would later need to face the crises of my life—all the fights still ahead with a racist system; with big-city politics; and even fights with my old man, my first role model.

"The cops shot a kid!" The cry was carried up the hall from up the block. People were shouting it all along 125th Street. Hitler, World War II, and everything else was forgotten. Some deep rage that had been seething for so long, perhaps unnoticed on the surface of things but felt inside every person in Harlem, was boiling to the surface. The response was chaos and looting that would go on for days. Whether or not a white cop shot a black kid, I didn't know, but it touched a spark that ignited Harlem—the city within a city that was my world.

I had been born there 11 and a half years earlier, in 1931, one of the babies of the Great Depression. But my father told me that I had one advantage entering this world: I was a Williams.

He didn't know where the name came from, or at what point in our Jamaican ancestry it was attached to my family, or by whom. But the name was a symbol of who we were. The name Williams was something we made our own, and what my father and his father and their ancestors had made of it was something proud, something to live up to. We lived in a United States at a time of deep-rooted and institutionalized racism in the North and legal segregation in the South—during the worst economic crisis in the nation's history. African Americans were at the bottom of things and had the furthest to climb. But none of that could change how we felt about ourselves, and my father impressed upon me that our family name was an emblem to rally around. I never thought of myself as better than anyone, but I certainly was no worse. At a time when most opportunities in America were closed to black people because of our supposed inferiority, to have such an unshakable attitude imprinted at an early age was an achievement, and it was my *father's* achievement.

My father did well by his family. He did *very* well when you consider the hard times, and the constraints put on African-American advancement in those days. But he moved on up, like the song says. He was 18 when he got married. He raised four kids in the Depression when he was still in his early 20s. He only had one wish: that his children would not have to duplicate his own tough experience. Unfortunately, I did. But when I became the first African-American fire chief of a major U.S. city, he was there to see it, and by that time he was an accomplished person himself.

But there would be scrapes along the way between him and me. Some nearly wrecked us. There was a little bit of snobbishness that my father got from his people, a little bit of superiority that those of Jamaican descent carried around in those days. It was a time when some light-skinned African Americans looked down on dark-skinned ones, and "passing for white" if you could manage it was a survival tactic for others.

In those days, Jamaicans—East Indians—would come to New York and colonize Harlem, and they felt they were better than American blacks. This is not to say that they didn't work hard. They did. They were driven by a desire to show people how good they thought they were. The Jamaicans didn't make an issue out of it, but they were always aware that American blacks had been slaves and had originated from somewhere else. It was the type of foolishness I would later see in upscale African-American society in Baltimore, a strange exclusivity in a community that desperately needed inclusiveness.

As a Harlem youngster, I simply knew Baltimore as a place where we visited relatives on our way to North Carolina, where my mother's people lived. My mother, Mary Elizabeth Barnes, met my father at New York City College, which is how I happened to be born in New York. Pops, as I called him, came from Jacksonville, Florida. His father, my grandfather, always retained a thick Jamaican accent. Pops did his damnedest to overcome that accent, and he succeeded, except for two occasions: when he got angry, and when he had a couple of drinks.

My grandfather was a little guy, 5'5". My father was also small in stature, but he was the strongest guy around. He was a man among men. Grandfather always wore a suit and tie. I didn't know what he did for a living, but he was a dapper dresser, accessorizing his suit with a vest and a bowler hat. He influenced my father, who felt the same way about being well dressed.

Pops had a little mustache and a dark complexion. He wore his hair close-cropped, without a part. He and my mother married in 1928 and filled our brownstone apartment with me and my three sisters: Gwendolyn (the eldest), Altomese, and Muriel.

My father was a scrappy little guy, and he would fight in a heartbeat, another trait that I inherited. He didn't engage in fistfights. A Williams wouldn't do that. His fighting urge was tempered by judgment. But it didn't matter how big someone was. If he said anything against Pops, his family, or his ancestry, that man would have a fight on his hands. Pops would be in his face telling him off.

One incident I remember involved the garbagemen. All of the tenants put their garbage cans in the alley for the city trucks to pick up. The garbagemen hauled them to the truck, emptied them, and then threw them back, denting them. These guys wanted to see how badly they could beat up the cans, so in six months, the owners would need to buy new ones. It was a game to them.

My father put up with this for a long time, then one morning he went out to confront them. From the window, I saw the courage of this slightly built man going up against these six-feet-plus guys. White guys. He just went after them, at a time when some blacks were physically afraid of whites. In many instances, a white could assault, and in some parts of the country, kill, a black person with impunity.

"What do you think you're doing, denting my cans?!" he raged. They listened to him, some insults were exchanged, but not once was my father worried about his own well-being. They saw that and backed off. That was the kind of guy Pops was.

They called me "Junior." I was a miniature version of my scrappy father.

But Harlem in those days wasn't really the "mean streets." It was the opposite—a wonderful community. It was also a famous place in the '30s, a mecca for African-American arts in the final years of the Harlem Renaissance, which introduced Langston Hughes, the great jazz musicians, and trendsetting dances and fashions of the day. By 1943, when the riots erupted, the tone had changed, from the gaiety of the Cotton Club to the dashed dreams Richard Wright wrote about in *Native Son*. But during the Depression, Harlem was a special world, and a good place to grow up.

Harlem might have been New York's African-American neighborhood, but you would have never known it from our tenement. It was a four-story brownstone, with two families per floor in two-bedroom apartments, and all races were living there. There was a Jewish family, an Italian family, some Jamaicans, us, and even some Chinese people. Living there, I learned tolerance at a very early age. We could fight each other. We'd call each other names, although we never crossed the line at racial slurs, perhaps because we knew we were a community in that building and we had to get along. We stuck together. Even though we could raise hell among ourselves, nobody could come across the street and bother anybody in our building. Let them try, and the kids of our tenement would respond as one body.

There was a fire escape running up the outside of the building. We played on it, which we weren't supposed to do because it was dangerous—we could fall and break our necks. But the fire escape was also our *heat* escape on those hot New York summer days. Or we would catch a subway and go out to Coney Island for a swim. A subway ride was five cents, and a couple of times a week it brought us to an integrated beach where all races relaxed together. Coney Island was the way I thought the whole world was—people enjoying themselves on the Ferris wheel and the roller coaster. We ate popcorn, frozen custard— vanilla in a cone—and cotton candy. The only way to cool off before air conditioning was common was to jump in the water and splash around.

We didn't lock our door when we left our apartment in Harlem. Nobody did. In those grim Depression days, people had to depend on each other for survival, and we looked out for one another. There wasn't much robbery in Harlem. In the time before drugs, crime was pretty much something that began and ended with gangsters. Dutch Schultz's gang tried to take over Harlem, and Dutch got "rubbed out" for his attempt. But there was an innocence, too, even in the operations of my grandma, who was the neighborhood numbers bookie.

Grandma's store was on 127th Street, near Eighth Avenue. A small place in the middle of the block, it was a candy store, and a great place for a kid. In big glass canisters she kept brightly colored peppermint balls, jawbreakers, and all flavors of hard candies. On the counter were boxes of the big candy bars you could buy for a nickel: Hershey's chocolate bars; Mr. Goodbar, the one with peanuts; and Baby Ruth, named after "The Big Bambino," who slugged home runs out of Yankee Stadium. Candy stores also sold tobacco and cigarettes, including my father's brand, Camel. That was a man's cigarette, and it might have been Pops speaking in the ad on the subway wall: "I'd Walk a Mile for a Camel." Or more likely he'd have *me* walk that mile, because I was the one who ran errands to fetch him things.

Since Grandma ran a candy store, it was customary that she provide a certain service for the neighborhood. She ran numbers. If they were doing it downtown, and just about every-place else in the eastern United States, we'd do it uptown. The people called them "policies." A customer came in to Grandma's, bought some candy . . . and bought some numbers. You'd choose the number you wanted, and if it paid off, lot-tery-style, you'd collect from Grandma. If you put down five cents, maybe you'd get back 30 or 40 bucks. That was big money during the Depression. People who won at numbers were admired. So if you put down a quarter and your number came up, the person who sold it to you had better pay off or you'd get mad. Grandma eventually came to a bad end, not because she refused to pay off, but because the numbers money she kept was too tempting for one robber. But that tragedy was still to come, during the war.

How did people pick winning numbers? Well, maybe the time of day would give them their numbers. Or people would wake up with numbers from their dreams. They'd count their kids' teeth, or the number of telephone poles they passed on the streetcar. Then they went to Grandma's candy store to put some money down.

It was a good life, in the late '30s and early '40s. We had everything we needed in Harlem, and we didn't need to go downtown for anything but the Rockettes. When I was a baby, they opened Radio City Music Hall, and when I was old enough, my aunt took us to see the Christmas show. At home we had a radio, and we'd listen to *Dick Tracy,* the fright show *Inner Sanctum,* and *Amos and Andy.* We didn't know that "Amos" and "Andy" were white guys acting black. We thought they were funny.

When I was a kid, we were all Negroes. If you called me "black," it was an insult. In the movies, the bad guys wore black hats. The guy with the white hat—the good guy—he would fight, and his hat would never fall off. We really thought that was special. Going home, we'd say, "How'd he fight like that?"

Or we were Colored. Colored and Negro, they sound strange today, but they were a lot better than the racial pejoratives more commonly applied to African Americans at the time. In the '60s, when "Black Power" came on the scene, it was hard for my generation to accept calling ourselves black, because of the bad connotations the word held for us from our childhood.

I WAS A MISCHIEVOUS KID. Trouble came to me naturally, and I'd defend my sisters against any slight. They'd come running into the house after some boys had chased them, and I'd run out and end up with a black eye. Then my father would come home, see I had a black eye, and I'd get a beating for fighting! It was beneath a Williams, this fighting, he said as he swatted my bottom.

A father "whupped" his boy with a belt in those days, and no one would bat an eye, but it triggered an early rebelliousness in me. I was just a little boy, and I couldn't analyze whether there might be a better way for Pops to make a point than smacking me around. I also didn't know then that being hit was sowing a seed for a more serious confrontation later. But I knew I didn't like the beatings, and they resulted in the opposite of what he wanted. I'd pick a fight with someone just for the hell of it, because Pops didn't want me to, and opportunities for brawls were everywhere. My sister Altomese was always getting kids upset with her. Boys and girls, they'd chase her home. I'd go out—I'd be somewhere between five and eight years old at the time—and if the girl chasing Altomese was my sister's age, she'd beat me up.

I liked to drive my sisters through the alleys and streets of Harlem in any thrown-together contraption I could make. I almost got sweet little Muriel killed that way, with the help of my cousins. We made a wagon out of a fruit crate and some planks—we got the wheels from somewhere and had ourselves a cart. I put my sister in it and gave the cart a shove to get it going down an alley, which had a slope. Nobody thought about how to stop it. Muriel found herself whizzing out the alley, over the sidewalk, and onto the street. We heard the screeching of car brakes, and thankfully, we ran out to find her unhurt.

I don't know if I got a beating for that stunt, but if I didn't, my father must have been out of town.

My father's sister—my aunt—and her son (my cousin) lived with us. It was my aunt's apartment, in fact. My father was constantly on the move between New York and Baltimore (where other relatives lived), and where my mother's kin lived in North Carolina. He was looking for jobs at a time when a third of America's workforce was unemployed, and Negroes were often the last in line to be hired. In New York, Pops worked on and off as a longshoreman.

But my father provided for us, and he did so well. I can't remember a time when the icebox wasn't filled with food—and he even owned a car, which was rare for an African American in those days. When Sunday came, we put on our best clothes: my sisters in their nice dresses, bows and ribbons in their hair; and me in my crisp suit, nicely starched white shirt, and long pants. In the summertime, I'd wear short pants. We were required to sit on the stoop after church, quietly. You sat, you didn't play, you behaved. If you went to the next stoop over, you were in trouble.

In addition to putting a roof over our heads during those hard times, and providing a little extra for trips to Coney Island, my father saw that we ate well. We must have liked the Catholics' idea, because every Friday it was seafood, some kind of fresh fish. Every Saturday it was hot dogs and baked beans. Sunday was the big dinner: fried chicken or roast beef, home-made rolls, mashed potatoes, and fresh vegetables. We were healthy kids. We ate a lot of fresh vegetables and little meat on other days. The grown-ups would have pork chops, but they wouldn't give us any. "You can't have pork; it's not good for you," they said.

I learned to cook watching my mother. She baked biscuits for Sunday-morning breakfast—some with a little sugar on top she would call "tea biscuits." We couldn't wait for those. My father had to have his homemade bread every day.

Other days, breakfast was cereal, eggs, and bacon. I grew to hate cold days, when it would be Wheatina, oatmeal, or Cream of Wheat. My sister would make it lumpy. What we didn't fin-ish for breakfast we'd have for lunch on school days. By then it would have congealed. My sisters would turn the bowl upside down, dump out the cereal, slice it up, and put it in a frying pan to brown it. With some maple syrup, it wasn't bad, but when I became an adult, I couldn't even look at that cereal, and I never made my own kids eat it!

When Pearl Harbor brought America into the World War, I was ten, and my friends and I all wanted to go out and kill this Hitler guy. We played soldiers while our relatives went off to fight for real. Two of my uncles went off to join the segregated armed forces. My father's youngest brother, Arthur, became an infantryman, and his experiences affected him mentally. We never learned exactly what happened, because when he returned home, he was a changed man—quiet and withdrawn. He would never talk about what he had seen, what he had done, or what had happened to him.

Harlem grew dark under blackout curtains that covered every window, and air wardens would go up to the roofs to look for enemy planes. All the neon signs along 125th Street were turned off so the German bombers couldn't pick out any targets. Pops had just bought a new Pontiac, and he put blue gels over the headlights to dim them for night driving.

He didn't know, none of us knew, that 125th Street was going to explode at ground level, and he'd be using his car to evacuate his family—not from invaders, but from the rioting.

IT WAS THE FIRST TIME I'D SEEN a community explode. I would witness it again years later; but then I would be in the thick of it, battling the flames. There were no flames during the Harlem riots of 1943. It was an occasion for looting. After word spread that a white cop had shot a black youth, a lot of people let their dissatisfaction boil over as rage. I didn't understand what was going on, but it was scary. My family members were law-abiding people, and our neighbors were the same. But I looked out the window and people were breaking into stores, grabbing what they could. I saw little kids pulling wagons stacked high with fur coats.

"Lord knows where those children got those fur coats!" my aunt said, joining me at the window. Then she gave me the same look my mother had given me, a warning not to dare think about venturing outside.

The very first day of rioting, my father decided we were going to get out—out of my aunt's apartment and out of Harlem altogether. But the death of his mother, which had shocked us, may have already put that idea into his head.

Grandma was murdered. A man came into her candy store, shot her, and got away with the numbers money. That was what we were led to believe, that he was after the policies take. The incident showed how the community was changing. The day that Grandma was shot, we locked the front door to the apartment for the first time, as if someone might come in and shoot us, too.

I don't know if my father sensed that Harlem would never be quite the same after he saw the riots break out. Or maybe he was frustrated that he never got the type of work in New York that would do justice to his college degree. But as the noise from the streets came up through the window—the shouts of people running and the breaking of store glass—he ordered us to pack our things.

When we were finished, it was nighttime. The electricity was still on, but with the wartime blackout in effect, the streets were dark and it was hard to see. But it was still noisy as my father led us out—lots of shouts and police sirens, and an occasional something breaking that made us jump. We loaded up the Pontiac.

We said our hasty good-byes to my aunt and my cousins and drove off into the night like refugees. I was very sad about Grandma's death, and now this, leaving for good. It was a jolt. Since we split every summer between North Carolina and Baltimore, I was used to traveling—but not like this. I was scared. After all, some worked-up people might stop the car and force us out. From out of the darkness someone might throw a stone at us. I checked to see that the windows were rolled up. My three sisters and mother were silent while my father concentrated on his driving. The radio was off, like he didn't want any distractions that might make him miss a sign of danger.

The proud thoroughfare of stores and nightclubs, 125th Street, was a wreck. Police patrols were out trying to control the looting. Up the block, a cop stepped in front of our car and raised his hand for us to stop. My father did so. He was calm, and he answered the policeman's questions. Yes, that was his car he was driving, he told the cops. "We're traveling, headed for Baltimore."

The cop was polite. He addressed my father as "sir." He had my father get out and open the trunk so he could inspect the luggage inside to make sure we weren't taking looted goods. In with the suitcases was something of mine that I was bringing along. It was my little red wagon, a Flexible Flyer.

The cop waved us forward, into the night. We headed west to the Holland Tunnel and drove beneath the river and out of the city. Then down the length of New Jersey to another river, where my father drove the car onto a ferry for the trip over to Delaware. When we got to the other side, I knew we had really left New York behind.

It wasn't long before we were stopped by some state troopers, for no other reason than because we were a black family in a decent automobile. The cop demanded my father's driver's license and car registration without saying why we were stopped. My father waited patiently, and you could tell from his tone of voice that the cop must have thought we were uppity Negroes he meant to put in our place. He gave my father hell. "You were driving too fast. The sign says 35. Not 37. Not 30. 35!" He left us with the impression he'd lock us up if Pops drove one mile above or below the posted speed limit. But from previous trips, I knew Delaware. It was terrible in those days. The cops would lock up black folks to intimidate them. I also knew that things weren't going to get better the farther south we went.

The next day we arrived at a place I always thought from earlier visits was a sleepy, dull Southern city: Baltimore. We had arrived for good this time.

FROM POPS'S POINT OF VIEW, Baltimore would have seemed like a logical destination. The war was transforming the city, making it an industrial center where people were drawn to factory jobs.

The state of Maryland's largest city had always been shaped by war and fire, from the time Lord Calvert, the Baron of Baltimore, founded the place and got a bird named after him. The settlement began as a tobacco port at the head of tidewater on the Patapsco River, a deepwater estuary of the Chesapeake Bay. The town contributed its seamen and a new-style naval vessel, the Baltimore Clipper, to the Revolutionary War effort, while its other ships were fitted as privateers, and preyed on any British vessel they could find on the high seas.

The British never forgave Baltimore for that, and after sacking Washington in the War of 1812, they were determined to burn the city to ashes, at a time when the fire department consisted of a hand-drawn wagon with a hand-cranked pump and some leather buckets. (As soon as a structure was alight in those days, it was considered lost, with nothing to be done to save it. All efforts were directed at keeping the fire from spreading.) But the British land forces were repelled, and Fort McHenry withstood a famous 30-hour naval bombardment, protecting the port while being struck by 15,000 bombs, whose "rocket's red glare" inspired a captive on one of the British warships, Francis Scott Key, to write the "Star-Spangled Banner."

Baltimore's merchantmen beat out competition from the Erie Canal by starting the Baltimore & Ohio Railroad in 1827. But the city hated progress of another kind, and the prospect of the end of slavery inspired people to riot when Lincoln was elected. Baltimore was an occupied city throughout the Civil War, and for years afterward the folks pouted about it, and progress was slow. It wasn't until the Great Fire of 1904 destroyed most of downtown that the modern, relatively bustling city was built on the ashes.

The city I knew from my first visits was the heavy-industry town that grew after World War I, exporting coal and Maryland wheat, manufacturing steel and refining oil. A lot of small industry remained, and workers—black and white—poured in, chiefly from the South and Southwest. The influx continued through the Depression, when the city's first real slums appeared. More workers came during World War II. The shipbuilding, steel, and aircraft plants were expanding rapidly to meet war production, and the year we arrived, 16 new industries were launched, and 90 existing plants expanded. A giant magnesium plant was under construction.

Arriving into this mix, Pops found himself a job as a special-delivery messenger. He mostly carried letters—some of them in armed forces envelopes carried the tragic news to families that their sons had died in battle. Pops got the job because in Baltimore, we found out, not many black people had cars. He was given the night shift, which meant that he slept during the day.

I thought I'd help him out. We were staying with my Uncle George—George Barnes, my mother's brother—at 1335 No. Mount Street. He went into the military as a radio technician in 1943, the year we arrived from Harlem.

One day, as Pops was asleep upstairs, I decided to wax his car. I'd seen Pops do it and thought there was nothing to it. The Pontiac was black, but all I had was brown polish—and it didn't bother me that it was *shoe* polish. To me, wax was wax. I didn't know the car was simonized, or what "simonized" meant. I just lathered on that brown shoe polish, not just on the fenders and body, but over the grille and chrome work. While I was working, the sun came out. It was one of those big hot Baltimore summer suns, and it started baking the polish. The car started looking messy, and I thought it was time to wipe the stuff off. But it wouldn't come out.

After he saw what I'd done, my father got the polish off with a lot of soap and water and cursing. He gave me a beating to remember, with no consideration at all for my good intentions.

One whupping I deserved was when we pushed my sister Muriel out the living room window. There was a large window looking out over the street, and a narrow bench to sit on to look out. On top of the windowsill were flower pots. We kids were jostling for seats, and Altomese and I wound up pushing poor Muriel right out the open window. It was fortunate we were on the first floor, but she got bruised and cut a little when she landed on the cement, and she cried at the shock. I didn't complain when Pops took off his belt. If you push your sister out of a window, you deserve to get whupped.

We settled into life in "Charm City," as Baltimore called itself for reasons I didn't immediately appreciate. To me, Baltimore was dull after Harlem. On New York's 125th Street, there was a lot going on. In Baltimore, living in a row house, there wasn't anything going on. I hooked up with some buddies, and for fun we'd walk three blocks to the railroad tracks and walk along the line. Maybe we would find an open boxcar and jump up to see what was inside. It wasn't exactly bigtime entertainment.

I settled into the routine of my new neighborhood. Every other week I went to the barber on Pitcher Street where the red, white, and blue pole revolved outside, and I paid 25 cents for a haircut. Nearby was the Jewish corner grocer, run by Mr. Baker. You could buy stuff there "on the book." Bread, milk, butter—families paid at the end of the week.

Every Sunday we'd take a ride out to the country to a dairy farm up in Loch Raven. My thrifty father would buy a big two-gallon container of milk, which would be gone by Thursday, when it had changed from milk to buttermilk. I hated the taste of it, but we had to drink it.

Friday and Saturday, the milkman dropped off a couple of quarts in his electric truck (in Baltimore, all of the milk trucks were electric). As a boy, I was interested in cars and trucks, and I was fascinated by the electric delivery truck, with its solid rubber wheels.

The iceman, Mr. Charles, was black. Like all ice wagons, his was drawn by a horse. From the back of the wagon, he chopped 100-pound blocks of ice into five- and ten-cent pieces. We put these in the zinc-lined compartment at the top of the kitchen icebox, which was the "refrigerator" most people had then. Mr. Charles wielded an ice pick like a master, and chop chop chop!—he'd cut off the size you wanted. As a kid, my responsibility was to empty the icebox pan of water after the ice melted. A block lasted a day. Sometimes my job was to take the little red Flyer, walk one mile to the ice house, and get a block of ice, which could weigh 15 to 20 pounds. In the summer, with the sun beating down, a quarter of it was gone by the time I got home.

I'd run after the iceman, shouting, "Hey, can I have a ride? Got something for me to do?" But it was the street peddler with the horse-drawn wagon who really caught my fancy. These peddlers were all over black Baltimore, and we called them "A-rabs"—I guess because at some point their carts, which were filled with fruits, vegetables, and odds and ends, reminded someone of an Arabian caravan. The A-rabs were all black guys, and they'd sing songs to get attention as they came down the street: "*I got potatoes, and vine-red tomatoes!*" The people would look out their windows and exclaim, "Oh, it's the A-rab!" Then they'd run down and purchase what they needed.

I helped Joe, an A-rab who'd go down to the Baltimore Inner Harbor in the morning, on his way to the fish market. All the A-rabs went there, along with the white guys who'd service the white neighborhoods in pickup trucks. The black guys would split up, some going to the east side, some to the west side, because that was where the black folks lived. You could always count on the A-rabs coming around with fresh fish.

Joe let me help out, so I'd sing for him, making it jazzy:

> *Watermelons!*
> *Here's your watermelon man!*
> *Good-time watermelon*
> *Get your watermelon!*

I'd help with purchases and tote customers' bags, helping out these peddlers who were a necessity for the black community. We had our corner grocers, but the A-rabs brought you the freshest stuff. Also, they were black. The groceries were all owned by white people who didn't live in the community, so folks felt that they might get a better deal from a black person.

The influx of African Americans and other workers into Baltimore during the war inspired the city to do something about slum conditions, so the officials pioneered one of the nation's first urban-renewal efforts, with a minimum-standard housing code being set. Construction began on the Gilmore Homes public housing project right across the street from Uncle George's house. These were for poor people, and permission to live there depended on your income. It was understood that the homes would be temporary housing for the tenants, who would improve their station, increase their income, and vacate the properties so others might move in. There was no stigma attached to living there, particularly during the critical wartime housing shortage. When we moved into Gilmore Homes, my father had left the messenger job for a better-paying position at Bethlehem Steel, although it was manual labor. A black man with a college education was lucky if he could wait on tables in Baltimore in 1944.

We would be at Gilmore for two or three years. You stayed long enough to get on your feet, then it was "get yourself out of here so this can go to a worse-off person." In later years, the city would be filled with judges and professional people who had lived in Gilmore Homes as the children of struggling families.

The homes were well-constructed concrete townhouses, with red brick, brown, or beige fronting. The tallest was four stories, with the high-rises coming later. They were nice landscaped plots, and everyone tended their gardens. We lived in a two-story row house, with grass lawns in the front and back. You cut the grass, planted flowers around your stoop (front and back), and like elsewhere in Baltimore—as well as back in Harlem—the stoop became the center stage for our lives.

We were Methodists, and the family sat together at the AMES Methodist Church on Baker and Calhoun Streets. After Sunday School, my sisters and I went straight to the 10 A.M. service, and by noon we were back home, sitting on the stoop. We stayed dressed in our Sunday finery, maybe reading the comics, and went back to church in the afternoon. Young people's activities, such as Bible reading and discussing the issues of the day, went from six to eight at night. It was a chance to give us something to do on a day when we wouldn't be allowed to go to a movie or play cards. Not on a Sunday! Bedtime was eight o'clock. Then up the next day for school at Booker T. Washington Junior High.

I got into the swing of Baltimore life with the adaptability of a typical 12-year-old. Summer was hot, and snow was not unusual in winter—sometimes up to three feet of it. In those days, you went to school anyway; schools wouldn't close for any measly three feet of snow! Baltimore looked beautiful, and people were safe. No one locked their doors, not even in the projects.

I liked the snow. We made snowmen in the yard, and I had a sled to pull my sisters up the street. There were fewer cars in those days to pose a risk, and we got rid of those that might have bothered us by using a hose to water down the street, or we'd open a fire hydrant. In minutes, the street would be a sheet of ice. The drivers wouldn't know what caused it, but they'd see the ice and detour to the next street. So we always had a good place to play.

Saturday was movie day. We went every week, hot or cold, rain or shine. After we finished our chores, the movie palace was our reward. Mother did the laundry while my sisters vacuumed the house. My job was to scrub the kitchen floor, the bathroom, and the windows. Mother had a job outside the house now. During the war, she was on the assembly line at Western Electric, making telephones, so there would always be money for her four kids' Saturday ritual. We made sure to get the chores done by noon so we could get to the movies by one. Just like I did in New York—when we went to the Harlem Theater, air-cooled in the summertime—I liked Errol Flynn and the swashbucklers, and that guy Clark Gable who got everybody wearing mustaches. There were even movies made especially for African-American audiences, but I never saw any of them. The only black actors we saw were in *Gone with the Wind* and *Casablanca*.

I liked music, too, not realizing how that interest would turn into my first professional career in a few years. I owe my musical appreciation to my father. Pops had an extensive record collection that he brought with us as we moved from place to place. The windup Victrola with the old-fashioned funnel speaker we had in Harlem was replaced by an RCA electric record player, but the records were the same: classical music, rhythm and blues, and jazz. We'd listen to Nat King Cole, Ella Fitzgerald, the Mills Brothers, and Louis Jordan. I couldn't afford to buy records, but my father did. His great collection was one reason I started to appreciate music so much.

Pops saw the value of music in my life, although we disagreed on the particular way to go about applying it. I was in the junior high school choir, singing baritone, and the Baltimore Boys Choir asked me to join. Pops insisted that I do so, as he thought it was a great opportunity. "It's a classy thing to get into the Baltimore Boys Choir," he said. But it wasn't the type of "class" I wanted. I liked *Handel's Messiah,* but I didn't feel comfortable with what I thought was the girly sound, all those falsettos. However, I ended up being in the choir for three years. I also stuck it out with the school choir under Mr. Burch, the choirmaster and conductor. He was a high-strung, nervous guy, and we wondered what was wrong with him. We wore little black coats, short like waiters' jackets, with bow ties.

The choir went on trips to concerts around the city, and school field trips acquainted me with the local historic sites. Our class went up to Pennsylvania, to Amish country, where the city boys and girls could see what farm life was like. Our family summer trips to Raleigh and Durham, North Carolina, had already filled me in.

My father also drove us up to see Gettysburg, site of the pivotal Civil War battle. I saw Fort McHenry, guarding Baltimore Harbor, on a school trip, but it was years later that I learned that one of its defenders against the British bombardment was a black man named William Williams. I've always wondered if I was related to him. He was a 21-year-old runaway slave who joined up with the 38th U.S. Infantry. He ran away from his Maryland slave owner in 1814 and enlisted as a private in the army. He must have looked promising to the recruitment officer, who didn't question his background even though his slave owner had the state covered with reward posters, and federal law prohibited the enlistment of slaves into the army because "slaves, being property, can make no valid contract with the government."

Williams got an enlistment bonus of $50, and he was receiving a private's wages of $8 a month when the 38th U.S. Infantry was posted at Fort McHenry in September 1814. Williams was one of the brave defenders during the British bombardment that held off the enemy, inspiring Francis Scott Key to write the poem that became the National Anthem. One of the shrapnel bombs "bursting in air" blew off Williams's leg, mortally wounding him.

No, we didn't learn about William Williams while touring Fort McHenry on our field trip from Booker T. Washington Junior High, even though we were a class of black children. Baltimore, I was learning through bitter and eye-opening personal experience, was a place that had different notions about the races than New York did.

There was no Coney Island in Baltimore, but there were two amusement parks, Gwen Oak and Park Circle. Both were in the city, and both were segregated, with no blacks allowed. They didn't open up for African Americans until the 1960s, after people who were trying to get in were initially locked up left and right.

But in the 1940s, it was true that African Americans, or Negroes, as we were known then, "knew their place." This was not to say we *accepted* our place. My father impressed upon me that we were as good as anyone. I was never afraid of any white person, but I wasn't foolish. I knew there were places where black people did not and should not go, where we were simply not welcome.

Another reason for tolerating, if not accepting, segregation was because what we had at the time wasn't so bad. Baltimore's African-American neighborhood in the '40s was a thriving community, with strong social ties mostly through the churches and our own newspaper, the *Afro-American.* Children were raised mostly in nuclear families living in proximity to relatives of their extended families. At a time of little crime and no drug problems, a strong work ethic prevailed. People knew a sense of pride, and public facilities, while inferior to what the whites had, were adequate. Whites had their movie theaters, but so did we, showing the same movies and selling the same popcorn. If Negroes weren't admitted to downtown nightclubs, well, the truth was, the music was better on Pennsylvania Avenue, the famous thoroughfare that was the commercial heart of Baltimore's black section. Certainly our church choirs were the best in the state.

But being a poorer area, the community was the type of place that the American Dream told us we should advance out of— and move on up. After the war, when people realized that segregation laws were hindering their progress, the Civil Rights movement really took off, and rightfully so.

During the Depression, when the entire country was poor, and during World War II, when we were united against Hitler and Tojo, Baltimore's African-American population put up with segregation, without liking it. But I was 12, and recently from New York. To me, the discrimination was insulting. I noticed that when I was with my mother shopping at a downtown department store, Hutzler's, she wasn't permitted to try on a hat she wanted to buy. It was a ladies' Sunday-go-to-church hat, and the saleswoman told my mother that she needed to know her hat size in order to buy it. Black people weren't permitted to try on clothes in downtown stores. If they did, the items would be considered soiled, and unfit for sale to white people. I remember being upset by that. I thought, *Do they think my mother's head is dirty?*

I looked around and didn't see any black people working at that big store except for the janitor and the elevator operator. The elevator man had the best job a black person could get there, but when I watched him close the steel mesh door, he seemed to me to be a man literally trapped in a cage.

In Baltimore, black people weren't denied the right to vote. Segregation was more subtle than in the Deep South. There weren't any signs saying "Whites Only." But I knew I couldn't go downtown to a movie. You also knew you couldn't go into certain neighborhoods. Fulton Avenue, two blocks from where we lived, was an all-white street that was the dividing line between where whites and blacks lived. In order to get to Druid Park, a large grassy space where the baseball diamonds were, we had to walk up Fulton. I remember the stares that my sisters and I would get from the windows where curtains were pulled aside as we walked up the street. My little gang of friends and I had to cross Fulton to get to the railroad tracks for our explorations. If white kids saw us, they threw stones, got into fights with us, and chased us back to our neighborhood.

But as I said, I wasn't afraid of the white gangs. In junior high, my attitude was, "If you bring me something, you can get it." That is, if you want to talk, we talk; if you want to fight, we can do that, too.

At home, they called me Junior. My friends had another name for me: Spunky.

I took after my scrappy father, but there were other important role models in my life. When Uncle Bob, my father's brother, came down from New York, we kids were always excited. He had a sense of humor and taught me the importance of being sociable on the job to make work go smoother. He told me how he liked to take his co-workers out to lunch. As an executive, years later, I'd find myself doing the same thing, and thinking about Uncle Bob. He'd sneak us out for ice cream and slip a little money into our hands—a quarter or even 50 cents, which was the equivalent of my weekly allowance. Pops would blow his top. "Don't you be spoiling my kids!" Pops was serious about being the only one to provide for his family's needs, no matter how small.

But it was Uncle Buddy, my mother's brother, who really impressed me, because he had a personality that showed me that in order to be a man, you had to look at life straight on. Uncle Buddy was a redcap, a porter with the Pennsylvania Railroad. It was a subservient job, but it was one of the best jobs a black man could have in the '30s and '40s. He was a redcap all his life, and he taught me that even though you may be a "servant," you can look any man in the eye. He also influenced my management style in later years, and taught me to go about my business not only expecting respect, but giving it to others. He also had a sense of fun about life, even when things were hard, and that rubbed off on me. I would also see this later in my own management style, when I'd kid around at the office and bring in meals for the staff that I'd cooked at home.

Uncle Buddy didn't let the times he lived in get him down. He should have been a big-league ballplayer. He was a large man, 6'2" and 240 pounds. He was a pitcher in the Negro League, with Baltimore's team, the Elite Giants. (The team name was pronounced "E-light.") He was good enough to go into the National League. He played during the war, and was still playing around the time Jackie Robinson first started with the Brooklyn Dodgers, breaking the color barrier in America's favorite sport. But by then, Uncle Buddy's playing days were numbered.

UNCLE GEORGE CAME BACK FROM THE WAR with his straight black hair and light skin, and the relatives all said I resembled him. In the navy, he'd been a radio technician, and he taught the technical aspects of radio to other operators. Back in civilian life, he opened Druid Radio and Television, one of the city's first stores dedicated to repairing that new marvel, the TV.

He had his naysayers, though. They'd tell him, "You're not going to get any business. Black folks don't own radios, and they're never going to buy TVs."

But lots of blacks owned radios, and Uncle George proved that when you have a skill that's in demand, customers will find you. White people from all over the city brought their bulky, round-screen TVs into his shop for repair. They constantly had Uncle George come to their homes, too—through the front door—at a time when television ownership meant constant adjustment of crude rooftop TV antennae. His shop prospered, and he branched out into refrigerators and household appliances. For the kids, he assembled trains, tracks, and little towns in the garage, all from scratch.

Uncle George was so knowledgeable that he actually built TVs from kits. In fact, the first television set my family owned was one he made. The first TV he built he put in the front window of his house on North Mount Street, the window we accidentally pushed Muriel out of. People gathered on the sidewalk and watched boxing—Joe Louis and others. It was amazing to look right into the ring at Madison Square Garden in New York when you were standing on a sidewalk in Baltimore. It was a new world. We had defeated Hitler, Baltimore had prospered from its war industries, and the big new plant was a refining center for high-octane gasoline. As I left junior high and entered Frederick Douglass High School, I wondered what place this new world held for me.

My father had his own ideas: I was to concentrate on my schoolwork, with no distractions. Scholastic achievement was a worthy goal, but the strict discipline he demanded was unreasonable. It chafed against a boy's natural desire to explore what he could do, and to be able to make mistakes.

I told my father I wanted a job. We weren't destitute, but my father considered my working some sort of insult against him. "No son of mine is going to get a job!" he shouted.

"Aw, Pops, can't I make a buck or two?"

"End of discussion!"

Some of the discipline I understood. My father was a stickler about homework. You had to do your school assignments before anything else—before you went out, before you sat on the stoop. I would later make this a rule for my own children. I also had to recite my lessons to my father to show him that I'd learned them and to prove I'd read the books. Later, I would read those same books to my own kids.

Pops had a whistle, and no matter where I was in the projects, when I heard that whistle I knew I'd better get home fast. My friends knew, too. "Hey, Spunky, you'd better get home!" I'd get there, and he'd send me to the store to buy the newspaper or his cigarettes. He'd read the *Afro-American* and *The Baltimore Sun,* and sometimes the Hearst paper, the *News American.* He insisted that I read the newspapers, as well as books, to keep up on current events, although he was never very interested in politics.

Dad bought quarter bottles of National Bohemian Beer, the type with the screw top. I wasn't any older than 14 when I started sipping that beer, and then I'd fill the bottle back up with tap water.

Pops would complain to Mom, "My beer's flat!" She'd say she didn't know what he was talking about. Then he would mark the beer bottle's level with a pencil. That made it easier for me, because I could fill it back up with water to that point.

Years later, we'd laugh about it. "Hey, Pops, remember when you complained how your beer would 'evaporate'? You knew Mom couldn't drink that beer. *I* was doing it!"

"I knew it! I knew that beer had to be going someplace!"

But there were other matters that weren't so funny, that we would later reconcile over but never laugh about. During my high school years, my father's natural desire for me to become a responsible man was enforced in some unreasonable ways.

One was the issue of my working. I didn't like to do things behind Pops's back, but that seemed like the only way to get a job because of his stubbornness. It started when I was 15, when I worked a little as a stevedore. After all, my buddies and I might need 50 cents for the movies. We went down to the Inner Harbor, to the docks where the cargo ships were tied up.

"Hey, boss!" We called the foreman who hired workers "boss"—not because he was white, but because he *was* the boss! "Hey, boss, we need some change. You got a job for us?"

He'd look us over, see if we were big enough to carry a bunch of bananas and not fall into the water with them, and holler back, "Get on!"

The banana boat would come in, and since there were no child labor laws in those days, I'd carry bunches of bananas up from the cargo hold until I made 50 cents' worth of trips. It wasn't work we *had* to do; we *wanted* to do it—to prove that we were independent men.

But soon enough, manhood would be thrust upon us, and all its responsibilities—and even dangers—would be ours.

❧ CHAPTER TWO ☙

Be-bop and Other Odd Jobs

"White flight" was already in full swing when my father moved us out of the projects and into a house on Fulton Avenue. We were the first black family in the formerly all-white neighborhood. The same white folks who stared with hostility at my sisters and me when we passed them on our way to Druid Park were leaving the area after unscrupulous real estate agents told them, "You'd better move—the blacks are coming." There hadn't been any black families considering Fulton Avenue until the Realtors panicked the homeowners into selling their properties.

My father was in charge of my life in just about every way. He bought my clothes the whole time I was at Frederick Douglass High School. He took me down to the men's and boys' clothing store, Tru-Fit, on East Baltimore Avenue. The year I joined the fire department, the store burned down, and five firefighters died. Today, such a loss of life would be unusual, but when that fire occurred, it was a more dangerous time, and a reminder to me of what I was getting into as a firefighter.

Doing that kind of work was the last thing on my mind when I was in high school. For one thing, there were no African-American firefighters. It was a white man's job, belonging almost entirely to the Irish, and entry was determined by patronage, nepotism, and race.

Not that I wanted to be a fireman. My impression when I was a kid was that they were a bunch of lazy guys. I would walk past a firehouse, and there they were, sitting against the wall, watching the people go by. They didn't look that bright, and in fact, they *weren't* that bright. You could be a firefighter with a sixth-grade education. I was better educated than they were.

By the time a boy was 16 in the 1940s, he was considered near adulthood, and his inner drive made him want to assume adult responsibilities. There were strict sexual morals, and most people believed that sex only came after marriage, which also hastened a boy's desire to live an adult life. I had friends who were impatient with high school and left to take jobs or get married.

My father would have none of that for me. He wanted me to get my high school diploma and then go on to college like he did. To drive home his point about what type of life I could expect without a diploma, he took me to his workplace the summer I was 15 years old. He taught me a lesson about manual labor I would never forget.

Crown Cork & Seal was the name of the factory where Pops worked making cork stoppers for bottles. The big Baltimore plants would allow their workers' kids to come in for summer employment. I was a husky boy, and they assigned me to the unloading of boxcars. Working at the plant was fine with me. In those days, there was no such thing as lying around all summer with nothing to do. I had always wanted to work, and here my father had arranged a job. What I was to discover was that his reason for doing it wasn't so I could earn some cash, but so he could teach me a harsh lesson.

A "hank," or bundle of cork, weighed a couple hundred pounds. All I did all day was walk up a ramp into a boxcar, put a hank on a trolley, and push it to wherever they wanted it. After three weeks, I'd had enough. The Baltimore summer heat and humidity made the physical labor worse. I felt like a kid who couldn't wait until school started again. I told my father I couldn't take it anymore.

"Then you'd *better* go back to school!" he said. "Because if you don't get a decent education, this is all you can expect out of life."

I took up every sport at school that I could—football, where I played tackle, and then basketball. My friends and I practiced our football moves on the streets and cement sidewalks—in our street clothes, without the leather helmets we had at school. I practiced for the softball team by playing stickball. We drew three circles in the ground, and that would be our diamond. At Druid Park, they had a diamond reserved for "Coloreds," but we couldn't use it because the Negro League played there, my Uncle Buddy's team. The black diamond was in the black section of the park. There was another diamond for white players in their section of the park.

I was on the junior varsity wrestling team; at 16, I weighed 160 pounds. I was on the boxing team, but wasn't any good at it and got pretty bruised up. For a couple of weeks until the bandages came off, I sounded pretty funny explaining, "I got my dose b'oke!" (Translation: My nose was broken.) But when it came to anything to do with sports, I'd put on the black-and-orange uniform of the Douglass Ducks, and I'd just do it.

The broad jump was my event on the track team, but I was seriously injured one day when I was just about to make a jump. My feet went out from under me, and I fell and hit my head. I knocked myself out and cut the back of my head open. Years later, I would wonder if a mysterious brain tumor found at the same spot had originated in that accident. The doctors said it had been developing for decades.

In academics, math was my favorite subject. I took Spanish, too, and already had a head start from the words I picked up from New York's Puerto Ricans. I used to like hearing them talk. But it was math—algebra, trigonometry, and geometry—that fascinated me. When my subsequent duties in the fire department included instructing new recruits, I taught them how to solve hydraulic problems with algebra. The last five questions on the department exams were math/hydraulic questions, and in many cases, how you did on these questions determined how you did on the entire exam and whether you'd be able to enter the fire department. Those separated the men from the boys.

The recruits would come to me, scratching their heads, all perplexed: "Hey, Lieutenant, how do I solve this math?" They knew I had a surefire method for problem solving. In algebra, you have to find the unknown. The unknown might be water pressure, the length of pipe, or the height of a building. "Nozzle pressure is 50 pounds per square inch, the fire is on the fourth floor, the pumper is parked 600 feet away. How much hose do you need?" I passed on some of my Douglass High math to help them out.

My interest in music got more serious, and I started playing instruments. There was always a piano in the house, and
over the years, I taught myself how to play. In junior high, I
was given a school violin, but I didn't care for it, so I moved
on to the cello. Then came the bugle, which I played in the
high school junior varsity marching band, wearing an orange-
and-black uniform with gold buttons, epaulettes, braids, a black-
brimmed cap, and leggings.

I didn't go to school looking like a bum either, because my
father insisted that I be well dressed. I wore a nice sports coat
most of the time, or a shirt and tie. I had one suit, a blue one,
my Sunday suit, and I learned to tie a tie by watching Pops.
When I started growing hair on my face at 16, my mother bought
me an electric razor, a Schick, which was a novelty in the '40s.

Outside of school, we didn't wear zoot suits, with the wide-
shouldered long coats, the baggy peg-legged pants, and the
watch chain that dangled to the knee, but "my boys" and I acted
like we did. It was in our attitude. My boys—Fred, Charlie,
Reggie—we were slick things. We were lovers for all the girls,
and the girls loved us. But it wasn't like today. Girls wanted to
remain virgins. The boys, well, we could *think* about it. The closest we got to sex was "dirty books," little comics where the char-
acters engaged in sex. These just appeared from somewhere and
circulated around. There was no sex education in schools; parents didn't teach anything except one lesson: "*You better not!*
You'd better *not* mess with no girls, you hear me, boy?"

Pops would say, "Any girl who would let you mess with
her is no good."

If one of my boys was lucky and got a date, he'd build it
up the next day. "I took out Sally. We went to the move-ies!"

"Oh, man, what happened?"

"Oh, I took her home to her place. Her folks weren't home. Man, she loved me!"

We whooped it up, enjoying the story, knowing he was lying. But poor Sally! Meanwhile, we didn't know what a girl *looked* like—it was all a lot of big talk. We didn't fool with any real bad girls, although there were plenty of opportunities in Baltimore, which was a port city. But we knew about the clap.

By my sophomore year, my father was working at Bethlehem Steel, and he brought me along that summer for another work experience. This time, I was assigned to the job *he* was doing.

Pops, a college graduate, was shoveling coal. The coke ovens had to be constantly burning to melt the ore, and a long line of laborers did the job. This was hard labor at its lowest. I went down there and worked alongside the men for four weeks. I started realizing a little more about what it meant to be "Colored." There were no whites at the coke ovens; it was all black men. (And every single person who worked in that area for any length of time came down with some kind of asbestosis. My father, too.) Shirtless and sweaty, we'd knock ourselves out shoveling coal into those furnaces, and by the end of the shift, we'd be grimy with a covering of coal soot. It was hot all year 'round at the coke ovens, but in Baltimore's summer, it was really hot. I had respect for Pops doing that— he showed me what he would do to support his family. We kids never knew what his job was like, since he'd be all scrubbed up when he returned home.

His lesson was, "Son, if you don't get your degree, you can expect to spend the rest of your life like this." A college degree didn't get Pops a good job, but times were changing, and there was hope for me if I finished my education.

Pops taught me something else about pride. Every day he would go to work dressed in a good shirt and tie. At the plant, he changed into his work overalls. When work was done, he'd be back looking his best.

But Pops's discipline grew more severe as I got older, until it was all out of proportion. As I mentioned previously, this would end up causing some serious problems between us. Up to the day I graduated from high school, my bedtime was nine o'clock, and he made it clear that he wouldn't tolerate vices such as smoking or hanging out with my friends. Girlfriends were a waste of my time, as far as he was concerned. For a boy who never got into trouble, and who was a good all-around student, athlete, and musician, I was kept on a very short leash, and it choked me sometimes.

The last week of high school, I decided to skip a few of the last days because I was graduating. I got together with my boys, and we headed up Pennsylvania Avenue to a pool hall. We were our usual slick things, swaggering up the sidewalk. I had my hat cocked to one side, gangster style, with a cigarette dangling from my mouth. Then I saw the Pontiac. Pops was driving, and he saw me the same time I saw him.

All I could do was swallow my cigarette, lit tip, ashes, and all. It burned the hell out of my mouth and seared my throat. Pops swerved over, the car hit the curb, and he jumped out. The way he looked at me you'd think I'd just murdered Grandma. He hit me upside my head, hard, but the sting of the blow was nothing compared to the shame I felt about being treated that way in front of my boys. I was 17, and he was acting like I was 7. He told me to get on home, and I left. I could feel my friends' eyes—they were embarrassed for me.

That's why I never told Pops about my girl. I was serious about her, and I knew that he'd say I had no right to be serious about a girl when I was 17.

Her name was Marjie. She lived on Myrtle Avenue, around the corner from the firehouse on Fremont. I met her through her sister, Doris White. Marjie was in the next class, so she was almost a year younger than I was. One day, I was thinking of visiting Doris, without any romantic interest in mind. A lot of my boys went to that area, and I said, "Hey, Doris, me and the boys are coming to your place to play some ball. I'll be around." When I dropped by, I saw that Doris's three other sisters were all very pretty like she was, with beautiful smiles. But with one look at her long black hair and her big brown eyes, Marjie stole my heart away.

Baltimore was a Southern city, and I was 16 going on 17 when I first set foot in that house, so certain proprieties had to be observed. I asked Marjie's father if I could come by from time to time to see everybody, "including Marjie." He gave me a long look, as if he was wondering, *Who is this guy coming here from uptown?* But then he gave his permission.

I got to know Marjie and talked to her about this and that, school and the movies. When the opportunity came up, I asked her to go to a hayride with me. City kids my age liked to go out to a farm in the Maryland countryside, and a farmer would take us out in a big horse-drawn wagon. The floorboards would be covered with hay, and we'd sit back, laughing and talking and watching the green hills go by. Maryland had some of the prettiest countryside.

Marjie and I had a good time, and her father even packed us a lunch, which said a lot. In those days, there wasn't a lot of hugging and declarations of "I love you" between parents and children—parents were more reticent. But they showed their affection with actions, like Marjie's father packing us that wonderful lunch. He went to the market and found the largest oranges I'd ever seen, and huge chicken legs he fried up in batter. "Hey, Marjie, where'd your father get these big chicken legs!"

Algie White, Marjie's dad, was a big man, and when Marjie's mother would get sick, he had to raise four daughters all by himself. One of his hands was as big as both of mine, so when he said, "I want Marjie back by eight o'clock," I was quick to say, "Yes, sir." And I brought her back by eight, because I didn't want one of those hands to whup me upside my head. If I had her back on her stoop a few minutes early, that was okay because we could talk, but not a minute later! Then it was home for my nine o'clock bedtime, which I thought was ridiculously early. The worst part was that if I came home one minute later, my father would smack me. I obeyed the curfew to avoid the humiliation of someone my age and size being smacked by his father for coming home at 9:05. That upset me.

Getting to know Marjie was great. Just when I thought I knew everything about her and she must have known everything there was to know about me, we'd make another discovery about each other. She was a lovely, sweet girl, intelligent and lively. My heart seemed to beat faster when I thought about her. It was true love, and I sensed that she felt the same way about me.

In 1948, the peace we were promised after the war with Hitler didn't happen, and we entered into a Cold War with Russia. Dewey's defeat over Truman for the presidency that the newspapers said would happen . . . didn't. But this thing I felt inside for Marjie, hey, this *was* happening! I knew we were meant to be together for a long time. I was crazy about her.

I started going to the Catholic Church when I met her—she belonged to the St. Pius parish. Pops didn't object. He felt that churchgoing was important, but he wasn't particular about which church it was as long as I was fulfilling the duty. I liked the Catholic Church. I found it mysterious (they spoke Latin, after all). It just seemed to have a certain mystique to it. Incense burned in the church, filling the whole place with a nice aroma. I didn't know what the priest was saying, but I *felt* the holiness.

I also liked the way the Catholic service was only 30 minutes long. St. Pius was a big church with a big congregation, and you'd get in and out in a half hour to make room for the next mass. It was efficient!

I also liked spending time with Marjie's father. Algie White influenced me by the way he looked at life and the way he acted. He was the type of man who looked you in the eye and didn't expect anything from you, but if you needed a helping hand, he'd be there. He was an all-around good man. He worked a sampling of the type of jobs available to black men at the time: He worked on the Baltimore & Ohio Railroad as a laborer, then he worked for Firestone Tire & Rubber Company as one of their first African-American supervisors. His crew's job was to unload liquid latex from containers. When he came home, Marjie and her sisters would help peel the crusty dry latex from their father's arms. He was strict, like my father, but he was a nice and gentle man.

I dated Marjie throughout the winter and into the spring, but with the end of the school year, I needed a car, since the senior prom was coming up. Marjie said she'd be my date, and I wanted some wheels. My father wouldn't let me work, so it seemed that there was nothing to do but go behind his back. I earned what I needed at the Regent Theater on

Pennsylvania Avenue, working as a candy hawker. I went up and down the aisle with a tray-load of Milk Duds and lemon drops, and people would buy from me instead of going out into the lobby. My mother knew what I was up to, but we kept it from Pops. He was doing night-shift work at the time and didn't know where I was.

After school, I went to the Regent, put on a bow tie, pulled the rack of candy over my shoulders, and started working for a commission of 25 cents on the dollar. A large Hershey's bar was ten cents, so a lot of hustling went into earning some money, especially when I had to contend with members of the audience who hollered at me if I got in their way. But it was fun, sort of a sport. "Get out of there!" they'd shout when I got in front of them. Someone would throw something at me, and I'd dodge it. All I was doing was trying to make a couple of bucks!

I finally had enough to buy a car: $25. I saw an old jalopy parked on the street with a For Sale sign on it: a big old 1935 Chevrolet, black. I found out that if you cranked it hard enough and pushed it long enough, it ran.

But I had to find a way to keep Pops from knowing about it and blowing his top. "You're too young to drive," he'd told me before. "A car is something you don't need." I parked two blocks away from the house, and I was careful when I drove around. But it was a great feeling, being behind the wheel of that Chevy. Very few black kids had cars in 1949. It didn't matter that my car was a piece of junk. All it had to do was last me through the prom.

I went to the Easy Method Driving School, where we practiced driving cars that had two of everything: two steering wheels, two sets of brakes, and two gas pedals.

The day of the prom, I was out driving, coming down North Avenue with my boys, approaching the intersection at 4th Street, when a car cut in front of me. I dented its fender, and the accident was considered my fault because my car struck from the rear. I made arrangements with the driver to pay damages of $50. I was thinking that that was a lot of candy bars I'd have to sell at the Regent. I had no insurance and couldn't tell my father. He didn't even know I had a license.

I wasn't going to let a traffic accident interfere with the fun my boys and I earned for getting through high school, though. We went on our way, straight to Robert E. Lee Park on Falls Road. All the kids were hanging out there, goofing off at the waterfall. It was a very tranquil spot, but the serenity was interrupted a little bit by my car. I drove down the hill to get to the parking area, and ahead of me was a big tree, a good three feet in diameter. The Chevy had mechanical brakes, which operated by a cable. Before I could make my right turn, the brakes gave way, and I went right into the tree. Both headlights broke. My boy on the right, Charlie, put his big head right through the windshield. Glass flew, but there wasn't any blood. He was okay. "Oh, man, who put that tree there?!" he said, rubbing his head. I put the car in reverse, backed out, parked, and got down to business, goofing off with my boys.

The police came and saw the car with the busted headlights. A cop called me over and told me in very clear language that I'd better have that car off the street by sunset.

That night was graduation, and I had my big date with Marjie. I had my tux, and she had a special dress picked out. I was thinking that I had to get that car fixed, fast. I hurried to find new headlight bulbs at the garage, but then I had more bad luck: It started raining. The car windshield used to be two pieces of glass, one on the driver's side and one on the passenger side. Now, Marjie's side was gone. I cut a length of cardboard and stuck it in place.

"Sorry about the car," I explained when I picked up Marjie at her house in the battered Chevy. "Charlie's big head busted that window." It was comical. In fact, that whole day was comical in the goofy way things go when you're in love. Marjie was happy, being driven to the prom in her date's own car, even with the cardboard window soggy from the rain. She was lovely in her prom dress, and I pinned a floral corsage on it for her. My boys whistled and said we were a beautiful couple. I hoped we'd be a couple forever.

Many seniors who graduated from Frederick Douglass High School in 1949 went on to be professional people and made something of themselves. I left with a letter from the band and one from the track team.

But my career took a back seat to my emotions. Things got worse with my father, until I had to choose between him and Marjie.

I don't think Pops had anything against Marjie personally, but he felt that any downtown girl wasn't good enough for me because I was uptown. Actually, he didn't want me to have a serious relationship with *any* girl, and he demanded that I stick to my nine o'clock curfew as a way to keep Marjie and me apart. I knew that he was deliberating messing things up between us. So, after graduation, I came home late more frequently. My love for Marjie outweighed any humiliation I felt as a result of getting smacked around by my father.

Tension was building up between my dad and me all summer. I was trying to date Marjie, coming home late, and still getting hit. "You're a Williams!" Pops would shout. "You've got to go to college!" He picked out a school for me, Morgan State, and I applied and was accepted. He gave me tuition money, but I held on to it. Another idea was in my head: to play music professionally. I would have liked to have talked to Pops about it, but I didn't dare. I wanted college, but I was also blinded by Marjie. If Pops had been reasonable, I might have held on to both. But he made me choose.

One night, he smacked me once too often. I came back at five past nine, and he let me have it. I couldn't take it anymore. I was almost 18 years old, a man, and it was ridiculous being treated like a kid. With that last hit, what he didn't want to have happen, happened, and it was like he was pushing me *toward* Marjie. I left the house where I had lived under the same roof with Pops all my life. I didn't say anything, and with my cheek stinging from where he hit me, I walked right past him and out the door.

I went to the house of one of my boys, Fred, and his mother and father let me stay with them. The next day, when Pops was at work, I came back, talked to my mother, collected my stuff, and left. He never contacted me.

I was so certain that what I was feeling was right that I didn't hesitate. I went to Marjie and asked her to marry me. "It's too hard, all these things keeping us apart," I said.

Marjie was 17, and her first reaction was that she was too young to get married. She was in the 11th grade, and she wanted to finish school. She knew her father would feel the same way about her completing her education, instead of running off with some knucklehead. But when I said I was afraid of losing her, that was all the convincing she needed.

We agreed that once the dust settled, Marjie would go back to school and earn her degree, which was something she *did* do.

We put our heads together and concocted a big lie.

Marjie told her father, and I told my mother, that I had gotten her pregnant. That was all it took to convince the old folks. They got together and talked.

"If she's pregnant, they get married," said Pops. That was the rule in those days. You couldn't bring a child into the world without the parents being married. It was unheard of, especially for two good kids like Marjie and me, who had never been in any sort of trouble. They took our word about Marjie's pregnancy; there was no talk about consulting a doctor. But I don't think my mother believed our story.

Meanwhile, in reality, I had never touched her. We were both 17, and virgins, when we were engaged.

Everyone settled into the idea that we were getting married, even if they didn't like it. We decided on St. Pius for the wedding service. I had meetings with the parish priest, who spoke to me about the responsibilities of marriage. On Thanksgiving Day, we had a full ceremony and did it up right. I was in my tux, and Marjie's sisters were among the bridesmaids. My boys were there, looking surprised. Marjie's father gave her away, and family and friends—whatever their misgivings—looked on as we took our marriage vows.

That night, we honeymooned in a room at a friend's house.

A kid would eventually be born to us, but long "overdue," if anyone was counting the months. Nobody ever confronted me about it, but I knew that they were all talking about me when I wasn't there. I think my father resented the fact that I'd pulled one over on him. But now that I was married, he would insist I take the responsibility seriously. Unfortunately, his way of giving lessons would cause more trouble.

I was 17, married, and I needed a job. What could a young black man do? Drive a truck—a small truck? Be a laborer? The winter of '49 to '50 was a cold one in Baltimore, and I spent it largely outdoors. I found a job delivering telegrams by bicycle. The pay was good, but the weather nearly froze me.

I started in December, delivering Christmas greetings. The company didn't issue me a uniform, but I wore a Western Union cap, with a black brim and the yellow company emblem.

In those days, the quickest way to get a message to someone was by telegram. It was also a ritual in show business circles. A place I was sent to a lot was the Hippodrome, the big theater in downtown Baltimore. I delivered telegrams to Frank Sinatra, Judy Garland, Tommy Dorsey, Tony Bennett, and most of the entertainers headlining the shows. I got a lot of good tips, but more than that, they reinforced the idea I got in high school that I wanted to go into music. *Someday, I'll be in a production,* I thought.

But not at the Hippodrome. At that time, blacks couldn't even go to that theater, unless you were sweeping up or delivering telegrams. But thank goodness they didn't call me "boy." Nobody I delivered telegrams to did that. They must have seen something in my attitude, not cocky, but expecting respect and giving it. If they had called me "boy," I would have corrected them by saying that my name was Herman.

Sometimes when it was real cold, I'd come home with icicles on my coat. At lunchtime, I ate out of a bag that Marjie filled with sandwiches and a thermos of coffee. I'd put the bag on the handlebars of the bicycle and go pedaling away. The bicycle had no speeds; you went uphill on leg power, not gear power.

But by the end of January, the cold weather drove me out of that job. I was also embarrassed to be a 19-year-old married man riding around on a bicycle to support my family. But I'd be more embarrassed *not* having a job, so I made sure I had another place to go.

My Uncle George knew someone at the Baltimore Soda Fountain Company, which distributed all the things a drug or department store soda fountain needed: syrups, cones, straws, and cups. For a while, I worked there loading trucks.

Marjie got a job working for the Glen L. Martin Company (Lockheed-Martin today), on the assembly line making airplanes. I went down to the plant, and they immediately gave me an impressive-sounding title, "plant engineer," and showed me the area of my responsibility. I was put in charge of brooms and brushes—I was a janitor. It paid 75 cents an hour. Marjie was getting a dollar an hour because she had a skilled job. But between us, we were doing all right.

We were both very sad when Marjie's mother died shortly thereafter. She had been hospitalized when we were married, and she passed away a short time later. But in the wonderful way that life sometimes offers compensation, Marjie's grief was offset by the child we were expecting. She was pregnant—for real this time. A baby was due in September.

I knew that the plant job wouldn't be my life's work. I was seeing what might open up next when I got a call from a singing group called The Swallows, made up of three guys from the neighborhood. They needed a bass player after the one they had got drafted into the Korean War. They knew I'd played bass in high school, my last string instrument after the cello. I played in a combo called The Six Sparks with my best friend, Fred, who played the piano. We'd play after school, on stage at school programs, and at some parties where we'd give our rendition of hits by Nat King Cole, The Ink Spots, The Mills Brothers, and other groups. Somebody in The Swallows remembered, and said, "Call Herman Williams."

I took my tuition money that my father had given me to go to Morgan State, headed down to the Royal Music Store on Pennsylvania Avenue, and bought a blond wood bass—brand new and as shiny as a silver dollar.

The Swallows needed someone fast because they had a gig out of town. I bought the bass, thinking, *Anybody can play behind guys singing,* and with that kind of confidence, I was off to Roanoke, Virginia, a couple hundred miles south of Baltimore. The gig was a segregated dance for blacks at the civic center. If whites wanted to listen to the music, they'd be up in the balcony as spectators. The reverse would happen if a gig were a white event. The police enforced these conventions where we played.

Baltimore had no segregated public facilities, but the same unspoken rules held in downtown nightclubs, where no black people were allowed inside. But a black person wouldn't have any reason to go because the music wasn't any good. Everything was happening uptown. On the other hand, whites would go uptown to *our* clubs. *Serious* segregation was what I'd encounter when I joined the fire department.

The Swallows had a couple of original songs, but mostly we did cover versions of popular Hit Parade songs, like the group's theme song, "When the Swallows Return to Capistrano." Before I joined up with the group, they even cut a few records with a Baltimore recording company. The bass man I replaced, a guy named June, wrote the songs.

Young as we were, audiences took us seriously because we were from Baltimore. The city had a reputation for good musicians and tough audiences that demanded the best.

John Coltrane was from Baltimore, after all. If you were a performer, you couldn't fool around like you could in front of an ignorant Philadelphia audience. You had to be at the top of your game when you played. If you were accepted in Baltimore at the three top nightclubs: the Comedy Club, the Avenue Bar, and the Zanzibar, you'd get recognition nationwide. Anyone who played an instrument came through there.

The Swallows were pretty good. Things worked out well in Roanoke, and I was accepted as a regular. The group's business manager was Irving Goldberg. A small man who wore black-rim glasses and a checkered coat, he owned a radio and TV repair shop, but he liked to tinker in show business. It was Goldberg who started the group four years before I joined. Goldberg started lining up gigs for us up and down the East Coast, and he arranged a car for us to drive. I loved playing music, but my first thought was to make money. I thought I could do better with The Swallows than scrambling after menial jobs.

Marjie had no problem with The Swallows, because at least I was working. Goldberg started by booking one-night stands, so I eased into the show business life. Or we'd get weekend gigs so the other guys could keep their day jobs. All of us were 16- to 20-year-old kids. Money Jackson was on guitar, Eddie Powell was on drums, and Randal Morris was our pianist. I had a voice, too, and did a lot of the singing: "Baby, It's Cold Outside." "Mona Lisa." Even be-bop tunes.

By doing weekend and one-night gigs, and janitor work at Martin, I managed to make enough money to support Marjie and our baby. When our little girl was born, we named her Marjorie. This little one did a lot to bring Pops back into my life. Once he saw his granddaughter, he softened up a bit.

Marjie's father was as proud as he could be, being Grandpa to such a beauty.

The time had come for The Swallows to spread their wings and take to the road. We quit our day jobs when Goldberg lined up a tour for us. We would be part of a revue going around the East, South, and Midwest, and between those dates we would be doing gigs on our own. Goldberg bought a brand-new car for us, a baby blue Hudson Hornet, which looked like an upside-down bathtub. But it could really move, with an inline six-cylinder engine, which was more powerful than a V-8. It was big enough for us and our instruments, except for my bass, which I had to tie on top. I would be the driver, because at 20, I was the oldest one in the group.

Before I left, I arranged to buy a house. The house was two bedrooms in the Cherry Hill section of Baltimore. It was a "fixer-upper," and I couldn't wait to get to work. Pops agreed to be co-signer for the property, which didn't involve him putting down any money. We were on pretty good terms, I thought. His grand-daughter made the difference. I didn't know then that he had different ideas about my going on the road.

We were out on the road from a week to three weeks at a time. Down to Miami, the Florida Keys, over to Mississippi, up through the Midwest. Another tour took us to Tulsa, Oklahoma, and back. Each trip was an adventure, and a chance to see new sights and people. It was springtime when we started, and the countryside looked beautiful.

But the traveling was tough. We'd play Pittsburgh, and the next stop would be Atlanta. I was driving down the Pennsylvania Turnpike, with the bass tied to the top of the car, and only hours before we had to get to Georgia. The wind kicked up and blew the bass off the roof. I saw it sail over the guardrail, and out of sight down a cliff. I couldn't pull over because the traffic was moving too fast. I just had a "There it goes!" feeling of helplessness. I knew that there'd be nothing left to pick up. The other guys sympathized, "Oh, man, look at that!"

In Atlanta, I had to buy a new bass first thing. It was there, on Peachtree Street, the main drag of downtown, where I really came face-to-face with the ugliness of racism. The town's segregation was bad enough—we'd eat at a restaurant, and even though it was a single building, it looked like a Siamese twin, with two doors, one for whites and one for "Coloreds"—and inside there were two counters, one for each race. Outside, we found that Atlanta's strict anti-jaywalking law gave the cops an excuse to humiliate black folk. The red light said, "Don't walk," but for some reason, Money Jackson, our guitarist, decided to cross the street. He went right past a cop, who turned and gave Money a kick in the behind. I was thinking that there was something wrong with Money if he couldn't see how things were, but I felt sorry for him when the cop kept kicking him, clear across the street to the other side.

I wanted to get out of town as soon as we finished our one-night stand so we wouldn't have any more problems with the police. The next stop was Jackson, Mississippi. We played in a barn in the middle of a cornfield. People came from far and wide to dance to The Swallows. That night was part of the touring review. We sang five numbers, and then the other acts went on. Ruth Brown, the singer, was on the bill, and so was LaVern Baker, who was popularly known as "Little Miss Sharecropper."

The bill would change often. In big cities, where we played mostly in civic centers, we'd be joined by the likes of B.B. King and Chuck Berry. Berry did the same songs (such as

"Maybellene") in the same style in 1951 as he would a few years later when he became one of the first rock-and-roll stars. But there was never any time to hang with the headliners. We would finish a gig at midnight, knowing we had to be on the road the next morning to travel to another one we had the next night. The life was difficult. People thought it was romantic, but it was really hard. I missed Marjie and the baby, so I'd write often, and telephone when I could.

It didn't help that Money Jackson just couldn't get it into his head how he was supposed to act in the Deep South. He almost got us killed. One night we pulled into a service station way out in the country. From the start, we made two big mistakes, and mine I attributed to needing to get to the next town as fast as we could to make a performance. First, we pulled into the station in a brand-new car, with Maryland plates to show we were Northerners (relative to Alabama, anyway), and then we failed to act subservient. Instead of being humble and sitting in the car so the old guy who ran the place could amble out and patronize us—"Hello, boys, what do y'all want?"— I hopped out, grabbed the nozzle of the gas pump hose, and started filling the Hudson myself.

There was a lot of role-playing back then, and if you didn't play your part right, you could get killed. Money didn't get it. He wanted a soda and just forgot all about the separation of races, how these back-yonder hillbillies wouldn't have a black person in their homes or stores. He just sauntered into the filling station office where the Coke cooler was, right in front of the grisly old proprietor in his greasy overalls, who just gaped at him in amazement. Money opened the cooler lid, pulled out a Coke, popped off the cap, and started drinking, *right there in the office.*

The man regained his wits and stood up. I watched from where I was filling the tank. My gut tensed when he reached up to the wall and pulled a shotgun down from its rack.

"Money!" I shouted. "Get outta there!"

At the door, Money came out, and complained, "Why? I ain't finished my damn soda!"

"He's got a gun!"

Behind him, the man came out with his shotgun, so angry that the words were sputtering out of his mouth. "I'm going to show you goddamn niggers, comin' here from up north, comin' in here like you own the place!"

I forgot about the gas hose, jumped in the car, and started it up. "Money, get in!"

He finally realized the danger. He dropped the soda bottle, which smashed to pieces, and ran to the car. I gunned the Hudson, pulling out. The nozzle of the gas hose jerked out of the tank and flopped around behind us on the ground. Gas was everywhere. The other guys shouted at Money to jump in as I drove off. He threw himself through the backdoor window, and he was still half out, his legs kicking in the air, when the gas station owner fired his shotgun. If the old guy had been a better shot, Money would have had his backside peppered with buckshot. But the charge went wild, hit a tree, and leaves and twigs rained down on us. I stepped on the gas and put those six cylinders to work. The powerful engine kicked in, and we rocketed into the night.

The other guys were hollering at Money, "Hey, man, you almost got us killed!"

I didn't stop until we got to our next date. CB radios were just coming in, and I was afraid the old guy had one and would call down the road.

There was a lot of responsibility being out on the road by yourself. We were entertainers and semifamous, but we were really just working-class boys. We toured eight months in 1950, traveling and putting on shows, and there was no time for romance. Girls hung around the bandstands, and they would holler and scream when we came on. It was flattering up to a point, but then we'd see how they'd go crazy and be just as loud for the next act that followed us.

We were a well-disciplined group, especially for three teenagers and a 20-year-old out on the road alone. It was a business, and we saw ourselves doing a job. We'd get to a hall, hook up our instruments, have a beer, and work until midnight or later. Then it was back to the hotel to get up early the next morning and move on to the next performance.

No one in the group drank or did drugs, contrary to the belief that all musicians had to be out there raising hell.

But it was an adventure, especially when the tour hit the big towns. We were asked to join *The Pearl Bailey Revue*, a tour that would take us to the biggest African-American venues on the East Coast. The Swallows played at the Earl Theater in Philadelphia, the Howard in Washington, the Royal in Baltimore (where my friends came to see us), and New York's Apollo Theater in Harlem. It was my first time back in my old neighborhood since my family had left eight years before. The familiar sights looked unchanged, including the legendary Apollo, and I was happy to be back in such an unexpected way. The great Pearl Bailey was the headliner, and at different times on the tour we were performing with the likes of Sam Cooke, Count Basie, and Johnny Ray. A young Aretha Franklin raised the roof with her gospel songs, and at another show we were with the popular Ruth Brown again.

The Swallows had to be good to hold our own in that company. I surprised a lot of people by showing how well I could handle the bass, and I was invited to play backup with the big acts. "You're pretty good, boy," Count Basie said, and they were fascinated by my being so young and playing such good bass. I was thrilled. It never went to my head, though, because the world beyond the stage door had a way of putting everything into perspective.

At some of the hotels where we played, the only way a black person was allowed in was if they were the entertainment. We found this in New Orleans, a very segregated city. The uptown area, which was black, was where the good music and the good food were. But Bourbon Street, which is a tourist attraction today, was just three seedy blocks of stripper bars in 1950. Blacks weren't allowed. The only way we were permitted to play at one of those bars was through special arrangement, and then we were told, "Don't look at the girls." We were told to play our numbers, get off stage, and disappear while the girls entertained the audience.

It was insulting, of course. How could you not look at the girls, especially when you're a teenager and they're stripping off their clothes? But we got through it because no one was paying much attention to us during the girls' acts.

We were learning how things worked out on the road. Our manager would send us telegrams with the names and locations of our next gig. We'd head down to the Florida Keys for some jobs, get on a boat, and for the first time in my life, I'd no longer be in the United States—I'd be performing in Cuba.

The club in Havana was a dive, and the hotel was a fleabag. But we got a little more consideration when I used my high school Spanish to "pass" as a Puerto Rican. My skin tone was lighter than the other guys in the band, and I had my wavy black hair slicked back. The act got us into a slightly better hotel. We always doubled up in rooms to save money, but we had our own beds.

I tried the Puerto Rican impersonation in Juarez, Mexico, and in Texas. I dressed in a white suit and mimicked a Puerto Rican accent from my memories of New York. It was a game, but beating the rules of segregation was a game, sometimes amusing but sometimes a necessity. My impersonation got us into slightly better hotels than the ones reserved for Negroes. The discrimination was less if I passed myself off as a Latino. It worked in Miami, too. I liked that town, which a half-century ago was undeveloped compared to today. You could drive down Main Street, the ocean off to one side, pull over, throw on some trunks, and dive in. I liked the white sands of Miami, as fine as salt. On the long drive over the new bridge to the Florida Keys, you could reach out the window and dip your hand into the water.

I would send money back to Marjie via telegram, or our manager Mr. Goldberg would send my pay to her. He was always fair, and he never cheated us.

When I would have a few days in Baltimore between legs of the tour, I would work on the Cherry Hill house. Pops had done some carpentry at his house, and I thought I had learned a little watching him. I saw him remove a wall from a stairwell once. He opened it up to make some interior space, and I wanted the same improvement for my rundown fixer-upper, so I started by knocking down the stairwell wall. I didn't finish the job before The Swallows went back on tour, though, and we were off on a long leg through the Midwest. I left a pile of rubble in the stairwell, expecting to get back to the job when I returned.

Pops was against my leaving Marjie and my baby and going on the road. He didn't consider a musician's life a suitable line of work. When Marjie and I got the good news that we were going to have another child, my father decided he was going to bring me home. He found a way to do it with the Cherry Hill house.

Pops hadn't put any money into the place, but as co-signer I suppose he felt a sense of ownership. He went in the house one day and saw the mess in the stairwell. I never told him what I was up to, but he could see from his own house what I was doing. With Pops, there was no holding back when he wanted to teach me a lesson. He went straight to the police and took out a warrant against me for malicious destruction of property.

He didn't really want me to get into deep trouble, but it was his way of making a point: Any type of hell might break loose, and where was I? In Texas? Cuba? Harlem? Anyplace but where I should be, in his view, which was home with my family.

Also, he had seen that month's *Jet* magazine. I had seen it, too, and I knew everybody back home had seen the item about my being romantically linked to a beautiful torch singer named Johnny B.

In the popular magazine's entertainment gossip column, readers were treated to this: *"Rumor has it that Johnny B has a thing with Herman of The Swallows."*

"Oh, man," I groaned when I read that. "My goose is cooked."

I knew what the reaction would be from my boys, and everyone else who'd be titillated in Baltimore: "Ooh, la-la!"

I worried about Marjie. What would she think when she saw it? It seemed that I'd been away from her about half of our married life. Everyone "knew" what wild lives musicians led, especially on the road. People didn't have a clue what a hard grind it really was, all the traveling that meant zero opportunity to socialize with the likes of Johnny B or anyone else. I *had* met Johnny B on tour, and we had performed on the same bill, but we weren't even acquaintances. It must have been a slow news week over at *Jet*.

When one of Pops's friends showed him the magazine, he hit the roof. But his extreme reaction, taking out a warrant for my arrest, almost backfired on him. Marjie got served with a summons, and she appeared on my behalf at the court hearing. The judge took one look at pregnant Marjie, saw that I was co-owner of the house I was supposed to be maliciously wrecking, and he gave Pops hell. The judge told him he was wrong to do that to his son, and he threw out the complaint.

I got a telegram from Marjie: "YOU MUST COME HOME OR NO HOME TO COME BACK TO."

I saw the message as a reference not just to a house but to our marriage. I didn't hesitate. I told the other guys I had to go. At the time, we were in Green Bay, Wisconsin.

"There's trouble at home. I've got to go back."

They were upset that I was leaving them shorthanded. "You can't do that, man! You can't just leave."

But for me it was simple. "My family needs me."

I hopped on a train, and in a couple of days I was back in Baltimore to find that the Cherry Hill house had been closed up. Marjie and the baby were with our friend Thomas Nimons. I never went back to the Cherry Hill house after that. I was too angry, and what little money I had put into it I wrote off as a loss.

We moved into public housing, to the Gilmore Projects that had been my family's home eight years before. As far as

I was concerned, Pops did what he did just to be mean, but a part of me must have been ready to retire from touring with The Swallows, because when I put down my instrument, it was years before I played that bass again. With all the running around we did on tour—enough to tire out even four young guys—and for the small amount of money we made, it was a waste of time. The adventure was there, and meeting those talented people was exciting, but Pops was right: I had a growing family that needed me to be with them. In the end, The Swallows got to be just a job for me, and I wanted a *better* job.

The trouble was, Pops didn't know when to leave well enough alone. I was back in Baltimore, home for good, but if he failed to get me into jail over the Cherry Hill house, he saw his chance when I got into a traffic accident.

I had bought a car, my first real one. Near Johns Hopkins Hospital on Broadway, I got a ticket for going through a red light, according to the cop who arrested me, which resulted in a fender bender with another car. I thought that there was some question about whether I ran the light and caused the accident, so instead of paying a fine, I chose to stand trial. Down we went to the courthouse. The judge agreed with the policeman, and he fined me $30. That was a lot of money in 1951, and I didn't have it. The misdemeanor was $30 or 30 days. They were going to haul me off to jail if I didn't pay.

I phoned my father at three in the afternoon. There was a long pause on the line, and then he said he'd come over. I was put in a holding cell, and the hours went by. Pops never came. I had this bad feeling that he was up to one of his old tricks. At six o'clock, I knew he wasn't coming. It was time for the lockup, and my fine hadn't been paid. The van for the convicts came, and I went off with the other prisoners to city jail.

When we were processed at the jail, they made me take off all my clothes, and they put me through an inspection. I was sprayed with disinfectant, the standard but humiliating procedure to make sure a prisoner was deloused.

I got into a fight the moment I got there. We were waiting for our cell assignments, and here I was a young 21-year-old surrounded by these older guys. My boys said if I ever got into jail I had to establish my manhood immediately.

The prisoners were shouting at me, "Hey, pretty boy!" It was a scene right out of a prison movie. This one guy said in so many words that he "wanted" me. He offered me soap, which I couldn't understand, and then he offered me candy, and I got the message. I laid into him. I knew I had to whup him. I didn't know if I would be staying a month in that place, so I had to stand up for myself.

Pops showed up late that night, after I had been locked in a cell. I was happy to get out of there, but I was angry because he had let things go too far. Parents always lectured their kids, "If you ever get yourself into trouble and land in jail, your butt's going to stay there so you learn your lesson." All parents said that, knowing full well they weren't going to let you stay. But not my father.

Just like he did with the Cherry Hill house, when he thought he'd found a way to bring me home, he'd gone too far again. I would forgive him because family ties weren't something to cut in those days, and we really did need each other. But I wouldn't forget. I also couldn't understand what "lesson" I was being taught by being made to go to jail. Not to get involved in traffic accidents? Not to challenge a traffic ticket? I was never clear about that.

But I had other things to worry about. I had to get a job. Good jobs were still almost impossible to find for a black man in Baltimore. The color barrier was everywhere, and it didn't matter that it was invisible—you couldn't get through it if you were African American.

In desperation, I even looked to the Korean War for a way out.

❧ CHAPTER THREE ☙

A Streetcar Named Bigotry

The Urban League of Baltimore was determined to bring down the color barrier that blocked African Americans from so many jobs. Entire professions and lines of work in the private and public sector were closed off to us. The National Association for the Advancement of Colored People (NAACP) was fighting discrimination in the courts. The Urban League, run by Thurman Templeton, was involved in the employment area, making jobs available not just for blacks, but for all minorities.

After World War II, there was a need to make the United States, which fought for democracy and was battling communism in the Cold War, more democratic at home. The Harlem riots showed that African Americans weren't content to live second-class lives forever.

In Baltimore, the Urban League broke open the taxi industry, and for the first time, black taxi drivers were seen on the
streets. At the time, African Americans with college degrees were
rare, and those who did finish college had a hard time finding
decent jobs. Either you were really accomplished, like a doctor or lawyer, or you were a laborer. There was nothing in
between. Baltimore was so choked by discrimination that a black
person couldn't get a job as a trash collector. That was a white
man's job. However, the Urban League was opening up opportunities that filled the gap between the learned professions and
the menial jobs.

All this activity meant that there were more work opportunities for people of color. And it came at a time when I was
scrambling for any work I could get.

At the army recruiting office, my application for service was
rejected. I was a strapping 21-year-old, and they needed men
for Korea, but I was married, with two kids. They told me that
I was ineligible unless Marjie and I were separated.

I was so desperate for a job that I even discussed the possibility of a temporary separation with Marjie so I could get into
the army. She gave me a look that showed that she understood
why I felt the need to propose such an extreme ruse, but in that
same look, she also seemed to be asking if I had lost my mind.
That ended that.

I saw an ad in the newspaper for a paper cutter at the
Howard Luggage Company. I went in to apply for the job, and
before I was through, I talked them into making me a leather
cutter. I could talk Lincoln off a penny, and they listened when
I spun a story that I was from Cuba. I thought because the trick
had worked before when I was with The Swallows, I might
try it again, so I spoke a little Spanish and passed myself off

as Cuban just to improve my chances of getting a job. It was like a game.

African Americans at Howard Luggage all worked as janitors, nothing technical. When I was put on the job as a leather cutter, I looked at what the other cutters were doing, and thought, *Hell, I can do this, too.* I got down to work, stretching pieces of leather over a table, and cutting out jigsaw patterns with an electric cutter. The pieces would go into a bin to be taken to the assembly line. The owner of the company noticed me. He was impressed by my work and asked my name. "Herman Williams, señor," I told him.

I was a thrifty person and always managed to save money. If I made 50 cents, I'd save a quarter. At Howard, I was getting 85 cents an hour, which was good money. All the other cutters were white, because it was a "white man's job," but we got along fine, because they didn't think I was "Colored." They asked me about San Juan, Cuba, the home I made up for myself. I had all the answers because I'd been to Cuba with the band.

It was a good thing that I saved what I could of my wages, because one day my boss got to talking about me with my Uncle George.

By the early '50s, Uncle George's list of customers who depended on his TV-fixing skills was extensive. One of his customers happened to be the owner of the Howard Luggage Company. He had Uncle George over to his house to fix his TV, and they started talking. My boss told him about this bright young worker he had. "He's Colored, but he's not."

"What's his name?" my uncle asked, just to keep up the conversation while he had his head inside the TV cabinet.

"Herman."

"Herman what?"

"Herman Williams," my boss told him.

Uncle George pulled his head out of the TV. "Herman Williams?! He ain't no damned Cuban. He's my nephew!"

I was fired the next day.

I went to my uncle, we had a beer, and we laughed about it, because I'd gotten away with something. I wasn't mad. I didn't expect the job to last forever, and because of discrimination, having that job for one day was one day longer than I was supposed to have it. I was young, and my whole life was ahead of me; and one boring, menial job was the same as another as far as I was concerned. If I had to pull some tricks to make things better, I would.

But my responsibilities were increasing. When Marjie's and my second daughter was born, we named her Clolita. Our families were delighted, and even Pops seemed to soften up a little toward me. By this time, my sisters were getting married, and Pops had a growing number of grandchildren. But all their children would be girls, and only mine would carry on the name Williams, if Marjie and I had a son.

I wanted a job that would last more than a few months. This desire happened to correspond with the Urban League's success at finally breaking the color line in public transportation in Baltimore. They arranged an historic agreement with the city to allow African Americans to drive buses and operate streetcars. This was a real breakthrough, because it meant that other city services would be desegregated eventually now that a precedent had been set. As for the black community, you wouldn't think that driving a streetcar was a prestige job, but the first African-American operators caused a sensation. Black people were happy to see black men at the helm of their public transport—and one of the uniformed drivers they would see would be me.

David Glenn over at the Urban League put out word that African-American men were encouraged to apply for the new public transport operator jobs. Notices went up around town, but at first there wasn't a lot of interest because no black had ever done this before. With no role models to follow, the only thing I knew about streetcars was how to jump on the back to get a free ride for a block back when I was a kid. I found out about the new opportunity when I saw a friend of mine in what we called a Trackless Trolley. This was an electric bus, but it had no engine. It was connected by an overhead rod to the same power lines used by the streetcars.

My friend David was sitting in the operator's seat, and I was so impressed when I saw him there that I ran out to the middle of the street and jogged alongside his window.

"You stole a trolley! Where are you taking that thing? What did you do with the driver?"

He grinned, "Oh, man, I *am* the driver! This is my first week."

"I want to do that!" I hollered, running beside him.

"Call Mr. Templeton at the Urban League. He'll set something up."

He clanged the bell, and off he went. So did I, to see this Templeton. Because I had a high school education, and was healthy, eager, and young, I fit the profile of the type of black man they wanted, and I was accepted. What followed was a 30-day training period. The guy who taught me was so light-skinned that I didn't know at first that he was black. Then he told me that when he was hired, they wouldn't let him drive a streetcar, which would mean interacting with the public, so they made him an instructor. In later years, he would become a manager on the line.

There was no practice area where we learned to handle one of the long streetcars that might have 80 people inside, including the standing passengers, so I trained right on the street. The job wasn't dangerous, but I was told that not everyone was cut out to do it. I found out why: There was a lot of stress involved. In addition to driving, you sold tickets, made change, collected money, punched transfers, watched the doors as passengers entered and left, and concentrated on traffic. Operating ten tons of moving machinery wasn't easy, and cars cut in front of you all the time, so you had to learn to brake this monster without throwing everyone to the floor.

My instructor taught defensive driving. He taught us how to anticipate accidents happening, and to be cautious. Particularly in residential neighborhoods, kids might be playing on the sidewalk, and they could run out between parked cars. You can't stop a streetcar quickly like you can a bus, so it took a long length of track.

At the end of the one-month training period, I was sent out on my own. I sat down on the operator's stool that was at the front of the streetcar, with no separation from the passengers, and prepared to meet the public. My uniform was a gray shirt and trousers, a straight black tie, black shoes, a gray cap with a black brim, and a badge that said **Baltimore Transit Company.** I was 21 years old, still young, and when the passengers started getting on, for the first time they were receiving their change from the hand of a black man. Some of them had never had physical contact with a black person before.

The stares I got ranged from surprise, distrust, or simple curiosity from white people—and generally the same reactions from black people. However, I think the distrust from black people had to do with the fact that I looked so young.

The working ladies on their way to maids' jobs in white neighborhoods said how cute I looked in my uniform, as if they were complimenting a schoolboy. Some of the other black passengers nodded their head at me to quietly show that my position was a source of pride for all of us.

My family was happy that I had a job that was steady, had a future, and paid well. They were also proud that I was a pioneer. But my mother cautioned me, "Never be so proud about being the first and only." It was her way of telling me not to get bigheaded.

If I ever was so foolish as to get conceited about my job, the old racist proclivities of Baltimore were there to slap me back down with a dose of reality.

Black streetcar operators and bus drivers did not go down well with a section of the public. Allowing us to operate public transport undermined the bigots' basic assumptions about black people—that we were too irresponsible to be in charge of big machines and people's safety. And how could a person from an allegedly lazy race keep to a schedule? How could we shift the gears of a bus when we were so, well, shiftless?

All these notions about African Americans were ridiculous, of course, and the bigots who held them probably knew it. But there was something else at stake, and that was the retention of privileges and the domination by whites of some jobs. When my black colleagues and I threw the throttles open on our streetcars, that was one less privilege to be had for white men.

This caused some dangerous resentment, as I found out the hard way.

I was on the 32 Line, going downtown. I steered the streetcar onto Linden Avenue, a white section close to the heart of downtown. I was approaching Lafayette Avenue, but before I got there, a guy attacked the car. Through all the usual "busy-ness" of operating a streetcar, I still noticed the guy sitting on the stoop of a townhouse a little ways ahead. What caught my eye was the concrete block on the stoop beside him.

He must have been sitting there for some time, until along came what he wanted, a streetcar driven by a black operator. I don't know how long he'd been waiting, because out of hundreds of drivers, there were maybe a dozen black operators.

It was a blue-collar neighborhood, and I knew that red-necks lived there, but I was still surprised when a cement block came flying toward the front of the car. Luckily, it smashed into the metal divider between the two front windows, dented it, and cracked the glass on either side. If it had been a little to one side, the block might have gone through the window and injured some passengers; a little to the other side and it might have hit me. That's what the guy wanted, to crack my head open.

The passengers screamed—some people thought I had hit something. I dropped the emergency brake, and by the time the car had stopped, the guy who threw the block was gone. I got out and looked at the damage. I saw the block, picked it up, and put it on the curb—there was nothing else I could do. I got back on the car, and you could cut the tension with a knife. Everyone knew that the attack had been aimed at me, but they had also been at risk.

All streetcar operators were also trained as bus drivers, and we were assigned to those routes as well. In the '50s, the street-cars had a streamlined look, rounded in front, and were heated by electric coils. The buses had air-conditioning, and I preferred driving them. I was a young guy, and I thought streetcars were for the old guys, out of style.

But on both vehicles, dealing with the public was a problem. For any operator, being your own bank (I wore a change machine on my belt so passengers would have the right amount to put in the coin box), punching transfers, and answering questions about routes made things hectic. But the white drivers didn't have to contend with situations such as the one involving those three white women at the bus stop at Park Heights Avenue and Ford's Lane one day. It was a suburban area, and when I opened the door to let them in, they looked at me as if I were an escaped convict. When they recovered, they waved my bus away. "That's all right. We're not riding with you."

I said, "You might as well get on, because the next two drivers are Negro, too."

But they refused. I closed the door and drove away. All I could do was shake my head and try to smile the insult away. I believed that being in good humor was part of the job, and the passengers deserved a cheerful driver instead of some grouch. But it could be hard keeping up the appearance.

I got into the rhythm of the job, the pace of the city's tracks and roads. Streetcars had their place in the middle of the street, where the track was laid beneath an electric line. They were efficient, and saved time if you had to get around the city. The law said that a car couldn't pass a streetcar if it was moving, and when more people started buying cars, congestion resulted. That was when the city started phasing out the streetcar line, only to have a change of heart in the '80s with a light rail line.

Sometimes a streetcar might jump the track at an intersection where the tracks forked off. This never happened to me, but two poles, front and back, which connected the car to the power lines, would come off sometimes. A rope hung from the poles to help the operator reconnect to the lines. Kids would pull the rope and cut off the power. It happened quiet often. I'd jump out, holler, pretend to chase them, and reconnect. You never went far from your streetcar—the passengers were there, as well as the fare money. The big responsibility was the "bank." I would be sent out with a certain amount of money after signing for it, and I had to come back with that exact amount, in addition to the fares in the coin box.

The streetcars had no speed limit. You didn't drive fast because you had to stop at every corner, but you could make 30 to 40 miles an hour on open track. In suburban areas, you could move along at 35 miles an hour, but the car would wobble and shake like an old ox pushed faster than it wanted to go.

When I began work in the fall of 1952, the operators were reminded to be careful about fallen leaves on the tracks. Wet leaves were like ice, they said, but I didn't believe it, so I decided to test it. I was on the 32 Line, which originated at the Belvedere Loop, a turnaround station where you drove your car around a circular track and ended up facing the street again. Number 32 was a main line from downtown, through open track to Woodlawn. Going to any destination and back was called a "run."

One time after the morning rush, I found myself on an open line headed for Woodlawn, without any passengers—just a lot of empty seats and the ads above the windows for Ipana toothpaste, Stopette Deodorant, and Wrigley's gum. It was a suburban area, where you could go faster, and leaves were everywhere. I got up some speed and decided to put on the dead-man (emergency) brake. While operating the streetcar, you had to keep your left hand on it all the time. If you removed your hand, the loss of pressure activated the brake. It got its name because in case the operator dropped dead, the car wouldn't run away.

They were right about those leaves! That damn streetcar slid for a half a mile. The funny part about it was that when the car finally came to a stop, there was a flat spot worn on all the wheels where they pressed against the rail when they locked up. When I started the car again, I had to listen to this clank, clank, clank! I reported the incident, like you had to do whenever you used the emergency brake, and made up some excuse. But I had a new respect for leaves.

Respect was something some of my passengers refused to give me, sometimes choosing another car over mine, but generally, I had good riders. There was an occasional drunk, even though drinking wasn't allowed on streetcars or buses. If the drunks bothered the passengers, they had to go.

With so much happening while you were operating a streetcar, the job was nerve-wracking, but it paid well. It was an hourly rate, so the more runs I took, the more pay I'd bring home. Home for Marjie and me and the girls was now a two-bedroom townhouse in Cherry Hill.

I'd grab every chance to make more money. The other drivers had a name for me: "Hoggy Williams." But the schedule made it dumb not to take additional runs. In the morning, I was assigned to 19 Line, the Belvedere Loop, all the way through the city to a section of the county called Parkville. I'd leave at 7 A.M., and be back by noon or one. Then I had free time, a layover, until 3 P.M. I no longer owned a car, and if I took a bus home to Cherry Hill, on the extreme end of town south of the city, by the time I got there I'd have to turn around and come back. Streetcars were constantly going in and out of the terminal at ten-minute intervals to serve Baltimore's 40 Line, so I'd take one of them to fill my layover.

Marjie stopped working at Martin Aircraft when the girls were born. She now had a job behind the counter at a soda fountain, making sandwiches at Read's Drugstore on the corner of Garrison Boulevard and Park Heights Avenue. It was a major intersection, and she and I would coordinate it so that at lunchtime I'd drive by in a streetcar. Marjie would always be ready. She had a sandwich made for me, in a paper bag with a soda. On cold days, there would be soup in there. Those sandwiches she made were humongous. She got on the car, handed me the bag, and gave me a big kiss. The passengers would smile, "Oh, isn't that sweet"—the streetcar driver and his pretty, young wife!

In 1953, the year my first son was born, all that driving earned me $5,500, at a time when the average working person's salary was $2,500. Despite the taunting I took and the troubles I had on the job, I was happy to have the income when Marjie became pregnant in the spring. In December, Herman Williams III was born. He was light in complexion like me, healthy and strong. I was proud to give him the name my father and I shared.

I was paid by check, which I deposited into my account at the Equitable Trust Company in Cherry Hill, and when I had enough, I bought a car. I had life insurance, but no health plan in those days. The car was a 1952 yellow Chevrolet convertible, a real beauty, and typical for the cars of that time—as big as a boat.

I worked to get the Cherry Hill house in shape for my growing family. The neighborhood was African American, middle class, although some parts of the area were poorer. It wasn't a bad neighborhood at all—in fact, we could leave the house with the doors unlocked. Our next-door neighbor was a dentist, Dr. McDonald. Two doors down lived a couple of teachers. Our two-bedroom house had a yard, and Uncle George sold us a Muntz TV, with a round picture tube like a ship's portal. We'd look inside and there'd be Lucy, or Ike getting sworn in after the first election when I was old enough to vote.

I got to know the tricks of the operator's job. I could even spot the T-men when they got on. T-men were safety inspectors—"spies," we drivers called them. Operators had to follow the schedule and be at a certain corner at a designated time. It worked a little differently than you might expect. If you were late to a stop, it was no problem. But if you were there early, the T-men would write you up in the report for having committed an offense. They thought that by going fast, you were passing up passengers. The T-men were particularly strict about uniforms. I got written up one time because my shirt wasn't gray enough. I brought it from home, but it wasn't the right shade.

On Line 13 in the afternoon, I'd get to Forest Park High School just as classes were letting out. There's nothing noisier than a streetcar full of kids. It didn't matter that they were white and Jewish—all kids loved to give the streetcar operators a hard time. They'd holler outside, scream at each other, reach through the rear window, and pull the pole down. It was fun to make the operator get out of his chair and go outside—especially if it was raining.

When we were kids in the projects, my friends and I would disconnect the back pole when a streetcar was going uphill. We thought it was hilarious when it would stop, stuck in the middle of hill without power. As kids, we would hop on the back of a streetcar and ride on the little ledge there. But as an operator, I saw how dangerous that was.

If I had remained with the Baltimore Transit Company, chances are that I would have risen to management, but I knew I wouldn't last on the operator's job. On the surface, I was a happy guy. I got to know my regular riders by name and face, and I always greeted them with a smile and an upbeat "Good morning!" But I hated the job. It was murder on the nerves. I never had an accident, but there seemed to be too many opportunities for those that weren't my fault, and I had to wonder what was behind them.

One day, a guy driving behind the streetcar passed me on the left side, the oncoming traffic side, which was not only illegal, but unheard of. He drove up a little way and stopped his car on the track only 50 feet in front of me. I didn't know if he was pulling a trick to intimidate me because I was a black operator. All I saw was that we were going to hit, and if I remained sitting on that stool, I was going to fly right out the front window.

I released the dead-man brake, got up, and sat down beside a passenger. The wheels were locked, screeching along the tracks. The passengers all looked at me. "What are you doing?"

"We're going to hit that car, and there's nothing I can do about it."

With the emergency brake on, the streetcar tried to stop, but we were coasting down the track straight toward the car. At the last minute, the guy must have seen this big trolley bearing down on him. He stepped on the gas and drove away. I got back in my seat and took control of the streetcar, but I realized how close we had all been to getting hurt. With no seat belts, we would have been thrown around upon impact.

About this time, I started drinking, not heavily, but more than I should have. I would never be drunk in front of the family, but I drank to relieve tension, which was a bad sign. I had firmly resolved to never take my problems from work back home with me, so I didn't talk things over with Marjie. Instead, I did what a lot of frustrated men of my generation did—I stopped by a corner tavern for a few drinks at the end of my shift.

One day in winter, I was operating the streetcar on the 32 Line. It was morning, and I was headed out toward the white suburbs. Most of the passengers were black women who were domestic servants and day workers going to their jobs. There was one white man I noticed, because he had been drinking, and even though it was cold outside, he opened a window so he could sit with his arm on the ledge, elbow outside.

The lady sitting next to him asked if he could put down the window. Cold air was coming in and freezing people. He wouldn't do it. At the next stop, the woman came forward to report him to me. I went back. "Sir, you have to put the window down; people are complaining." He didn't look at me when I spoke, and I returned to my seat to get the car to the next stop on schedule. The woman came forward again with the same complaint, and I went back a second time. "Sir," I said, "people are cold." He just sat for a moment, and then he said, "Beat it, nigger."

The streetcar's window operated manually, by cranking. I reached over and cranked it down to the top of his arm. Not all the way down, and not touching him. If he wanted a frozen elbow, that was his business. He didn't say a word, and I drove on to Gwen Oak Junction.

The guy stood up and headed toward the front of the car like he was going to get off. I stopped, opened the doors, and he turned to me. He spat in my face. I got hit with a mouthful of saved-up saliva. Then he ran out.

I set the brake and left the car right on the corner. I chased him down Gwen Oak Boulevard. I was going to catch him, and part of me wanted to tear him to pieces. I was young, and big, and if I'd caught him, I would have shaken the hell out of him. He had a good start on me, and as I was running, I came to my senses. If I was to do anything to him, even shake him a little, I would be fired.

I wiped my face and went back to the streetcar. There was still a load of passengers. They had watched the chase, because everyone wanted to see what was going to happen. The ladies shook their heads. "Oh, that's a shame," they said. "Sorry."

I started up the streetcar and resumed the run, thinking that it couldn't get any worse than this, but I was wrong. Racism knows no shame. There would be one final bad incident that would convince me that I had to get out of streetcar driving, but by that time, I had somewhere else to go. It was a place I never would have imagined going before: the Baltimore Fire Department. When that step was taken, it would be the culmination of years of effort by generations of lawyers, civil rights leaders, and activists. The combined work of the NAACP, the Urban League, and progressive white politicians led to the breakdown of one of the most stubborn color lines in the city, the all-white fire department.

From its founding in 1859, the Baltimore Fire Department had never seen a black firefighter. The department was predominately Irish, and jobs were secured through family connections. To show how racist the department was, when I arrived in Baltimore in 1943, the firemen had a tradition of blackening their faces and staging minstrel shows for their charity ball.

The fight for black firefighters had already been going on more than 20 years when I was driving a streetcar. The Baltimore Urban League began the struggle in 1930, and 14 years later, an African American named Trust Brown passed the civil service examination required to enter the department.

He was followed by 13 other black men, who also passed the civil service exam by 1947. The Board of Fire Commissioners (the Fire Board) didn't approve the hiring of any of them.

The firefighters' union opposed African Americans on the grounds of segregation. Firefighters lived together in station houses, and the union's all-white membership wouldn't tolerate sharing living space with blacks.

But by 1952, three factors pushed the goal of African-American firefighters toward fruition. The first was politics. When my family arrived in the city, Baltimore was seeing the largest gain in nonwhite population of any major city in the United States. Blacks were still in the minority, but between 1940 and 1950, the number of nonwhites grew by nearly 100,000 to 266,053, while only 31,000 new white people raised the number of white residents to 724,000.

The mayor at that time, Tommy D'Alesandro, wanted to court the black vote for his 1951 reelection, and he made civil rights one of his campaign issues.

The second factor that hastened the acceptance of African-American firefighters was an increase in the number of firemen who were needed to run the force. In 1952, the city was warned by insurance underwriters that unless the number of firefighters increased, fire insurance rates would skyrocket or be canceled. The business community was understandably upset by this, so 200 firefighters were required immediately.

Part of the problem was that four out of five (white) men who took the civil service entrance exam to be firefighters failed. Instead of opening the process to qualified and educated African Americans, the firefighters' union tried to lower the test standards. As it was, the department accepted guys with only a sixth-grade education.

Third, the firemen already working were demanding shorter hours. They were putting in 67 $1/2$ hours a week. Their union wanted this reduced to 48 hours.

David Glenn at the Urban League, who helped open the streetcar jobs, put out notices that black men interested in becoming firefighters should prepare to take the civil service exams. I was among the 30 or so guys who went downtown to the Civil Service Commission on North Calvert Street. I got out of a streetcar run to take the test.

A few weeks later, each of us received a letter from the commission. The message for all of us was the same: Every one of us had failed. But that assessment was an insult to our intelligence. The exam had been so simple that it was impossible for all of us, or *any* of us, really, to fail.

The story made the newspapers, and the reports hinted that something fishy was going on. As a result, we were all called back to take the test again. This time, we all passed. That was in the fall of 1953, but we weren't admitted into the department.

The Urban League sent the newspapers three reasons why the fire department should be integrated: "(1) More men will be available to make our city safe at a time of manpower shortages; (2) the city would be able to avoid penalties from the National Association of Fire Insurance Underwriters; and (3) the 95-year practice of excluding Negro men from the Fire department will end."

The Baltimore Fire Officers Association submitted their own statement at a meeting of the city Fire Board, which ran the department and agreed with the association: "Resolved, that because of the manner in which the working conditions and hours of employment of the department are at present conducted, it is deemed inadvisable that members of the colored race be appointed to the Fire Department of Baltimore City at this time."

This had been the same response to the notion of hiring black firefighters in the 20 years since it was first raised: Now was not the time to continue this stance.

The NAACP threatened to sue the Fire Board, Mayor D'Alesandro threatened to fire the Fire Board, and in May, an African American scored first place in the latest round of civil service examinations. It seemed impossible that an African American would not soon join the force. But what type of force? In the newspapers, there was debate that the department might be run in a segregated fashion, with white firehouses and black firehouses. Everyone knew that segregation meant "separate and unequal." How could a vital public service such as fire fighting be implemented unequally?

Meanwhile, a family tragedy struck to remind me how much I wanted to get off the streetcar line: My mother died. She was young when she left us, only 43, but she had stomach cancer. In a short time, her black hair turned completely white. She was ailing, and we knew that she didn't have long to live. A tumor grew, and even though she put on a little weight at the end, which indicated that she might be recovering, she died at home.

I was operating a streetcar that day. The supervisor drove out in his car and stopped me en route. I will never forget where I was, at Liberty Heights and Garrison Boulevard, or how the intersection looked. There was a store on one corner, a firehouse on another corner, and a church opposite. It was a summer's day in August.

The supervisor got on the car and said in a flat voice, "I got a call at the office that you should go home."

"Did something happen?"

"Your mother died."

That's how I learned about it, from this man who showed by his tone of voice that he resented having to come down and look after a streetcar until another operator arrived. He was one of those people who looked at me and only saw a nigger. There was nothing in his heart to allow compassion for my loss.

I was struck hard by the news, but I was also angered by that man's attitude. I left immediately and went to my parents' house. My anger was such that when I arrived, and someone said something to upset me, I put my fist through the front-door window. Maybe it was my father or someone who asked what took me so long to get home, or maybe they said it was too bad I wasn't with my mother when she died. I felt guilty about that.

I was also despondent because I had taken the test to join the fire department, and if I did succeed, my mother would never see that I was making something of myself. In those days, a guy going into the fire department was a big deal. Now she wouldn't share in that. And that damned callous supervisor, like so many of the people I had to deal with . . . I punched the door window right out and cut an artery. I would carry the scar for the rest of my life.

My mother was a beautiful, fair-skinned woman. She shared the secret of my drinking Pops's beer, the driving lessons and the car I bought in high school, the movie job, and other things I had to keep from my father. Telling her made me feel less guilty.

Now I was a man, and I had a wife to tell things to, but I would miss Mom very much.

THE PUSH TO ADMIT AFRICAN AMERICANS into the fire department became too great for the union and the Fire Board to resist, and they finally had to concede to the inevitable. In October 1953, the first ten black guys who passed the civil service exam were chosen to enter the department's training program. I was selected to be in the third class, so I quit the Baltimore Transit Company. My income would be slashed by more than a third, from $5,500 to $3,500. That was a big pay cut, but there was compensation: the idea of being part of a pioneering effort, and proving the worth of my race to skeptics.

But being admitted to the fire department didn't mean that blacks were accepted. In many ways, the fight to prove our value and dignity hadn't even begun.

❧ CHAPTER FOUR ☙

Firefighter
(Engine Company 35)

"**H**ey, Jim?" a white firefighter shouted to another guy the minute I walked through the firehouse door.

"Yeah?" came the reply in a tone that was anticipating a good joke.

"You know that fire last week at Cherry Hill? You know that nigger we found hanging by his toes?"

"Yeah?" The other guy could barely control his laughter.

"It was a good thing we got there in time, or that fool nigger would've fallen on his black ass and broke his head!"

Everyone at the all-white firehouse had a good laugh at that. I thought, *What a bunch of damn hillbillies.*

Except it wasn't an all-white firehouse anymore. February 8, 1954, was my first day with the Baltimore Fire Department, and I was reporting for duty.

The only thing I was certain about was that there were no guarantees. I didn't know how long I would last, but I was determined to see it through. Thirty days of training would fill Mondays through Fridays. On Saturdays, the recruits reported to the firehouses where we would be stationed at the end of training. I was assigned to Engine Company 35.

Recruits would later be taught at a special Fire Academy facility, but for us, training was carried out at Engine Company 36 on Edmonton Avenue in northwest Baltimore. There was a hose tower for rope training and rappelling off the roof. We used it for a fitness exercise, when we were told to run up its four stories hauling the hose over one shoulder. Studies were divided between classroom instruction, exercises, and practical hands-on simulations, called evolutions. In these sessions, we practiced putting out fires, raising ladders, and extending hose. We were taught the basics, such as first aid, and how to loop a hose under one arm.

We raised a ladder with the standard two-man team, one to butt the ladder, putting his foot down to anchor it, the other to lift it up. But that drill taught us the object of most of the training: teamwork. We saw that we'd need to rely on each other. Lives would be saved or lost depending on how we responded. That was why discipline was so important in the fire department, we were told, and why it was a semimilitary organization. You had to obey orders.

There was no other profession where a worker would find himself in front of a building engulfed in flames, where his boss would tell him, "Get inside!"—and he'd run to do it.

Right from the start, there was tension between the 20 or so white recruits and the 10 African-American recruits. Just about every white guy who came into the fire department had a relative who was already a firefighter: a cousin, uncle, brother, or father. It was a family business. If you got in, you took care of your own. The white recruits were being coached by their relatives. They were given tips on training, and the resentment toward the new black firefighters held by the established firefighters rubbed off on them.

All firefighters needed to wear the regulation protective clothing, called turnout gear, which you quickly put on when the station bell clanged and you "turned out" at the fire truck, prepared to go. This consisted of the heavy trousers, boots, big jacket, and helmet with the familiar wide brim that extended far out in back to deflect embers away from the neck. The white recruits were given used turnout gear by white firefighters from the station houses. Or their relatives would lend them money to buy new gear. The black recruits were shown no such consideration. We showed up in dungarees, galoshes, and whatever heavy jacket we could find. We looked motley, unprofessional, and the white guys snickered at us.

The captain, battalion chief, and two lieutenants who ran the training were neutral rather than hostile toward the black recruits, at least to our faces. I liked the captain, John O'Malley. He was fair, and he encouraged us. He taught the evolutions, the "how-tos" of fire fighting. He was also in charge of calisthenics. In the yard, in the February cold, he'd have us do jumping jacks and push-ups for a half hour, and he'd do them right along with us. When we were finished, and panting for air, he'd get down and impress us by doing a one-arm push-up.

O'Malley was mild-mannered, while I was a show-off. Because I still had money saved from my streetcar job, I bought turnout clothes the second week. Some of the white guys still didn't have their gear, and they resented me because when we were given hose training, we got wet, especially when the hose got away. We'd wrestle with it as it snaked around like a wild animal, spraying everything. There I was, all dry, and the other guys were soaked.

One white guy, a bully type, decided from the start that he was going to take me on. He turned a hose line on me, and I didn't like that. With enough water pressure coming out, a line of water could really hurt you. The water might have knocked me down if I hadn't been alert. We got into it right there, and fists were flying. The other guys separated us because we could have both been suspended and lost our jobs. There was some name-calling, but no racial slurs. Nobody wanted to cross that line.

I also stood out by driving to training every day in my yellow Chevrolet convertible, bright with chrome and long as a boat. When I'd leave, a half-dozen African-American guys would pile in, and we'd go to a bar, but I guess the white guys didn't like to see us having a good time, because one afternoon, when training was over and I sat in the car waiting for the other guys to join me, I smelled something. At first I shrugged it off, thinking it was some of the flammable liquid they used for training. We were sitting there talking as the engine warmed up in the February weather, and I smelled something again. I got out, went around back, and saw an oily rag tied around the exhaust pipe. It was smoking, close to bursting into flames. I yanked it off and stomped it out. Those guys were trying to set the car on fire.

On Saturday, I reported to my assigned firehouse in the Brooklyn section of the city. The department policy was to place firefighters close to where they lived, and my Cherry Hill house wasn't far. A second African-American firefighter was sent to Firehouse 35. Wade Marand-el was his name. He said he was Moorish. Wade was tall, soft-spoken, on the thin side, and he could be moody. But when his back was up against the wall, he'd fight. We would be tested soon enough.

Our first minute at the firehouse, when the white guys greeted us with the "joke" about the black fire victim, Wade and I just looked at each other like, *Can you believe this?* Who knows how long that guy was saving up his "wit," waiting for us to walk through the door.

Wade was assigned to Truck Company 35, part of the five-man crew that ran the long hook-and-ladder truck. The same number of men were in Engine Company 35, the "pumper" vehicle that hooked up to water hydrants and pumped out water to the hoses. While the hook-and-ladder guys were punching holes in the roof to ventilate a building, the engine company hit the fire with water. I was put in the engine company.

In order to fight fire, you needed equipment, a helmet, and protective clothing. That first week, the only store in town that sold firefighting gear was low on stock, so I couldn't buy anything until my second week. We were also required to purchase our own dress uniforms. My first day at Engine Company 35, we had an alarm. I only had my rubber galoshes and an old navy pea jacket that my Uncle George had given me. No helmet.

I was only on the job a few minutes when the gong sounded. I jumped up on the truck and held on to the hose as we raced out. It was my first time riding on a fire engine. There were no closed compartments on the trucks in those days, and it was freezing cold. We went out to semirural Curtis Bay Avenue in South Boston where a barn was on fire. Flames shot up from burning hay inside. Now that I was faced with the reality of fire, I thought a person had to be crazy to run into a burning building. I only had on a flammable jacket, leather gloves, and dungarees. Ordering me inside the barn would be putting me in danger, but the lieutenant in charge gave the order. I was told to help with the hose line.

Gas masks were hardly used then, and none of the firefighters had them on. I coughed from the smoke, and my eyes watered. I saw the lieutenant walking around unaffected, like his nose was equipped with a filter. I asked him why the smoke wasn't bothering him. He pulled out a red and yellow foil package and said, "You chew this tobacco, it coats your throat and stops the smoke."

I knew this was b.s., but he was letting me in on a secret: Real firemen didn't wear gas masks. I made a mental note to get some chewing tobacco, just to be one of the boys. After the action of fighting the fire, the reality of life at Company 35 for an African American hit home when we returned to the station.

The fire department had decided against segregated stations because there wasn't time to set them up. The firehouses would be integrated. But I found out that "integration" in the Baltimore Fire Department meant stiff and absolute segregation. The Urban League might have gotten us in, but the department wanted us to know we weren't welcome.

Company 35 was a typical fire station, really just a garage to house the fire apparatus, with living quarters. The main room on ground level was where the trucks were parked and maintained. The captain had his office on the ground floor, and the desk where the alarms came in was there. The firefighters slept upstairs, where the bathrooms were, and they descended when the fire gong was pulled by sliding down the famous brass pole. Downstairs was the kitchen area where the firefighters made their meals, and a dining area.

Company 35 was a two-company house, an engine company and a truck company. Some stations were single-company houses. Ten firefighters were on duty during a shift, along with three lieutenants and the captain.

After the first fire run, I went up to the bunkroom. I saw the welcome they had prepared.

There was one bed in the corner I knew had to be mine. On the bed board, someone had placed a sign saying "RESERVED."

In the bathroom, another sign was hung over one of the sinks: "RESERVED."

And on one of the toilets: "RESERVED."

I took down the signs, one by one, and not knowing what to do with them, threw them in the locker I'd been assigned. I was determined to use any sink, bed, or toilet I wanted. I was a firefighter, the same as the other guys.

The next day, the signs reappeared. Bed, sink, and toilet: RESERVED, RESERVED, RESERVED. This time it was Wade who took them down and tossed them in his locker.

The signs were there the next day and the next. After a month, Wade and I had a growing pile of signs in our lockers. We shook our heads, and wondered, "Where do they get all these signs?" There seemed to be an endless supply.

As long as I was with Company 35, I'd have that slap in the face for a greeting every time I arrived at the firehouse, signs meant to segregate me into one bed, sink, and toilet that no white person would then want to use.

Not one thing happened in any firehouse without the knowledge and approval of the top-echelon authorities. The signs were being hung in every firehouse in the city where African Americans were posted. They weren't legally mandated by law, and this meant that they were ordered or at least approved by the fire chief and Fire Board. If the higher-ups had that attitude toward us, I knew that the bigoted firefighters could do as they pleased.

I could tell that the white firefighters were annoyed that I was taking down the signs, but they didn't say anything. They didn't speak to us at all other than in the line of duty. There wasn't one nice white guy in Company 35, or at least not one who was brave enough to *act* nice toward us. All of the white firefighters had the same negative attitude toward us, and they stuck together, including the officers.

In the dining area downstairs, Wade and I were supposed to eat at our own little table, like a kiddies' table away from the big table where the white guys ate. We weren't allowed to sit with them, and at that point, I didn't care.

Wade had a drinking problem, and it wasn't helped by the stress of our reception, which never let up as our training ended and we became regular firefighters. He sometimes reported for work half-loaded, so he'd go upstairs and lie down. The white firefighters would play cards, but they wouldn't invite me to join them. So I read the newspaper. But I had to buy my own— I wasn't allowed to read the firehouse newspaper.

We firefighters would come back from doing a job in the winter with icicles hanging off us from the water that sprayed back and froze on our clothes. More than anything in the world, a firefighter wanted a cup of coffee when he got back to the station. But there was none for me. I wasn't permitted to drink the firehouse coffee.

All these things were denied to me because I was excluded from a firehouse tradition called the Coon Skin. I was put off by the name at first because I thought it was a racial slur. But it turned out that the name came from the costume worn by Davy Crockett. There was a popular TV show about him at the time.

All firefighters contributed a little money to the Coon Skin, and funds were drawn from it to buy newspapers, coffee, food— anything that was needed. The guy who went out with the Coon Skin money was called a Trapper, like Davy Crockett, who sold pelts. His main job was to get things free or at a discount. He'd go to a grocer, buy two pounds of coffee, and the grocer would give him four pounds of coffee. Merchants loved to help firemen because they felt we'd respond faster if there was an emergency at their premises.

Wade and I weren't invited to contribute to the Coon Skin. That meant that we couldn't partake in the things the Trappers brought back.

It was an unwritten law at any firehouse that the person who had the last night watch made the first pot of coffee in the morning so it would be ready when everyone woke up. The length of a watch depended on the number of men at a house. With ten men in our two companies, and a night shift lasting from four in the afternoon to six in the morning, a watch would be around an hour and 20 minutes.

If I had the last shift, I didn't make coffee. I just refused. The captain came down, rubbing his hands, and he couldn't wait to get to that coffee on a cold February morning.

It was a little payback time for me. The captain went to the stove and picked up the pot. He expected it to be full and heavy, so he put some strength into his lift. The pot flew up, right into his face, and he hit himself. He turned to me, "You didn't make coffee?"

"No, I don't drink it, I don't make it," I replied.

He didn't say anything after that, because he knew what was going on—he knew everything that was going on at his station—and he didn't want me involved in the Coon Skin.

Ranked above the captain was the battalion chief. When he came around for inspections or announcements, firefighters addressed him as "Sir" (if they didn't, they could be put on report). A firefighter could also be put on report for "refusing to pass the time of day," the term for not speaking to a superior officer when addressed. And, you could get punitive action for forgetting to salute, or not lining up when the battalion chief or sometimes the fire chief arrived. The gong (it was not called a bell) was "thrown," and you lined up with your cap on, your hose strap in your pocket, and keys to the house and the book of rules in your hand. The hose strap was a short length of rope a firefighter always carried to attach a hose to the side of a ladder so it wouldn't get away when you trained the line of water on the flames.

I had a nasty battalion chief who took pleasure in belittling me. He was the kind of guy who would line up the men twice a day, morning and night, not to see if everyone was there—he knew who was in the house—but to see who was drinking. I was now taking a long bus ride to work. Because I was making much less money in the fire department, I lost my car when I couldn't keep up the payments. For the night shift, I would come in and work a couple of hours on my knees scrubbing the apparatus floor until the gong was thrown and we lined up for the battalion chief.

Sometimes he looked at me, irritated. "What are you doing here?"

"Working, sir."

"No, you're not. You're off! Get out of here."

They would schedule me for off time, but nobody would tell me beforehand. So I would come in and work for two hours (free to the department), only to be sent away.

As far as vacations were concerned, I could apply if I wanted to take the kids somewhere, but if this battalion chief saw the application, he'd hold up the paper and tear it up right in front of me. Then he dismissed me with one word: "Denied."

I just held in my anger. The fire department was a semi-military organization, and it was like I had a sadistic commanding officer. Wade had a little different way of coping. I wouldn't make coffee, but he would. And when he brewed coffee, he put in anything he could find that didn't belong there. He'd spit into the water some of the time; he'd even spice it with a little piss. He wouldn't put in enough so that anyone would notice, though, and the white guys would come down all groggy from waking up, liking the coffee because he made it when I wouldn't. Wade would sit back and laugh at them.

I brought in my own coffeepot and frying pan. I had to use my own utensils, and I brought my own mug. There were mugs provided for all the firefighters, and they had a special mug for black firefighters, also to be used if another black firefighter was attached to the station to fill in for someone. White firefighters would share their mugs. Of course they wouldn't touch the "black" mug. If a black man accidentally drank out of a "white" mug, it would be gone the next day.

Of course, you could go out and work with these guys, rescue people, and risk your lives together. But as soon as you got back to the firehouse, they started up with the same old b.s.

I've always said that a fire department reflects the larger community it serves. Company 35 conformed with Baltimore's attitudes of 1954. If I wasn't accepted inside the firehouse, I couldn't expect to find respect out on the streets. There were decent white people in Baltimore in 1954; there have always been decent, honest, unbigoted white people in the city. The bigger problem was with the custom of segregation, doing things the way they'd been done for generations. But there were also a lot of racists, and a lot of neighborhoods you wouldn't enter if you were an African American.

Shortly after I was assigned to 35, and before I lost my car, I was driving to work on Hanover Street. I was in my dress uniform. The rules required a firefighter to go to and from work in his uniform to identify himself as a firefighter. (He'd also be less likely to stop by a tavern and have a beer, because he might be identified.) The uniform was a blue serge suit, with a blue shirt, tie, and cap. Police officers wore badges, but firefighters didn't; badges were reserved for officers.

Heading to the station, I saw a nasty accident. A boy not older than 12 was riding a bicycle, and he collided with a car. His bike flipped, and he hit the ground hard. I was trained in first aid, which was one of the first things we learned. I pulled over, ran to the kid, and saw that he was bleeding from a bad wound on one arm. The bone protruded. I knelt down, took hold of his arm, and stretched it out in preparation for a splint. "Lie still," I said.

The boy was groaning, and his eyes opened. They enlarged when he saw me. "What the fuck are you doing, nigger?!"

I had to work fast. He was bleeding, and I needed a bandage. I took hold of his shirt and tore it.

Once he started cursing at me, he never let up. "Nigger, get your hands off me!"

By this time, a crowd of people had gathered. None of them offered any help. I was the only black person there. He appealed to them, "Make this nigger stop!"

The boy's fury was such that it was like he was blaming me for the accident. I wrapped up his arm. He screamed, "Nigger, get away from me! Don't touch me, you black devil!"

Someone called an ambulance. I stayed with the boy through all his ranting to make sure he didn't hurt himself more. The ambulance arrived, and the crew dismissed me. "Okay, we got it."

I walked away, drove to the station, and changed clothes. I was shaken up by the violence of the boy's hatred toward me, and by my disgust with the crowd for not urging the boy to quiet down so the fireman could help him. But they just gawked.

An hour later, the captain called me. "Did you give first aid to a kid this morning?"

I admitted that I did. Reporters were phoning the firehouse, and they wanted to know who the black fireman was who came to the boy's rescue. Because I was wearing a uniform, witnesses knew I was a firefighter. There weren't many black firefighters, so the reporters just called the three stations in the area. Both the city's newspapers ran the story.

The battalion chief was furious about the favorable publicity given to a black firefighter. He threatened to put me on report on the pretext that I failed to inform the captain that I was involved in an incident. The rules said that anything you did as a firefighter, you had to report. I knew this, but at the time, I just wanted to forget the whole ugly incident.

The battalion chief must have realized that it would look bad if he disciplined me after I helped that kid, and he never carried out his threat. He probably made up for it the next time he rejected one of my vacation requests.

SOME MEMBERS OF THE PUBLIC would curse me even if their property was at stake. My job on the fire engine was the same "low man on the totem pole" work all the newcomers on the pumper rig had to do. I was the leading-off man, the one who attached the pipe to the hydrant. The glory job was on the other end, with the firefighter who held the pipe nozzle and fixed the water line on the fire. That job came with seniority.

After attaching the hose to the hydrant as the leading-off man, so named because I was the first off the truck at the scene, I ran back to help with the hose. My job was to "follow the line," to be with the hose and stay by the officer in charge to follow his orders.

At the sight of me, one homeowner got purple in the face with anger. "Where does that nigger think he's going?" We were in the Brooklyn section, where people would never have a black man in their homes. The house's owner shouted at the captain, "Make him stay outside!"

This would happen from time to time. I didn't like the abuse, but it didn't keep me from doing my job. The captain would either send me back, or he would ignore the protest if the job was a big one and he needed me.

A German philosopher named Nieztsche once said that anything you endure that doesn't kill you will make you stronger. I was 162 pounds when I joined the fire department. In 30 days, I weighed 210. It was mostly muscle. My body was responding to the physical training after a year or so of sitting in a streetcar or bus driver's chair. My jacket size expanded to 46, and my neck grew to 17 1/2 inches. It was as if I was reacting to the tension going on around me by putting myself in fighting condition.

The time between fire runs—and we never knew when someone would pull one of the city's hundreds of fireboxes and we'd have to jump into action—the firemen did chores. Polishing the brass was an important task, not just to keep the nozzles and other gear on the apparatus bright, but to reduce the friction when the men slid down the pole. On his inspections, the battalion chief would put on a white glove and run his finger down the pole. If it came back green or black, he'd give the commanding officer hell. The Baltimore humidity caused the brass to tarnish quickly.

One morning when Wade was upstairs in the bunkroom, chores were divided up, and his truck company had just finished making the beds. Those of us in the engine company finished cleaning downstairs. It was one of the times when Wade and I were assigned to the same shift, so I went up to see him. Some of the white firefighters saw that we were together that day, and they were prepared.

There was a pool table in the bunkroom, and Wade and I were standing ten feet away from where four white guys were talking around the table. All of a sudden, one of the guys turned to Wade. "Did you call me a motherfucker?"

Wade kept his anger in check, and he said coolly, "No."

The guy was out for trouble, and he wouldn't settle for less. "Yes, you did. You called me a motherfucker!"

They locked eyes, and Wade answered, "I said no. But if you *think* I called you a motherfucker, it must mean that you *are* a motherfucker, motherfucker."

The guy reached down and cocked his hand to deliver a big haymaker punch. With all his strength, he brought up his fist, swinging. Wade caught his fist, did some fancy footwork, twisted the guy's arm, and dropped him. He hit the floor hard.

Wade said to me quickly, "You with me, man? 'Cause we got something going."

"I'm with you."

Surrounded by the white firefighters, we stood back to back, our fists raised, ready for what was to come. One guy picked up a pool cue. Wade and I stared at the other guys. They saw we were ready for them, and they saw what was in our eyes. Two guys ran away, down the stairs. Since they couldn't beat us, they were off to tell the captain that two niggers had gone crazy in the bunkhouse. The guy on the floor who threw the punch started crawling away. He reached the pole and slid down like a snake. That just left the guy with the pool cue. Wade told him where he was going to shove that stick. He put it down and hurried down the stairs.

Wade and I relaxed and shook our heads. But we knew it wasn't over. A minute later, the captain came up to investigate. "You guys are troublemakers!"

"Captain, they started the fight."

He gave us hell anyway. There would be no fighting in his firehouse, he said. He also told us that he didn't like our attitudes, which was code in those days for saying that we didn't know our place.

The white firefighters didn't get the same lecture. I knew it was only a matter of time before the incident would be repeated.

By this time, I had moved my family several times around Cherry Hill; sometimes we stayed with friends. For a while, we were living in a two-bedroom apartment on the second floor of the projects. The last apartment we lived in had a coal furnace in the basement, and it was the tenants' responsibility to buy coal to keep the furnace burning. When it was very cold and we ran short, I took the kids' red wagon and went down to the railroad tracks. I'd cover a mile of track and pick up coal that had fallen from the trains transporting anthracite. Then it was back home with my little red wagon full of coal, doing what I had to do to economize.

During the hot Baltimore summers, we threw open the windows and turned on an electric fan to stir the air. Baltimore had several parks, and on the hottest nights, the neighborhoods would empty out and people, white and black, went to the parks to sleep under the stars. Nobody worried about getting mugged or molested.

If I'd expected to drink less now that the streetcar job was over, I was wrong. Wade and I never became close friends, since he was so quiet and withdrawn, but because we worked together, we'd hit a tavern after our shift and try to forget about the treatment we had to put up with. When I was driving a streetcar, I drank beer to relieve pressure. The fire department turned me to hard liquor. I drank Old Overholt and Pikesville rye. I got off work, and I wouldn't go home until I had a drink. Wade and I both lived in Cherry Hill, and if necessary, we could walk from Brooklyn. We would sit on the step of a liquor store and drink straight out of the bottle, out of a brown paper bag. We'd talk about the b.s. at the firehouse, what we had to put up with every day, and the growing pile of RESERVED signs in our lockers. None of the other guys ever warmed up to us. They were united in trying to wear us down so we'd quit.

In the '50s, unless you got so drunk that you fell on your face every night, no one thought you had a drinking problem. I wouldn't get drunk, but it was a shame that I had to use booze to keep the anger I felt in check. And I was developing an attitude that if anyone messed with me, I would mess *them* up. That was dangerous, because if the white firefighters decided to provoke me into fighting and they succeeded, I could get fired.

A year went by, and the firefighter's routine became familiar. Moments of firefighting action were followed by a lot of idle time doing chores. Firefighters put in four daytime shifts in a row, took off a half-day, and reported back that night for four night shifts, after which they'd be off for two days. Day shifts were 10 hours, and night shifts, when we slept at the firehouse, were 14 hours. You were allowed to go to bed after 9 P.M., and someone would rouse you for your watch. At 6 A.M., 12 blows of the fire gong would wake everybody up. Every firehouse in the city did this, waking up the neighborhood as well. The gong would be pulled a second time at six at night.

The city was connected by a system of 122 fireboxes. These were located about one on every block. When someone pulled a box alarm, an electric current was sent to headquarters, and the box number lit up on a board. An alert was sent out to all the firehouses indicating which ones were to respond. A single alarm was the smallest incident, and one engine company responded. This could be a car accident, a call for medical assistance, or an investigation into a dangerous situation—even a cat stranded on a high tree branch.

A one-alarm fire required the response of four engine companies and two truck companies. A two-alarm fire brought another truck and another engine company. On three alarms, another truck company responded, an additional company was called for a four-alarm, and so on. It could go "as high as high," depending on the severity of the blaze.

The fireman who had the watch sat at the ground-floor desk, and when news came in about a fire, he alerted the company. Above the desk was the alert board, a grid where pegs showed all the city's fire companies. Red pegs designated the truck companies; black pegs were for the engine companies. When an alarm came in, the smaller of the station's two gongs sounded, and a tickertape machine began punching out holes on a tape that ran across the back of the desk, the number holes corresponding with the number of the firebox. For some reason, the tickertape machine was called The Joker. The gong banged out the firebox's number with one to nine strikes, pausing a beat between numbers. Meanwhile, a loudspeaker would alert the watchman through the department's radio system, "Alert box 1429." And later, "Company 25 is out on service to Bank Street and Ballou." The watchman pulled the corresponding peg and placed it in a box that indicated the companies out on runs. The sequence of gong strikes was repeated four times, and by the fourth sounding, the fire trucks would be out the door.

When our own company was called, the watchman would throw the big gong to alert the firehouse. The gong was giant, two feet in diameter, and could be heard all through the neighborhood. At the top of his lungs, the watchman hollered, "Turn clothes!"

We firefighters threw on our clothes, slid down the pole, and jumped on the trucks. It was adrenaline time. By the fourth time the sequence of gong strikes sounded, the big station doors were opened, and we would be racing out into the night to whatever life-threatening situation or false alarm awaited us.

That was why I was very lucky I wasn't seriously injured the time the white firefighters pulled another one of their tricks. The gong went off while I was asleep. Instinct took over when the racket of the bell sounded and woke me up. To save time, I slept in my firefighting gear, my "turnout clothes." I kept my boots side-by-side next to the bed, so when I sat up I could slip my feet in. I wasn't completely awake until I hit the pole.

I got up when the gong sounded and swung my legs over the side of the bed. It was a good thing I didn't press my foot down too hard. There was a lightbulb inside one boot. I didn't have time to think; I just pulled it out, put it on the bed, and ran for the pole.

When I returned from the run, the bulb was gone. It was then that I was hit by what they'd tried to do. When a thing like that happens, it takes something out of you. It was cowardly. They didn't like me because I was a black man, but instead of confronting me or throwing a punch, they did that. I had a wife and small children to support, and here they were trying to cut me, cripple me.

I was angry, sure, but a part of me wanted to break down and cry. But it never occurred to me to quit.

My end at Company 35 came a year and a half into my life as a firefighter.

In September 1955, all over the southern United States, schools were opening one year after the Supreme Court made segregation in public schools illegal by ruling on *Brown v. Board of Education of Topeka, Kansas*. I read in the newspaper that Dave Garroway, the host of the *Today* show, would be devoting the program to the progress that had been made with integration.

I turned on the TV. I knew it was "their" television, because the white firefighters had chipped in to buy it. I would have contributed, too, but they didn't ask. That would have meant I could join them to watch.

I just thought, *This isn't a private club; it's the ground floor of the firehouse.* The TV was mounted on the wall behind where the fire trucks were parked. I switched to the *Today* show, pulled up a chair, and sat down to watch.

Immediately, a guy came up, stepped in front of me, and without saying a word, he switched the channel. He turned on a show more to his taste, *Mighty Mouse.* Instead of watching the news, the TV was showing a cartoon.

I stood up, went to the set, and switched it back. I sat down.

The guy returned and switched back to *Mighty Mouse.*

I got up a third time and turned the channel back to the *Today* show, and this time I kept my hand on the knob. The guy walked up, and I could tell that his anger was ready to boil over. But so was mine. He took hold of my hand and tried to pull it away. I balled my hand into a fist, punched him in the jaw, and knocked him down.

The lieutenant ran out of his office there on the first floor. He saw the other firefighter down. "Williams, I'm putting you on report!"

When charges were placed against a fireman, the battalion chief had to be notified, so he showed up to verify the charges, and the lieutenant gave him a one-sided account, making me out to be the instigator.

There was no union to champion my cause. African Americans weren't permitted to join the firefighters' union until 1961, six years in the future, and only after a long court battle.

But the battalion chief didn't want to press charges, which would have led to my suspension. He told the lieutenant the incident would make the newspapers. He knew what the story would be, too: A racial fight broke out in a city firehouse caused by a dispute over the Supreme Court's anti-segregation ruling.

The battalion chief did not want to fire me either. Despite all the tension and the unrelenting animosity from my co-workers, I showed up without fail, and sober. I carried out my work diligently, never complained, and I knew the job. I was young, didn't get sick, and only pushed back when I was pushed first.

And so, I became the first person in the fire department to get "shanghaied." I was sent away, banished from Company 35. On September 14, 1955, I was assigned to Company 57. It was a much longer bus ride for me, and there was no guarantee that I wouldn't be jumping out of the frying pan and into the fire at this new station.

I never counted how many RESERVED signs Wade and I took down from the bed board, sink, and toilet. From time to time, we cleared them out of our lockers. But at three a day, from the day I entered that firehouse to the day I left, I would have amassed 1,791 signs.

But there was one consolation: Firemen were notorious gossipers. Everyone in the fire department now knew about Herman Williams—and how you couldn't push him around.

❧ CHAPTER FIVE ☙

"Wooden Apparatus, Iron Men"
(Engine Company 57)

Engine Company 57 was located at Curtis Bay near Baltimore's Outer Harbor. It was a long bus trip to the docks from where I lived in Cherry Hill. At this firehouse, they'd never had an African-American firefighter.

Some of the white guys had the same attitude as their colleagues in Company 35. They didn't want a black firefighter in their house. But they didn't know what to do about it. The kitchen was downstairs, which was typical for a firehouse, and there was a long dining table. I came down the stairs, and the first sight that awaited me was that table. It had been "segregated." One end was cordoned off with a line of bottles and condiment jars. The ketchup and mustard, the sugar bowl, salt and pepper shakers, and the relish bowl were put in a line to section off the far side of the table. I was to sit at that far end, and for a few days, I did. It was miserable to be quarantined like that.

Then I thought, *To hell with this.* There were usually only three or four people eating at a time, so there was plenty of room at the "white end" of the table. I joined the other guys. I didn't complain to the captain; I just did it. The other guys looked at me like I was crazy. One of them tried to get the words out, but couldn't, "Herman, uh, aren't you supposed to be—"

I cut him off. "No."

He went to the captain, who asked him, "What do you want me to do about it?"

That was Captain Martin Klensmith, and before I'd come to the house, he lined up all the shifts. He told them a Negro firefighter was coming, and he made it clear that he wouldn't tolerate any discrimination from them in any form. That was important, because it set the tone. There were no RESERVED signs at Company 57, and stunts like the segregated dining table were soon history. Some of the guys were dyed-in-the-wool racists, but there would be no fights set up to get me kicked out of the fire department, like at Company 35.

Another thing that worked in my favor was that everything that happened in the fire department, everything that was said, was known to every firefighter in an instant. We had a saying, "Telephone, telegram, tell a fireman." I'd never seen anything like it, but if you wanted to pass on something fast, you told a fireman. (I say "fireman," because women would not enter the department until 1981.) A guy would get on the phone, "Did you hear . . .?" If somebody didn't know something, he made it up. All of it was to excite or agitate the other guys.

I had a reputation that was going through the department that here was someone you didn't want to mess with. "Herman, he'll knock you down . . . you better not bother Herman."

But when they got to know me, they saw that I wasn't a hothead. I was someone who treated others with respect, and expected respect for himself.

I had a bed in the bunkroom of Company 57 like every-body else. I joined the Coon Skin, and never again had a problem with coffee. I was also free to do what I wanted in the kitchen. I started cooking for the first time in a big way. I pre-pared meals for the shift side-by-side with the other guys. One of us would peel potatoes; another guy would cut onions for making soup. Three or four of us would be busy at one time. Firehouse food was simple: spaghetti and meatballs, meatloaf, hamburgers. The burgers we called "belly busters." The recipe was this: Take a fist-size ball of ground beef, flatten it, and work in minced onion and garlic. Fry it, and pour on gravy. Belly busters were too big for hamburger buns.

We always made mashed potatoes, and peas straight from the can. Some days it was chili, and always a lot of hot coffee drunk out of old mugs, all stained and cracked.

The white guys liked my cooking, and it helped ease my way into life there. But if Company 57 was a comparatively civil firehouse, it had to be. Nowhere was a good working rela-tionship between the firefighters more important than at Curtis Bay. This was in the heart of Baltimore's industrial area. We were reminded daily of our need to depend on our fellow fire-fighters. The area was filled with chemical plants, and chem-ical fires required every available man to work to his utmost, with no conflicts. In those days, when we could bust our bellies with hamburgers and meatloaf every day and be unaware of the consequences to our arteries, industrial safety standards were also primitive. The mortality rate among firefighters was high, and reflected the danger of the job.

The Davis Chemical Company was one of the plants near the firehouse. There was a sulfur mill on the premises, and at least once a week there would be a fire in that building, as the sulfur dust would ignite. For days prior, the dust would drift up and collect in the ceiling rafters 20 feet in the air. Without proper ventilation, the dust would accumulate until a spark set it off. Then the dust would rain down like fiery snowflakes.

Responding to a chemical fire, we used foam, a kind of soap solution. Water would just spread the burning chemicals. The idea was to blanket the flames and suffocate them. The department had special chemical wagons, and one was stationed at Company 57 because we were at the Curtis Bay industrial area. The two firefighters assigned to the chemical truck had an aerator, like a blender. From five-gallon drums, they poured the foam solution into the hopper to so-many parts water, supplied by our pumper truck. A hose coming out the other end was trained on the fire.

At Company 57, we had to have a knowledge of toxic chemicals, and every officer carried a book called *Chemtrac*. All the chemicals and their properties were listed. In the course of fighting various kinds of blazes, we learned what type of chemical fire, like a gas station fire, you could actually put out with water. The force of the water line knocked out the flames.

We entered Davis Chemical and hit the burning sulfur with a hose line. The fire rained down like water. Some of the burning flakes fell on me and stuck like glue to my shoulders. I beat out the flames with my gloves. The sulfur rain was very thick, and some flaming particles went down inside my glove and stuck to my skin. It was a dangerous situation because those particles could blow down your neck. Firefighters didn't usually go to the hospital. You did your job, and either you got injured or you got killed. That was the attitude. Today, a firefighter would be required to go to the hospital to have an injury examined. At the Davis Chemical fire, I just took off the glove, washed the burn with water, and put on a Band-Aid. I'd have the scar for the rest of my life.

Firefighters had this attitude that we were tough and nothing could bother us. Each fireman was issued a gas mask, but no one wore it without a direct order, and those came very rarely. I saw on my first day on the job that the attitude was: Real men don't wear gas masks. None of the firefighters wanted to be thought of as "Sissybelles." It was the same in other cities, where firemen were called "Smoke Eaters."

Some of the danger came from antique equipment. Firefighters had a boast: "Wooden Apparatus, Iron Men." Amazing as it seems today, firefighting ladders then were made of wood, and they were flammable. I was attached to the engine company, but our chores included helping maintain the apparatus of the truck company. There was the big 100-foot ladder, or "Big Stick," which could be extended upward to seven floors. (For this reason, fires couldn't be fought as effectively above the seventh floor of a building, and ladder-assisted rescues weren't possible. This is still the case today, and it's something to keep in mind when you reserve a hotel room: For safety's sake, consider a room no higher than the seventh floor.)

A hook and ladder consisted of the engine cab, and a trailer for apparatus that was so long that a tillerman sat in a seat at the rear to steer a second set of wheels when the driver in front made a turn. A hook and ladder was generally a rescue wagon, made by American LaFrance, a U.S. company that also made the pumper trucks. Ground ladders, carried by hand to where they were needed, were strapped to the sides, and compartments held various tools, such as ceiling hooks. The duty of the fireman who rode standing on a step at the left rear was to use the hook to tear down a ceiling to ventilate a room. The man standing on the right rear step handled an ax, which was kept in another compartment. We had to keep the ladders clean by stripping them down and putting on new coats of clear shellac. We had no chemicals or sandpaper to do the job. Instead, we smashed bottles and used broken pieces of glass.

From the first horse-drawn fire trucks at the time of the Revolutionary War, the firefighters' apparatus was always elaborately decorated. The scroll work, lettering, and trim lines were beautifully etched in gold leaf. Firefighting apparatus was considered prestigious for any community to own in the old days. During the Civil War, horse-drawn fire wagons were confiscated by both sides when a town was captured. But the reason for all the frills wasn't decorative. The gold leaf was reflective material, and it made the apparatus stand out in sunlight or artificial light. This was also the reason for all the brightly polished brass, so the speeding machine could be easily seen and people could get out of the way.

The fire department kept a painter on the payroll whose only job was to redo the gold leaf. He was retired in 1971. By then, reflective paints and materials made gold leaf obsolete, and powerful batteries permitted an array of flashing colored lights on the front, back, and sides of the trucks.

LaFrance introduced the modern cab-forward style of fire truck in the late '40s, for better driver visibility. Mack made the Bulldog truck, with the engine compartment in front of the cab; Seagrave was the third maker of fire trucks. All these companies regularly upgraded apparatus to incorporate improved technology.

Some apparatus lasted forever. The Baltimore Fire Department's Water Tower One, a 65-foot-tall pole with a nozzle on top first went into operation in 1898. The tower, later mounted on a 1936 Mack truck, was still in use in the 1950s. The tower was raised by hand cranking. We also hand-cranked some of the World War I–vintage fire trucks to get the engines to turn over, such as the department's 1917 Mack, the first generation of motor-driven fire apparatus that combined pump, hose storage, and a chemical/water tank. When I joined the department, these had become second-line equipment, maintained in reserve for when they were needed.

The pumper truck was used to transport hose. When we returned from a run, all the hoses had to be scrubbed and then hung to dry in a tall hose tower attached to the firehouse. In Baltimore's humidity, there was a danger of mildew. Hoses had a rubber inner lining, with a nylon outer layer. If left wet, an acid would form to corrode the rubber. Today, a better grade of nylon and a different composition of rubber does away with drying. After a fire is put out, the hoses are neatly stacked back onto the trucks at the scene. The hose tower has become a relic of the past, but can still be seen attached to most city firehouses.

I was the company newcomer, so I was still the leading-off man, but I got the timing and the acrobatics down to an art. When we arrived at a scene and saw that the fire was a magnitude that we would need to use a large hose connected to a hydrant rather than a smaller hose that drew from the truck's tank, I would grab several folds of hose while the truck was still in motion and jump off as we passed the hydrant. I would make the connection to the hydrant outlet as the truck continued moving forward, with the hose unraveling behind it. The truck would stop at the scene before the slack was taken up. The pump operator took the other end and connected it to the engine's intake valve.

A second hose was connected to an outlet. A pumper engine had up to four outlet valves, two per side. The hydrant fed water into the engine, which pumped out 750 gallons per minute to the hose that was trained on the fire. (Today, 1,000 gallons per minute is standard, but trucks can pump up to 1,500 gallons per minute. A million gallons of water might be used putting out a big fire.)

All of this putting-in-service was accomplished quickly, as fast as we could run.

You "trained the line," or aimed the stream of water, at the seat of the fire, and not at the flames. Flames were just rising gas, and the water went right through, hitting whatever was behind and not the object burning. I learned in a closed area to twirl around the "line," or water spray, to hit both the burning objects and to dissipate the dangerous gases above.

We worked in tandem with the truck company, which was the first to arrive at a dwelling fire because they had the rescue equipment. That company's job was to ventilate the building, knocking holes in the roof or opening windows to allow gases to escape and providing a route for the fire to follow. Fire follows the source of oxygen. When the oxygen is used up, the fire "lays low," smoldering until a well-meaning but ill-advised citizen kicks in a door, and an explosion caused by backdraft conditions results. The building will instantly ignite, and the good citizen may be knocked back to their death.

The truck company also went in to search for trapped people, while we in the engine company trained the line on the flames. It was essential to keep below the flames, which rose and could trap anyone above them. People trapped above the flames were taken out through windows by firefighters who led them down ladders.

There were two things that you see so often in the movies that you expect to see at every fire scene, but which I never witnessed in my entire firefighting career:

1. *A firefighter carrying someone down a ladder or out of a building slumped over his shoulder.* A firefighter is burdened with too much equipment to carry a person over his shoulder. We hauled 70 pounds of equipment, including an oxygen tank, on our backs. It was enough for a firefighter to carry himself. We led or dragged people out.

2. *A rescue using a net.* The nets were attached to the hook and ladders, mostly to keep up a tradition, but they were so dangerous that no one ever thought to use them.

Curtis Bay had ships old and new docked within Company 57's area of action. Early on, I almost got killed on a ship fire. It was an older vessel, with a wooden deck, berthed at Hanover Street. The fire was in the hull, consuming the cargo, so the usual precaution of fighting a fire below the flames wasn't possible. The fire was so intense that it started breaking up through the deck. The men spread out, and suddenly, the deck gave way under me. I was falling, and then miraculously I stopped in midair. But I felt the most terrific pain in my groin, so bad I thought I was going to pass out.

I was straddling the hose, which had stopped my fall. My legs had been on either side of the hose when the deck collapsed. The hose now ran across the hole, from one side of the deck to the other. I found myself suspended in midair, and riding the hose, I could look down on the fire. When those hoses were expanded with 100 pounds of water pressure, they were as hard as concrete. The wind was knocked out of me, but the other men pulled me out.

The people I risked my life for at Curtis Bay didn't know or care about those dangerous moments. For example, on Independence Day, Company 57 was participating in a parade down Patapsco Boulevard. We were in our dress uniforms, our blue serge suits with the shiny brass buttons, and I was riding on the back of a vintage pumper truck.

This was an all-white area, far from my home in Cherry Hill, but I wanted my kids to see their daddy in the parade. Sure, their old man encountered bigotry every day, but it was the Fourth of July, when the country celebrated its ideals, and we were all Americans first. I saw my pretty wife, Marjie, and the kids in the crowd lining the sidewalk. Marjie was pregnant with our fourth child, who was due soon. She waved at me. Marjorie, who was six, was holding up little Herman, who was two and a half. Clolita, my five-year-old, was also there, and my entire family had big smiles on their faces for their father. I was so proud and happy to see them; I smiled and waved back.

It was a mistake, because it roused the bigots. If I had just stared ahead with a stony profile and made myself inconspicuous, I might have gotten through without an incident. But I dared show my pride, my joy at seeing my family, and that drew attention to me.

"Hey, nigger!" The shouts never stopped down the length of the parade route. I wondered if the kids heard.

"Get that nigger off that truck!" The catcalls were full of anger. After people saw an African-American fireman in "their" parade, some of them were furious.

It was a bitter Fourth of July, and I had to wonder about a country that prided itself on that day for being a beacon of liberty, and then treating some of its people with such hatred. I never asked the kids if they heard the racist insults, because I was still trying to leave all that ugliness outside when I came through the door of our home. I didn't know yet how to talk about such things; I didn't know how to explain racism to my little children.

That July of 1956 ended happily when my second son was born. Marjie and I called him Montel. He was another handsome, healthy baby boy, and my heart was full of a father's pride. My wife and children were my purpose for living. They were the reason I put up with abuse on the job.

But it was growing increasingly difficult to keep my disappointments and anger from showing at home. I finally saved up enough to buy a secondhand car, and to cool down after a shift, I would sit outside the house in the car, drink rye out of a bottle, and eat a bag of peanuts before going in. That became my routine.

When I returned to music, it was for the money, and not as a means of regaining the good ol' times. Especially after Montel was born, I was determined to get us out of a rented house and into a home of my own, even if, as I told Marjie, I had to build one with my own two hands. That vow would prove prophetic, but first I needed some extra cash.

Shawn Lewis and The Pyramids was the name of the group. I became one of The Pyramids. Lewis was a supermarket manager; in fact, everyone in the band was a responsible person.

They were looking for a bass player, so when I got the call, I thought first thing of Marjie, and the trouble my playing with The Swallows had caused.

I asked her, "Can I play with these guys for a weekend?"

She said it was okay with her. There would be no touring involved, but the occasional local gig turned into regular weekend bookings. I ended up playing with The Pyramids for 20 years.

We played at strip bars, where the patrons were all white, and just like in New Orleans, we were told, "Don't look at the girls." This was on Baltimore Street, a section called The Block. It was seven or eight blocks of nothing but strip joints, where Blaze Starr, the world-famous stripper, got her start. But how humiliating that was, being told to keep my eyes off the strippers in case anyone in that white audience might think I was having lascivious thoughts about "their" women.

The Pyramids were pretty good. We played Top 40 hits, and we were constantly booked. Being on stage in our snazzy uniform (a burgundy blazer with black trousers) gave me confidence, and as a result, I would never fear talking to groups in the future.

I was the singer in the band, and as my assurance grew, I started imitating people. When we did Nat King Cole, I sounded smooth. Then I'd really give it up for an Elvis song. Chuck Berry, The Platters—we'd cover everybody.

Every Friday and Saturday night, we'd play at a party or social function. When I was scheduled to work night shifts on weekends, I'd trade the shift with someone else, or I'd use my vacation time. I used up most of my vacation time that way.

The guys at Engine Company 57 knew that I played music. They asked me what instrument I played, and I told them the bass. It was a mistake. I could never let my guard down. Those guys just didn't get it about racism and treating others with respect. Racism comes from ignorance about other people. One day, I learned just how ignorant my co-workers could be.

I was on the firehouse apparatus floor when they called me from the basement, "Hey, Big Herm, come on down here." I went down to the eating area by the kitchen.

This one guy had a wooden barrel he'd found somewhere, and he had a broom sticking out of it. He was banging on that broomstick like he was playing bass strings, going "Dum-dum-dum!"

He was in blackface. His skin was smeared with grease, and he was grinning through it as he imitated a black man scatting.

The other firefighters were ringed around him. They were throwing pennies at his feet.

I gaped at them for a moment, not believing what I was seeing. Then my anger at the insult took over. I picked up the barrel, and threw it the length of the basement. It smashed against the wall.

The white guys pretended they didn't understand why I was upset. "Hey, Herm, can't you take a joke?"

But to me they were like thieves, trying to steal my manhood, my humanity.

I felt a deep sense of isolation. I felt alone there, surrounded by men who didn't see me as a man like them. They actually assumed I would share their view that black people were ridiculous, and fair game for jokes. We could go out to answer alarms, risk our lives saving others, and save each other, but when we got back to the firehouse, the separation, not physical but in every other way, returned.

From the top down, there was an attitude in the department that African-American firefighters didn't have to be held to the same standards of consideration as white firefighters. Things that would never be asked of a white firefighter were forced on black firefighters without a thought. In 1957, a large winter storm dropped two feet of snow, and cars were buried under snowdrifts. The evening the storm hit, I looked out the window of our Cherry Hill apartment and I knew that I'd have to get an early start. The buses wouldn't be running, and I would have to walk to Curtis Bay. I got started at half past three in the morning. I was due at the firehouse at six, as usual. I fought my way five miles through the driving snow and got to the station on time.

Every day, the battalion chief came around to pick up the station's report, but he wasn't going to do it in the big snowstorm. He let the report wait. Anyone with sense would have done the same. The whole Eastern Seaboard was hit by the storm front. But at our firehouse, the captain got nervous. There was quite a lot of fear in those days in the fire department. The lieutenant feared the captain, the captain feared the battalion chief, and he, in turn, feared the fire chief. Firefighters summed it up by saying, "Crap rolls downhill."

And I was at the bottom of the hill. "The battalion chief's got to have these reports," the captain told me. He ordered me to go downtown to headquarters and hand-deliver them. There were nine other men at the station, but I was singled out to go back out into the storm.

It took me hours to get downtown. I crossed the Hanover Street Bridge, and the wind cut through my clothes. I felt so disgusted that I turned down a Good Samaritan who pulled over, rolled down his window, and asked, "Can I give you a lift?" I just waved him away.

I arrived at headquarters, and the battalion chief looked at me in disbelief.

"You mean to tell me you walked all the way here? This could have waited until tomorrow." Hearing him, you would have thought that it was my idiotic idea to go out into the storm. I turned around and made my way back to the station.

Summer weather could be just as brutal. In Baltimore, the temperature was always in the high 80s or low 90s. Turnout clothing was heavy, and a firefighter had to wear all of it for protection. The turnout pants and jacket weren't made of asbestos, which was used in insulation, but canvas, and heat proofing came from multiple layers. Firefighters accepted that in the summertime you were hot, and in the wintertime you were cold. Fighting a fire, we were typically out there for three to six hours. In the winter, you turned into an iceman. Firefighters walked around like zombies, caked in white. In the summer, putting out a fire at a dump or at a chemical plant, a Baltimore firefighter finished the job soaked to the skin—but from his own sweat, not the hose spray.

"Wooden apparatus, iron men." That's the motto that applied to us. But a firefighter had to be tough for another reason: We had to face more than danger. Every fire run brought you face-to-face with human suffering. You might be confronted with the possibility of your own death and injury, but your job also required you to face the horrors that struck other people. Some things we saw were out of a nightmare. In the days before counseling was available to us, such sights would cause emotional problems for some firefighters. No wonder we took refuge in booze and machismo, because the unspoken code was you never talked about what you saw. You went back to the station and forgot about it, or you made a joke—no matter how close you came to your death that day, and no matter how many people's corpses you pulled from the rubble. All those innocent people who were charred and mutilated, and you thought, *Nobody should have to die like that.*

"My daughter's missing! My God, man, can't you help?!" We heard it so many times, but it always hit you hard in the gut. And every part of you wanted to help. So many firefighters lost their lives by recklessly rushing into a building to go after a missing person. In my early years as a firefighter, every day was hell, and I saw a lot of death. It was like a war experience, especially on the night shift, when you wouldn't know if you'd come back home alive.

You learned the unspoken language of fire fighting: There were certain sounds you'd get to know and listen for. Was a wall about to collapse? Was the floor going to give way beneath you? You knew if a building was going to collapse by the creaking of wood. You could tell what you were in for by the color of smoke: white, gray, black, or brown. You could see the building "breathing," literally expanding and contracting. Smoke would go out, and then weirdly, it would be sucked right back in, like the building was inhaling. This was a backdraft—the most dangerous condition. You knew that if someone opened a door when a top floor wasn't ventilated, the place would explode. You prayed that no one would make that mistake. Sometimes something would go wrong, a fireman would open a door, get blown off his feet, and be killed.

The smell of death was in the air, and we would get to know it. Driving to a fire, pulling into a block and approaching a building, there would sometimes be the stench of burning flesh. You knew right away there was a body. I would never get over that. The mortality rate was high with civilians. They'd be smoking in bed, in a chair; or cooking. The smell would permeate your clothes. Along with the smoke and the toxic fumes, the smell of death would linger in your lungs long after the fire was extinguished.

You pulled up to the scene and people would run up to you, screaming, "I can't find my child!" "My mother's in there!" "Save my husband, he was asleep!" The terror on their faces would erase any shred of bigotry they might have felt by looking at me, clutching me, forgetting in their desperation that I was a black man.

I'd break through a window. Everything would be murky in the darkness and swirling smoke. I'd glimpse a doll, a baby doll, and my boot would kick it while I lifted the hose to hit the flames. But the doll wouldn't react like it was plastic. I looked down. It would actually be a baby, a dead baby. I'd say a prayer, "Please, Jesus, no more . . ."

I'd crawl on my belly. You were taught to crawl, like a snake; you couldn't see a thing. The smoke would block out the light. That was when I might bump into a body—a woman, her eyes open and staring, lifeless.

At one fire that I specifically recall, I was crawling on my belly, and a closed closet door was ahead of me. But something told me to open it. There was a kid inside who had gone in to hide from a fire, and he was dead. The fire had sucked out all his oxygen, sucked it out of his lungs. It was like I could feel my heart break.

I couldn't tell my family about what I went through. If I'd told them how Daddy spent his days and nights, they'd be scared and wouldn't sleep. Maybe they wouldn't let me go to the firehouse and be afraid when I went to work. So I'd sit in the car out front, take a drink from a bottle in a brown paper bag, and eat a fistful of peanuts. What could I say to Marjie? You heard that war was hell, but fire fighting was also hell, and it was something you did every day, in peacetime.

I had a duty to serve all those panicky people. Mothers pulling at my clothes, "My child! You have to save her!" Firefighters reacted to that. They tried to get into a flaming building where they shouldn't go. Mortality was high among firefighters.

Resuscitation was mouth-to-mouth; there weren't any plastic pipes like there were later on. You put your mouth over the unconscious person's mouth and blew. You smelled the smoke coming out. Then you'd get out of the way fast, because nine times out of ten, they'd vomit. You carried them out the best way you could, depending on whether they were conscious. Usually you dragged them out. It wasn't pretty like in the movies.

I lifted weights—I had to, because I was an emergency worker. But there was something else going on. I was building up protection against everything that was happening to me on the job. At some point, the frustration and emotions spilled over into my home life. I was short with the kids and had mood swings, like Dr. Jekyll and Mr. Hyde. Going from the disrespect I was shown at work, I would try to put on a happy face at home. Sometimes I'd miss a beat, and the wrong face showed through. But Marjie was patient; she seemed to understand. If she was worried, she never let it show, and that helped me a lot. I couldn't have functioned without her love and support. As a result, I grew more devoted, more dependent on her. Me, the big, macho fireman—I never thought of another woman. What was the point when I had Marjie?

I did everything I was supposed to do at home. I played with the kids and made sure they did their homework and chores, but part of my mind was still at work, where I was treated like a nonentity. The contrast was almost too much. My kids looked up to me as if I were an all-powerful, all-knowing god, the way little kids usually think of their father. But in the department and to a lot of the public, when they didn't need me to save lives, I was treated like dirt. Like at the Fourth of July parade: *"Hey, nigger, what are you doing on that truck?!"*

That dead boy in the closet wasn't any older than my son Herman. His eyes were open, gaping at me.

The guys at the firehouse—they were looking right at me, too, talking to me, but I was invisible to them. They didn't see me any more than that boy did.

IT WAS FRIDAY NIGHT, AND THE BATTALION CHIEF was at the fire-house. In-house training was every Friday, and the officer-in-charge went over points with the men. The battalion chief did his inspection, but this guy was sneaky. He would sit in a chair beside one of the fire trucks and lean against a fender casual-like. When he thought nobody was looking, he'd reach down and rub his finger under the fender to see if it was clean. We were required to keep the apparatus clean on the bottom as well as on top.

There was a simple reason for this cleanliness. During runs, the undercarriage would pick up foreign objects, such as nails and debris, but we would never be told the reason for any chore, so unfortunately, we didn't know. You were just told to do everything a certain way. It was the same thing with shining brass. This wasn't busy-work, or something we did just to keep things looking nice. It was done because in the summertime when the brass turned green, it would be harder to slide down the pole. The fire department was a semimilitary organization, but it was detrimental to all of us when we were treated like dummies who had to follow orders but not be given the simplest of explanations.

As for the sneaky battalion chief, the next Friday I was ready for him. I thought, *I'm going to fix this SOB.* I knew he was going to pull that same trick again because he always pulled his chair up to the same place. I wouldn't have minded an honest inspection; we did our work, and we kept the equipment clean. But I didn't like the subterfuge. I took a graphite oil gun, which dispensed lubricating grease, and squirted it under the fender.

The battalion chief put his chair beside the truck like he always did. He leaned back against a fender and started talking. Then he put his finger under the fender. Everybody knew what I'd done, even the lieutenant, but they didn't like him either. He pulled out his finger, looked at it, didn't say anything, but pulled out a big old white railroad handkerchief and started wiping.

He never tried that trick again.

IN THE AFRICAN-AMERICAN CHURCHES OF BALTIMORE, the congregations would pray for the black firemen. They were proud of us, and they knew that we faced danger on the job and discrimination in the department.

It was no secret that not a single African-American firefighter was permitted to be in the firefighters' union, Local 734. In theory, there was nothing to prevent us from joining. All a new firefighter needed was an application from the union steward, to be co-signed by three firefighters who were union members. Then the entire union membership voted on the application.

White firefighters breezed through the process. When they became union members, they had access to information and contacts beneficial to their careers in the department.

Some stewards refused to hand out applications to black firefighters. If an application was obtained, it would be impossible to get three white firefighters to sign it. They knew they could be blackballed, because the full union membership was dead set against black members.

African-American firefighters needed representation, and in 1956, we decided that the only way to get it was to form our own union. But a department rule forbade membership in any other union other than Local 734.

For this reason, we formed not a union, but a "social club." The Social Association of Fire Fighters (SAFF) was put together by Charlie Thomas, who went to New York to get advice from an old-timer in the black union movement, A. Philip Randolph.

The department wasn't concerned about the SAFF because the top brass genuinely thought it was a social club. Unfortunately, the African-American firefighters seemed just as confused. There were 179 black firemen in the department by 1956, but few joined SAFF at first. I joined, but I knew it was only a step toward the goal of a real union. Thomas had the idea of working with the Negro American Labor Council and getting the AFL-CIO involved.

The year 1956 was also when the Urban League pressured the department into banning the RESERVED signs that enforced segregation in the firehouses. An executive order was handed down by the acting fire chief, Charles Thiess, but it was ignored by individual house captains.

That same year, Baltimore's Equal Employment Ordinance was passed, and SAFF was able to register its members' grievances about our exclusion from the firefighters' union with the Baltimore Equal Employment Opportunity Commission. The commission, the NAACP, and the AFL-CIO all came on board to give advice about a lawsuit to force the union to open up membership. The court case began in 1959, and I was one of the main movers behind the suit. We had a good lawyer, Ken Johnson, who later became a judge.

The bigoted union just didn't want us, and they tried every trick in the book to keep us out, but the lawsuit energized African-American firefighters to the possibility of representation and improved conditions. Many black firemen joined the SAFF.

When it came to doing the job, the action part where all firefighters worked side-by-side made it worthwhile, but it wasn't enough to end the segregation or the white firefighters' attitudes. But for a few moments, good sense and brotherhood would take over. White and black, firefighters had to work as a team. For me, not having to look over my shoulder all the time to see what trick or disgrace was being cooked up next, and knowing instead that my back was covered by the other guys, was a pleasure, and it made me sad to have to go back to the firehouse.

The moments of action were times when an African American could prove himself a hero. It was an answer to the prayers of the good ladies at the churches, provided that we survived.

One day in 1958, I was standing in front of Company 57, and I saw a motorized crane coming down the street. I remarked to some of the other firefighters standing there, "That guy's driving too fast." I could see that the big crane was bouncing on its supports.

Sure enough, about five minutes later we got a call to respond to Cabin Branch Creek in Curtis Bay. We raced there at once, to this small body of water about ten feet deep. Because it was part of the industrial area, the creek was polluted with all sorts of stuff that made the water brackish, almost black, since the chemical companies dumped in their toxic waste and raw sewage. There in all that glop was the crane. It had flipped over and lay on its side. The driver must have really been going fast, because the crane landed 25 feet from the roadway.

"I knew it!" I shouted over the siren. We jumped off the truck and went down the embankment. Two guys were in the crane when it left the road. One was riding in a chair outside, up in the back. His job was to lower the mechanism when the crane encountered power lines, and he was thrown clear. But the driver was trapped inside the cab. The other guy had swum out to help him, and the tide was coming in. The co-worker was holding the driver's head above water.

A fireman named Andy Kovoski was with me, and our first instinct was to go in after them. We pulled off our boots, dove in, and swam out in our clothes. We found the driver almost completely submerged. He was conscious, but in great pain. "What's going on?" I asked his partner. "Why won't he come out?"

"His foot's trapped under the steering wheel!"

The cab door was open. "Let me see what's happening!" I dove under, but the water was so murky that I couldn't see my hand in front of my face. The pollution felt like acid on my eyeballs. I had to grope around, over the foot pedals and gear levers. I found his foot, but his ankle was twisted, wedged beneath the steering column.

Every time I touched his leg, he'd holler and scream. I came up for air and saw that a crowd was gathering on the embankment. The captain was also up there. They called the rescue wagon, and when it showed up, a discussion ensued onshore about tying a rope from the crane to the truck to keep the crane from slipping further. I didn't see how that would help, because the real problem was the rising tide. Andy had the driver's head raised as far as he could manage. We only had a few minutes.

The driver was a big guy, 250 pounds. Whenever I went into the water to try to free his leg, he would scream and wince so violently that Andy had a hard time keeping water out of his mouth. I came up. There were a hundred people on shore. "We're going to have to cut this guy's leg off, or he dies," I said.

I went down and felt some space behind the column. I always carried a knife—most firefighters did. The knives were used in bedroom fires to cut open mattresses. Mattress fires were tricky, and we had to make sure they were truly out and there was nothing smoldering that could catch fire again. I came up and said to Andy: "I'm going to get his leg out one way or the other. Get ready."

I said to the driver, "I'm going to yank your foot out, or I'll have to cut it out." I went under again. This time, I felt some space behind the column. I twisted his ankle hard. I was underwater, but I could hear him scream. His foot came free.

I shot up and spit out a mouthful of foul water. Andy and I pulled the big guy higher so his head was well clear of the creek's surface. The rescue team brought out a basket, and they swam him back to shore in it.

I suddenly realized something. "Andy, how the hell did I get out here? I can't swim!"

When we first arrived, I didn't think, I just dove in. I now managed to dog-paddle back to shore. I came out of the creek covered with tar and chemical slime. It was a new experience for me, although in semirural Fairfield where there was no sewage system, I saw firefighters running through the fields and fall into cesspools. I now knew how they felt. It was all part of the firefighter's life.

The battalion chief had arrived, and he'd seen the rescue. He issued an order. "Captain, I want this written up for citations."

"What about me?" the captain asked.

"*Only* the men in the water."

There was a ceremony, and Andy and I got medals. Photographers took pictures of the fire commissioner pining a medal on my chest, and it made the newspapers. I was glad it wasn't the fire chief, who was a mean, racist bastard. I thought the commissioner was an all right guy. It was a proud moment.

IN CONTRAST TO THE FILTH AND RUBBLE we encountered fighting fires and performing rescues, the firehouse itself had to be immaculate.

A principal job was the floors. We used brown soap and lye. One guy cut up a half-dozen soap bars into chips, put them in a big bucket, set it on the stove, melted the chips, and poured lye into the brew. We used this concoction to scrub the floors. Today, they'd fine the fire department for polluting the harbor, because after scrubbing, we'd hose down the floor to wash off the soap, which went into the sewer and into the bay. You could eat off the apparatus floor.

But I hated washing floors. I wanted to get out of that in the worst way. Escaping those chores would be one of the rewards I'd receive if I could make an ambition come true: I wanted to become pump operator. Pump operators didn't do the lowly chores; they were responsible for the engine apparatus.

There were no African-American pump operators in 1959. It was the top job on the pumper engine, and an examination was required for the promotion. I'd been in the fire department for five years and had four children to support—little Marjorie was already nine. Instead of looking outside the fire department, I thought I should stay where I was and advance my way up.

That was the American way. You worked, learned, studied, became skilled, and moved on up to the next level of responsibility and rewards. The trouble was, the fire department wasn't ready for an African-American pump operator. And they'd let me know it.

"THE SIX SPARKS"

"I mean, we are somewhere", was the statement made by Herman, the organizer of that popular singing group of harmonizers "The Six Sparks."

They are booked for the entire spring season. These dates include engagement in New York. For this summer they have planned to travel from state to state.

The members of the group are: Herman Williams, Talmadge Nimmons, Alphonso Foy, Nathaniel Butler, Charles Prettyman, and Windell McNeal.

Playing with The Six Sparks in high school.

1951: Performing front and center with The Swallows
at the world-famous Apollo theater in Harlem.

Another
Swallows gig.

FIREMAN CITED—Fire Board Commissioners President William Hilgenberg pins a Meritorious Service Bar on Fire Fighter Herman Williams, Jr., 27, of 3024 Southland Rd., Cherry Hill, Baltimore. Mr. Williams was one of four men cited for the rescue of an occupant of a mobile crane which ran off the highway at Pennington Ave., an upset into a creek. Working under five feet of water, the firemen released the pinned driver and placed him on a metal stretcher which was hauled to safety. Mr. Williams has been with the department four and a half years. He is assigned to Engine Company No. 57, located at Pennington Ave. and Filbert St.

Receiving a Meritorious Service Award for diving into
the polluted Cabin Branch Creek and rescuing a crane worker.

Moonlighting with The Pyramids in 1965.

The billboard that was part of the fire prevention campaign
that saw fire-related deaths in Baltimore go from
an average of 50 a year to 19 during my tenure.

On duty at the scene of a fire.

With Mayor Schmoke (photo by R. B Chapman,
courtesy of the Baltimore mayor's office).

With Mayor Martin O'Malley
(photo by S. E. Cuffie, courtesy of the Baltimore mayor's office).

Cooking at a benefit for the fire department.

Riding proudly with Marjie at the city parade.

A family portrait from the '70s. Clockwise from top left:
son-in-law Ronald Hines; daughter Marjorie; daughter-in-law
Milagros; son Herman III; son Montel; daughter Clolita; Herman;
Marjie; Marjorie and Ronald's daughters, Rene and Michelle.

Announcing my retirement in 2001 with Mayor Martin O'Malley
(photo by Amy Davis, courtesy of *The Baltimore Sun*).

Proud parents
with son Montel
upon his gradua-
tion from the U.S.
Naval Academy.

Marjie and I celebrating our 45th wedding anniversary with
daughters Clolita and Marjorie.

A portrait of proud parents with Montel.

Herman III
with one of his
wire sculptures.

Another picture with Montel.

Traveling at last: New Orleans.

Enjoying Paris.

Our trip to South Africa.

❧ CHAPTER SIX ❧

Front of the Truck

It was 5 A.M., and we were working through the burned-out remains of a bar. At times, fire fighting could be like police work, when you look into the dark underbelly of society. It was obvious that she'd been stabbed, this woman in the rubble. She was white, young, and (we later learned) had once been beautiful. We found her after we put out the fire.

We were "overhauling," what we called the after-work to make sure the fire was completely killed and wouldn't flare up again. We stopped as soon as we found the woman's body. The captain called the Fire Investigation Bureau (FIB).

The FIB usually went to a fire scene after the fire was out to determine its origin, where and how it started. If evidence of arson was found, it became the responsibility of the police arson division to catch the perpetrator. A firefighter couldn't arrest or detain anybody. If someone died in a fire, culpable homicide was added to the arson charge.

At first, we didn't see a murder weapon, even though we went through the debris, brick by brick. But then we found a knife. By that time, the police had arrived, and they were pleased with the find. The operation showed the need to take care with cleanup after a fire—no dumping things left and right. The police later let us know that the bar was set afire to hide a murder.

Every so often, we ran into a lot of arson. It was a way for people to dispose of their problems—but it was a dangerous way. Sometimes the perpetrator would die in the blaze, like that guy we found behind a door, his corpse frozen in place with his arm raised still holding a match he intended to throw on the gasoline he'd spread. But the lit match ignited the fumes before he could throw it. Firefighters worked with the police to get to the bottom of every case.

We returned in the apparatus to Company 57 to hang the hoses to dry, scrub ourselves down, and have some coffee. Then I hit the books. I was studying to take the pump-operator exam, and the captain was more than happy to give me help. He allowed me to use his office to review procedure manuals and technical books—his own books.

He was doing this for one reason: He didn't think I would ever become a pump operator. He even humored me by allowing me to drive the engine truck to a fire scene. The pump operator, who was known as the "engine man" until 1958, had a prestigious job because he drove and maintained the apparatus and possessed specialized knowledge.

The captain knew something I didn't: The department top brass and the firefighters' union didn't want an African-American pump operator, and they were prepared to repeat the same tricks they'd used six years before when they delayed the entrance of blacks into the fire department.

The captain had another reason to keep me happy with pump operator training without having to worry that I would get the job. The firehouse already had two pump operators, one on each shift, and they weren't going to retire anytime soon.

But then another shift was added at all the houses throughout the department. There was an immediate need for 59 new pump operators, one per engine company.

Hundreds of firefighters took the test. There was a written section, where you displayed your knowledge of engine maintenance and vehicle repair, and a performance test. I felt that I did well on both. One of the practical tests was drafting water, or pumping water, out of the harbor. That was a specialty of mine because I'd practiced at Curtis Bay.

The list of those who passed, with their rankings, was issued. The newspapers got hold of it and published the names of the top 59 scorers who had earned promotions to pump operator.

I was listed, just barely, but I was still there plain as day. I came in 58th.

But my jubilation was premature.

The reality that they might have an African-American pump operator hit Company 57 like a ton of bricks. Suddenly, all the help I got—the driving lessons, the instruction, the books, all that goodwill—vanished.

The lieutenant made his views clear: "As long as I'm lieutenant, no nigger is going to drive me."

At headquarters downtown, somebody let the cat out of the bag, and it was discovered that this Herman Williams on the list was black. I got a call, the type of call a lowly firefighter usually didn't get. It was from the executive secretary of the Fire Board. We all knew him as THE man. He was the businessperson in charge of everything, and the real administrator of the department. In those days, the fire chief was more of a figurehead. The chief could come in to work at ten and leave at two. The Fire Board ran the show.

"Williams, there's been a mistake."

It felt like something had dropped inside my gut, because I knew at once that I was about to get robbed of a position I had worked hard for and had earned. "Sir, what mistake?"

"This list the newspapers ran, your name shouldn't be on it."

"Sir, how could this happen?" But he wouldn't give a reason. He said he was sorry if I got my hopes up.

But it wasn't a matter of hope, I thought. I was already listed for a promotion; it was a fact. The executive secretary of the department was really telling me that I was wrong to have *any* hope in the first place.

The executive secretary was true to his word about my being out. Whenever there was a promotion in the fire department, a general order went out to every firehouse. In morning and afternoon lineups, the order was read by the officer in charge, so everyone knew what was going on. The general order went out about the pump-operator promotions. All the names were read except mine.

Everyone in the company knew I had been listed originally. I didn't get any congratulations when the newspapers ran the list because they were in shock. But they were aware, and to have the revised list read to all of them with me being excluded was humiliating.

That should have been the end of it, as far as the fire department brass was concerned. But they didn't figure that I knew something about big-city politics.

It was a time when a few behind-the-scenes string-pullers could dispense favors and correct wrongs. Baltimore had a few of these "godfather" types, who weren't involved in organized crime but were politically connected and looked after neighborhoods or ethnic groups. They listened to people's problems or requests, then they picked up the phone, connected with the appropriate city or union official, and called in a favor. They could get things done.

I knew enough about this trading of favors to know that if I ever needed one, I'd have to build up some credit first. I contributed to political campaigns and charities whose patrons were these powerful players. I didn't have a lot of money to give, but I gave consistently, and I got on the right lists. After a while, the politicians' staffs would know they could call Herman Williams for a five- or ten-dollar donation. I was too busy playing bass with the band when I wasn't on the job to attend fundraisers, but my motto was, "You're running for council, I'll buy a ticket. You're running for mayor, I'll buy two tickets." It helped that I usually picked the right horses in the election races.

The African-American community had its "godfather" in Willie Adams, a big guy who dressed impeccably, looked at you closely, and listened just as attentively. His expressions went from grave to jovial. He had a big, good-natured laugh. I went to see him and explained the problem with my revoked promotion.

To my surprise, Adams sent me to another political insider, Irv Kovens, who was Jewish. Like Adams, Kovens knew how to turn the wheels of city machinery.

I sat in his office and explained, "I strongly believe that the only reason they didn't take me is because I'm Colored."

A well-dressed man like Adams, Kovens sat behind his desk and nodded his head in agreement. He was a man of few words. He didn't need them; he knew what buttons to push. "You go to your job. I'll take care of this."

By the time I got to the firehouse, it was done. I got another call from the executive secretary of the Fire Board. His tone was, Gee, the strangest thing just happened: "You know that mistake on the list? We got it all straightened out. You're promoted to pump operator."

Victory was sweet, and I was elated. He added, "You stay right where you are, at 57."

The reason I was reassigned to my firehouse, I soon found out, was that the department brass wanted to keep quiet that there was now an African-American pump operator. I did get the promotion, but in a break with procedure, no general order went out to announce it. Without the general order, no one knew officially that I was promoted. They kept me at the same station so the news wouldn't get out.

And the underhanded approach made it easier for the lieutenant to again say, "As long as I'm a lieutenant, no nigger is going to drive me."

He meant drive the engine truck. I'd been looking forward to that duty, being behind the wheel of that big red machine, racing down the street, flashing the lights and wailing the siren. *Everybody get out of my way—this is an emergency!*

I knew the job, but on our very first alarm, the lieutenant ordered me to the rear step of the truck, to the "back of the bus." It was 1959, and we thought Rosa Parks had put an end to such discrimination several years before in Montgomery, Alabama. But the reality still existed in many forms elsewhere. While I stood on the engine's back step, some white boy drove, so young that the acne blazed across his face like a three-alarm.

This was an illegal breach of department policy, which said that the pump operator always drove. When we got to the fire, the lieutenant ordered me to get to work operating the pump.

The "driver" hopped out and took the hose. The lieutenant could no longer order me to go inside a burning building because I had to operate the pump. This involved monitoring the gauges that showed intake pressure from hydrants and outlet pressure, and keeping the required balance. About 100 pounds of pressure came in from a hydrant, which had to be regulated so that 60 pounds of pressure came out of the hose nozzle. You had to do the hydraulic calculations to make that happen.

Being denied the right to do my job and being sent to the back of the truck was a humiliation. It was worse knowing that the guy in the driver's seat didn't have my experience. It was a miracle we didn't get into a wreck, and for a while there, public safety was in jeopardy. But we managed to get back to the firehouse, with me riding in the rear.

This went on for a few weeks, but I kept quiet. I knew I was the pump operator, and it was just a matter of time before proper procedure was reestablished. I didn't give in, but I bided my time. Somebody must have told the lieutenant he was going to get into trouble and was setting himself up for something big. The trick the fire department pulled to deny me my promotion never hit the newspapers, and this new twist of not letting me do my job would have been embarrassing for the department if some reporter had caught wind of it.

The day came when the lieutenant didn't order me to the back of the truck. I took my rightful place in the cab, and he sat silently beside me. I switched on the siren, got the light array twirling, and drove the engine out of the station.

I was finally at the front of the bus.

Four months later, the department legitimately and properly promoted a second African American to the pump-operator job. A general order was distributed to all the stations, and there was my name. They sneaked me in for the record as having been promoted.

By then, everyone in the department knew anyway by way of "telegram/telephone/tell-a-fireman."

It seemed that anything these guys could do to make me a second-class citizen, they'd do. But I had to wonder about the intelligence of those guys. Here they were humiliating me, but their lives were in my hands. What if they were in a burning building, in the fire room (where the blaze was), and the pump shut down so they didn't have any water? How stupid was that? Fighting fire, everyone's safety depended on everyone else.

I WAS NO LONGER WASHING WINDOWS, scrubbing floors, and polishing brass. My full-time job was to maintain the engine company apparatus. I lubricated and cleaned, and kept the pump mechanism working and ready to go. A pump operator had to be a mechanic.

The engines from the 1920s that were second-line equipment were more than 40 years old when I maintained them. The 1922 Ahrens-Fox was a classic, a museum piece even then. Nobody else knew how to keep her going.

Chemical fires were like any other conflagrations: Once they cooled off, by water or other means, they stopped. It was the gases coming off the chemicals that ignited, and these had to be dissipated. My engine was equipped with a gooseneck nozzle, which sprayed water up so it fell with more force. The truck's main hose had a $2^1/2$-inch opening, the standard fit for hydrants. A hose with a larger $4^1/2$-inch opening was used to draft water out of the river or bay.

A pumper engine was a mobile water carrier. The five-man crew that went with her was made up of the pump operator, the officer, the leading-off man—the youngest guy on the team who hooked the hose to the hydrant—and two hose men, one who held and aimed the nozzle, the other who held the hose behind him and followed him wherever he went. The truck tank carried a limited amount of water, depending on the size of the truck. Hydrants might or might not have enough pressure to do the job. If more pressure was needed to get at a fire on a high floor, I would kick in the engine-powered pump.

After the Baltimore Fire of 1904, which destroyed the entire downtown area, the city set up a pumping system to maintain 100 pounds psi (pressure per square inch) through nine miles of water main that fed all the hydrants in 170 acres of downtown. The system was used until 1966. For large downtown fires that were beyond the capability of an engine like mine, the department kept four high-pressure hose companies.

Baltimore had a very old housing stock, much of it dating from the 19th century. These were the classic Baltimore-style row houses, with the fine marble stoops in front. But the wooden structures could be as flammable as the chemical companies that went up with such regularity at Curtis Bay.

For example, a smoker would fall asleep in a chair and let the cigarette in his hand touch the chair fabric. That cigarette could be smoldering for hours, and while that was happening, gases would rise up. They'd be trapped by the ceiling and built up in the confined space of the room waiting for someone to come in. A person would open the door, oxygen would rush in, the person would turn on a light, a spark would ignite the gas, and there would be an explosion. The whole room would light up. (This is why if you're in a burning building or you smell something burning, you must *feel* a door before opening it. If the door is hot, keep it closed!)

To prevent more pockets of gases from exploding, the truck company was the first to get to work when it came to ventilating a building. While they were up on the ladders, the engine company had to be careful not to knock one of them with the hose spray. The civilians expected us to hit the fire with the hoses first thing. They complained angrily when we held off to let the hook-and-ladder men knock holes to draw the fire. But without proper ventilation, there would be the danger of a backdraft, the explosion that came when a surge of new oxygen from an opening door triggered trapped gases.

This happened to me. Engine 57 arrived at a burning house, and we took the rear of the building. My old company, 35, was in front. The building hadn't been properly ventilated, and when 35 came in, we came in at the same moment. The fire ignited with the introduction of oxygen, and a solid wall of flame came up the hall toward us. I knew that if the building had been ventilated, the fire would have gone upward, not horizontally, directly toward the opened doors. Fire always follows the path of least resistance, and gases rise. Luckily, we could hear the roar of the flames through the smoke even before we saw them. Everyone dropped to the floor. The explosion passed over our heads.

But perhaps my scariest moment as a firefighter came at a chemical plant called the Food Machinery Company. We didn't know what went on inside—it was some kind of secret operation. But every so often they'd have an explosion, followed by a fire. At the station, we'd hear the factory's warning siren, and then *blam!* Outside, it looked like an atomic explosion, with a giant orange fireball rising over the roofs. I was doing some engine maintenance one time when I heard that siren. I braced myself, and then I heard a loud explosion.

Even before the alarm came in to the station, and the gong was pulled for us to go into action, we knew. We immediately suited up and responded.

When we arrived a few minutes later, people were running out of the company yard. "Don't go in!" they shouted. "There may be a second explosion." But in a situation like this, where hesitancy could cost lives, we still had to go in. I was frightened because no one knew if there would be another explosion.

We hooked up to the standing pipe attached to the building. As the pump operator, I stayed with the truck, monitoring the gauges and making adjustments to keep the pressure up. But another serious explosion would have incinerated the truck.

I could smell burnt flesh. Then we saw him—a fellow who was working in the laboratory. We didn't know what he did, but we later learned that he'd caused the explosion. It was so powerful that it blew him through a concrete wall, across the yard 20 feet, and into a wire mesh fence. We saw his body embedded in it.

It was scary waiting for more explosions, which fortunately didn't come. But after we put out the fire and I drove the engine away from the rubble that was once the factory, my foot was shaking on the accelerator.

I WANTED TO DO BETTER FOR MY KIDS than my father had done for me. Not that he did poorly, I just wanted to do better. As a parent, I found that you did everything by pure instinct. The kids had to do their homework before watching TV. I didn't think about it; I just laid down the law.

Marjorie, Clolita, Herman, and Montel were four lively kids. They all found their own things to excel in at school. Marjie and I went to see them at their recitals and plays, and we cheered them on at sporting events. At Christmastime, we hung up stockings over the fireplace, and I filled them up and put their presents under the tree after the kids went to bed. I once went all the way, dressing up in a Santa Claus costume to surprise them.

I took them on local trips to the beach, to Baltimore's museums, and day trips to the many historical sites the region had to offer. We went to Washington, D.C., for the monuments, to Harper's Ferry in West Virginia, and to the Gettysburg battlefield in Pennsylvania. I would also encourage the kids to go to the library.

But I wanted my children to know a life different from the inner-city existence I'd always known. Times were changing, the suburbs surrounding Baltimore were growing, and I wanted the American suburban ideal pictured every week in *Life* magazine for my kids. Glen Burnie was a location in the southwest outskirts of Baltimore where I heard that housing sites were available. One day, Marjie and I drove there from Cherry Hill, and I saw a sign on a tree that said "Lot for Sale." I said to Marjie, "This is a nice spot to build a house."

She agreed, and we started saving up until we had $1,500 for the 1/3-acre plot. There was electricity, but because it was out of town, the area had no sewage or water. We would have to install a septic tank and dig a well, operated by a small electric pump. And, of course, I would need a house to complete the *Life* magazine picture for my family.

I built the house myself. It was 1960, and I joined a majority of voters who put John Kennedy in the White House. It seemed like the dawn of a new era, and I was sort of a pioneer myself at the fire department. But discrimination in attitude and deed never really let up in the firehouses toward African Americans throughout the '60s. For me, construction work was a means of escape, as well as a way to enhance my income later on.

One of the lieutenants at Company 57 was helpful. "I know this guy named Biddy. He can build you a house. That way you don't have to get some big-time contractor who will stick it to you."

Biddy Walker was an old, grizzled German. He chewed tobacco, and his mouth was always working beneath his snow-white beard. He had chewed tobacco for so long that the sides of his mouth were stained brown. He had an old black dog about as old as he was who was always at his side.

I met him at the Glen Burnie plot, and he asked me why I'd called him. "I want to build a house here, ranch-style."

He looked at me suspiciously. "How many children you got?" I told him, and he laid down the law. "Four?! You don't want no ranch! You want a Cape Cod, with an upstairs for a growing family."

He was such a character that he spoke to me like I was a damn fool, *not* because I was black, but because he felt I had brains but I wasn't using them. I had to like this irascible, blunt-spoken guy, even when he proved to be a very difficult taskmaster.

I asked him, "Who's going to build this house?"

"You are."

"What? I don't know how to build a house."

But he ended up *making* me do the work. Maybe he saw that I didn't have much money to hire workers, but he also had the *confidence* in me that I could do it. And I had confidence in *him* because everyone I talked to said that Biddy was good. He wasn't a good businessman, though. His office was his shirt pocket, where he kept all his papers and contracts on teeny pieces of paper.

There never was a blueprint or drawing of any kind. We simply drove by other houses that Biddy had built and compared them. "Your house has to have a two-car garage," was one of the things he told me.

I drove out after work and cut down all the trees myself to clear the lot. I did this with an ax and cleared the roots with a pick and shovel. That old pioneer spirit possessed me, preparing the ground for the homestead!

Then we started digging the basement. Guy, Biddy's son, came with a backhoe tractor and dug out a big hole.

When it came to buying building supplies and meeting the other expenses of the house, I was short by $5,000. Marjie suggested, "Let's go see my father." Algie White was one of the best men I knew. He had a lot of integrity and was a real role model for me. He wasn't rich, but Marjie felt I should talk things over with him. I didn't want to, but I put away my pride, and we drove over.

"What do you need?" he asked. I told him the amount, and without pondering a moment, he said to Marjie, "Bring my checkbook."

I was floored. "I'll pay you back in two months."

"Forget it." I was really moved by his confidence in me.

The foundation excavation was a big job. I hired Herman Clemens, the second African-American firefighter to be assigned to Company 57, to help me, and we were working the same shift. When he arrived at the 57, the firefighters started calling me Big Herman, and him Little Herman.

Biddy laid out a foundation trench with pegs and string around the basement excavation. The rectangular frame that would hold the wall foundation ran 12 inches wide, and 12 inches deep. "I want that hole dug by the time I get back," Biddy ordered, and drove off in his pickup. It was June, and stifling hot. We worked with a pick and shovel. I'd never done work so strenuous in my life. By the time he got back, we were just about lying in that hole.

When Biddy returned, it was 6 P.M. The sun was a bronze furnace in the summer sky. He took one look at the foundation trench and turned right back around. "I'll come back tomorrow. We'll pour cement."

The truck came and poured the cement for the foundation footing. The concrete blocks for the basement walls went up next, and I started seeing a house come together.

The house would have a brick veneer over a wood frame, so we started making the frame. The work was hard, but the feeling of accomplishment kept me going. That and Biddy pushing us along. A truck pulled up and dumped a pile of lumber. Biddy sawed one piece and told Clemens and me, "Cut every piece of wood this size!" We each had a saw and got to work. Biddy marked every piece with an X. "I want four nails at each X! You don't have to think where to put them!"

He hated the way I swung a hammer. "Who taught you to use a hammer? You don't shove a hammer; you throw it! You look at the nail, and you throw it!" I tried it his way, but twice he came back, cursing. "Goddamn it, I showed you three times how to use a hammer, and you still don't do it right. Get off the job. You're fired!"

"But it's my house!"

"I don't give a shit. Get out!"

Needless to say, I started learning how to hammer properly after that.

I began the cigar habit because of him. At first, Biddy gave me some tobacco to chew. "Try this." I chewed it. But when I went off one day and bought some, he complained, "Don't use that. It has too many chemicals. Try this."

He pulled out a King Edward cigar. I started chewing on that instead. In later years, I'd be given fine Cuban and Dominican cigars. I'd take two puffs and end up chewing the rest.

The house started to come together. We put in pipes and a water heater, and a company with a big drill made the well. Then the septic tank was put in the yard. One thing Marjie wanted was a fireplace in the living room, with buff-colored brick around it. We installed an oil furnace in the basement and put shingles on the roof. When we were done, I'd learned how to build a house from bottom to top. Biddy even made the kitchen cabinets. We didn't fool with the electricity, but brought in an electrician.

The kids came out to watch. Herman and Montel ran up to play in what would be the attic. There was no ceiling, yet, but they were excited: All that space, inside and out, after the series of cramped apartments we lived in at Cherry Hill.

I was working below and heard a crack. I looked up and Herman's foot was sticking down through the ceiling.

I hollered, "Stop fooling around up there before you break your necks!" I knew how to get my kids' attention.

I was from the Old School that held that if you spared the rod, you'd spoil the child. When I was a kid, if you did something wrong, my father pulled off his belt and *whupped* you. *Bam!* At school, the teacher had a big old ruler. "Hold out your hands!" *Bam!* Then she would call my mother. When I got home, I'd get another sock for misbehaving at school. *Bam!* Then my father would come home, hear the news, and *Bam!* However, when I look back, I can't say that that way ever solved anything.

I thought that I could talk Lincoln off a penny, and I could in a lot of situations, but I think that sometimes my kids would have preferred that I slap them upside their heads than talk to them. I could preach about right and wrong, but I could see that they wanted me to *shut up!*

Later, when I advanced through city service and had to supervise workers, it was the same thing. I called workers in for a disciplinary hearing, they stood in front of my desk, and I sat there and lectured them. I could see their expressions after a while: "Hit me, fire me, shoot me—just shut up!" I made an impression so they wouldn't repeat their mistake.

Construction of the four-bedroom house took three months. We put in a lawn, so I went down to Sears and bought a garden tractor. We put in bushes and hedges all around. The appliances were installed; as well as a ceramic floor for the kitchen, slate floor for the dining room, draperies and curtains in all the rooms—and then it was time to move in.

There were shopping centers all around, and the kids did everything that average American kids did. They went to movies, played school sports, and watched *The Flintstones* and *The Bullwinkle Show* on TV. I couldn't watch much TV because I didn't have the time. I mostly watched the news. But not at six in the evenings. That was dinnertime with the kids. I'd hear what they did at school, and we'd talk about current events: the Space Race, Cuba, the Berlin Wall, and the Civil Rights marches.

Marjie had a car to pick up the kids after school activities, and she would pick up the neighbors' kids, too. The area started to develop, and about two years after we built the house, the county came through with water and sewage.

I was literally helping the area grow. When I was building our house, people came by, thought I was a contractor, and asked Clemens and me to build for them. We started by building a house right across the street. When I finished with my house, I owed Biddy some money. He worked for $3 an hour. He was such an honest old guy that at the end of the week he'd give me his hours, and he never added an extra minute. I ended the job owing him $2,000.

"All right," he said, "you can work it off." I went into partnership with him on the other house construction jobs. I built my house in my off-hours, and I started working the same way with Biddy.

"How do we keep track of the time?" I asked.

He broke off a piece of slate rock and nailed it to a wall. "Write on that when you come in."

I got to work. Like most Americans alive at that time, I remember where I was when I heard the news that President Kennedy was shot. I was building a house, up on a roof nailing shingles. By the end of my partnership with Biddy, I'd built a couple of dozen houses with him.

Playing with The Pyramids was another source of income I still needed. But there was some shame in it. I always regretted that I never went to college. The Pyramids played at social functions, and the guests would be people I knew from high school and the projects who now had their degrees. They were in the professions, doctors and lawyers. They'd made something of themselves. For me, the novelty of being a pioneer African-American firefighter had worn off, and I was feeling like an ordinary Smoke Eater. I knew I would never be invited to those glittering social functions; I was just there as the entertainment.

When I played my music, I tried to disguise myself. I wore sunglasses so fewer people would recognize me, and I just went home when the gig was over.

By then, I knew I was going to be a firefighter for the rest of my life, so I didn't do anything to jeopardize my job. I was no jive-talking musician. I never wanted to bring attention to myself or embarrass my family. I had to credit my father. I did believe that stuff about Williams being a name you had to respect.

I hid behind dark glasses because I didn't want anyone to know I was playing. There was a stereotype about musicians in those days—that they were irresponsible, drank, and ran after women. At social functions where we were playing, I felt embarrassed when I knew people from school were talking about me. "Oh, look, there's Herman up on the bandstand. He's a musician. Probably drinking, got all the girls."

They didn't know I was making more money than most of them in my three jobs. I wasn't about to give up the music income, and as the '60s went on, The Pyramids never stopped getting gigs. The music changed, and so did our outfits. In place of the first band uniform—the burgundy blazer and black trousers—we wore dashikis. I put on my mellow voice to sing our cover versions of Johnny Mathis, Otis Redding, The Temptations and The Spinners, then revved it up for Sam and Dave and James Brown.

I was now well into my 30s, and I felt that I should have advanced further in the fire department, but I was held back. The advances people of color made in the 1960s seemed to make us more impatient for what was rightfully ours. Dr. Martin Luther King, Jr., was a great man, and he was bringing good things to our people. But there was so much further to go, for me and all other

African Americans. I would feel the discrimination every time the fire department held its annual Memorial Day remembrance.

A prayer service for firefighters who lost their lives in the line of duty was held in various churches every year in the early spring. Everybody who was off-shift was expected to attend. The battalion chief came around the firehouse. "I want everyone in church tomorrow."

At the church door, they'd take down your name. If you didn't show up, the next time they did your efficiency rating for the year, the battalion chief would take into consideration your "cooperation," and you'd be marked down. Or you could apply for a vacation and be turned down.

All of the city firefighters would parade to church. It was an impressive display. People in the neighborhood where the service was held came out to watch. Sometimes 2,000 firefighters marched in lines down the street in our dress uniforms. Because we didn't have any marching training, it could be funny. Guys were looking at their feet, and double-stepping to keep up.

The parade and service didn't bother me, but what followed was depressing. A religious retreat was held every year, and all of the white firefighters would go. No blacks were invited, not a single one of us. The firefighters' union was fighting our lawsuit in court to keep African Americans out of the union. So they'd do their praying, a bunch of bigoted firefighters, and then on Monday they'd come back and mistreat their black co-workers. I couldn't understand these guys being so "religious," but never extending the hand of inclusion to us.

In 1961 and '62, not a single African-American firefighter who sought a promotion received a maximum efficiency rating. But 68 percent of white firefighters, over two-thirds of those applying for promotions, were given maximum efficiency ratings. I knew it wasn't because the African-American fire-fighters were inefficient. Part of the problem was that these ratings were based in part on written examinations, and copies of the examinations were provided to white firefighters because the questions were written by their superiors in the firefighters' union, the one that black firefighters weren't permitted to join.

There was a lot about the fire department that didn't make sense, and most of it had to do with continuing to do things the old way, even if they went against common sense. These could be major issues, such as depriving the department of valuable manpower by thwarting the advancement of African Americans; to small things, such as the business of thawing out frozen fire hydrants in winter.

The procedure was that during cold weather we'd go around to inspect the hydrants. First, we'd shovel snow from around the hydrant. Then we'd put a flaming torch made of oily rags around the bonnet, or lid, of the hydrant. Every time I did that I thought how dumb it was, because the temperature would be 30 degrees, and the hydrant was going to freeze again. Sure enough, a half hour after we left, it froze. It wasn't until 1989 that the Manual of Procedure (MOP), the fire department's bible, was changed, and it instructed firefighters to put oil on the hydrant bonnet after thawing to prevent refreezing.

It was that same lack of common sense, suppressed in the name of tradition, that later caused the city so many self-inflicted problems because its firehouses weren't representative of the community they served.

African Americans made up an increasing percentage of Baltimore's population during the 1960s. In 1970, with almost half of the city's population composed of African Americans, only 14 percent of the fire department's employees were black.

It stood to reason that people who determined that the city's fire department was disrespectful of its African-American employees—or saw that they simply weren't being hired—would feel that the department had little respect for Baltimore's black community as a whole. Anyone watching America's other cities burn in race riots, from Watts to Detroit and elsewhere, wouldn't have been surprised by the eruption that hit Baltimore when Martin Luther King, Jr., was assassinated.

By that time, I'd found a way out of the tension of firehouse life, as well as the feeling of inferiority that caused me to hide behind dark glasses at The Pyramids' gigs to escape the notice of my accomplished former classmates.

If you did a job well, you'd eventually be noticed by the people who needed you, no matter what your race. That's the way America works. I was a good pump operator, so the battalion chief in charge of the department's Fire Academy asked me to teach pump operation there.

Some black guys who had entered the department after I did were getting promoted, so I was getting angry at myself for not getting the same recognition. When I saw the chance to be a lieutenant at the academy, I went for it. I stopped working for Biddy and devoted my time to studying. In six months' time, hitting the firefighting books until I could quote the data in my sleep, I was ready for the exam. A general examination for the fire lieutenant position had 100 questions, but for lieutenant in the Fire Academy, it was 120 questions.

I passed, and this time there were no tricks, no subterfuge to block my promotion. I was 36 years old, and when I transferred out of Company 57, I was old enough to pass my years of knowledge and acquired skills to new recruits. After 13 years of daily fire fighting—the risks and drama, the racial tension and all the chores—I was ready to assume a new role. I would be a teacher.

I went into the assignment without prejudice. I would teach black and white recruits equally, even if I thought that the white guys might eventually join a union where they'd be working *against* the interests of the black members. Our lawsuit had been successful, and the union had been forced to pry open its doors to African-American members. At first, the union tried to force all black firefighters to pay back dues from the day they joined the force, which for me would have been seven years' worth of money to an organization that had tried to keep me out all that time. We would have nothing to do with such a deal, and the requirement was dropped.

By 1965, most of the African-American firefighters had joined Local 734, but our numbers made up less than 10 percent of union membership, and our interests—especially our complaints with regard to discrimination—were ignored.

But there was always a possibility that as a teacher I could make a difference, perhaps positively influencing the white guys' attitudes. I was sure going to try.

❧ Chapter Seven ☙

Training the Line

By 1967, the Civil Rights movement had instilled confidence and expectations in a new generation of African-American men who joined the fire department. Some of the young white recruits had also been affected by the changes of the 1960s, showing a newfound respect for blacks that their elders had not known—and those who didn't knew that the days were over when they could walk all over us.

The name "Big Herm" was retired. The recruits called me "Lieutenant."

The Fire Academy wanted an African-American instructor, and they also needed someone to teach pumps. For about a year, I was an instructor, and then after passing the exam to become a lieutenant, I left Engine 57 and taught at the academy on a full-time basis.

The classes were composed of 30 recruits or more, and they came in and learned it all. There was textbook instruction, but my teaching was hands-on. I had an easy method for cutting through the formulas to make things simple. For example, nozzle pressure is very important when you're fighting a fire. It's not a matter of just opening a hydrant and finding that the force you need is automatically there. I taught the recruits that the way to calculate pressure is to, essentially, feel the hose. The hose was like a living thing, especially when it got away from a green recruit and snaked around, spraying everything in sight. With practice, a recruit could tell by the hardness of the hose if the pressure was sufficient. Out in the field, there was no time for a paper and pencil, where you could calculate the number of hose sections you had. A single section was 50 feet—the elevation of the nozzle and the engine pressure.

I treated all the recruits the same. "I kick them all in the butt!" I told Marjie.

She knew when I was kidding. "Not too hard, I hope!" If any woman could read her man like a book, it was Marjie. If I was now a lieutenant in the fire department, it was due to her support. During my first decade and a half with the department, the stuff I'd had to put up with could have turned me into a heavy drinker like Wade. As it was, I drank too much, but Marjie's patience saw me through. Every time I drove away from our house, there she was at the window. She'd wave, and I'd wave back—every time, even if I was just going on an errand. She didn't have to do that.

The devotion she showed me reminded me that I was a lucky man to be married to her and have four good kids. Every marriage requires work, and I wasn't the easiest person to put up with, unlike my wife. She was always cheerful, outgoing, and charitable. I've heard her question some of the things people did, but she was never harsh. When I made mistakes, she was a saint about them. I've always loved her for that.

At the academy, I was the recruits' first exposure to the fire department. I was aware of that responsibility. The "military" part of the organization—the lining up, drills, and saluting—was one aspect, but teamwork and cooperation also comprised part of the training. In just about every class, at least one recruit would drop out. We'd have to get rid of one or two others because they couldn't cut the mustard. It was demanding training, but it wasn't meant to torture anyone, and my goal was to get the recruits excited about the job of fire fighting.

For the first time in my career with the fire department, I was in a position to exercise some influence and do some good.

The first thing I did as a lieutenant at the Fire Academy was warn recruits about the unnecessary destruction of property. That had always bothered me, all those years fighting fires and seeing how some of the truck-company guys would attack houses. I noticed that the poorer the house, the less regard the firefighters had for it. Property owned or occupied by African Americans was treated with little respect, and carelessness while ventilating a building would cause a lot of damage. This led to resentment toward the fire department. It all came down, again, to respect—giving it and receiving it. A time was rapidly approaching when some firefighters' disregard for the community would lead to a dangerous situation.

I told the recruits to use common sense, and to remember that a building is someone's home or business. "You don't always have to break a window to ventilate a room; you can just as easily raise the window."

Teaching responsible attitudes was high on my agenda. I personally never considered fighting fires to be fun, because other people's property was being destroyed. Every fire was a personal or business loss for someone. Fires were always traumatic, and they changed lives and cost lives. I liked fire fighting because I liked helping people. I would hear the firefighters at the station houses—either young guys who were gung ho or older guys who were bored—say, "I hope we have a run tonight." And I would think, *You mean you hope someone's going to be in trouble!*

Racial tension was present at the Fire Academy, but it was kept under control. However, one incident did occur during Fire Prevention Week. Baltimore's fire department, like many city fire departments, sponsored a public-information campaign during Fire Prevention Week. At the Fire Academy, we used the training facility to put on what we called among ourselves a "Thrill Show." To the public, we called it a "safety demonstration" to show the destructive power of fire and the modern methods of fire fighting.

Teachers brought children in by the busload to see the recruits go through their training. We'd bring out the apparatus, and raise the hook and ladder's Big Stick, or main ladder. The recruits would scramble up and train hoses on a fire we set in a mock building.

Each year, the highlight of the "show" was when the captain in charge of the academy put on a fireproof asbestos suit and walked through fire. He was a white officer, because there were no African-American captains at the time. His outfit looked like a baggy silver space suit (with a visor for looking out), and it completely covered him. The captain had been doing the stunt for five years, but it was a risky operation. We lit debris on the ground, the flames shot up, and the captain entered the conflagration. While he was making his way through the fire, I stood nearby and held a hose in case something went wrong.

The flame temperature exceeded 2,000 degrees, and any material, even asbestos, could withstand direct contact for only so long. The suit started to burn, and patches burst into flame. As soon as I saw this happening, I turned the water stream on the captain. The impact of the water on the burning suit and the surrounding flames caused an explosion of steam, and the captain was nearly cooked like a lobster in that suit.

He wasn't injured, but when we got him away and he threw off his headgear, he was angry. I'd never seen a man so "steamed." He seriously thought I was trying to get him. "Why'd you put that water on me?!"

I didn't answer, because all he had to do was look at his charred suit to see the trouble he'd been in. It was my job to douse the flames, and anyone else would have done the same thing. But the captain reacted as if I had it in for him. Always below the surface there was a suspicion that some black-on-white or white-on-black animosity was at work when a conflict arose.

As for the firewalking stunt in the asbestos suit, that was the end of it. In future "Thrill Shows," it was dropped.

For the recruits, I was the first black teacher some of these guys had ever had. But if they had a problem with me, they kept quiet for the most part.

IN FIRE FIGHTING, THE SMOKE SMELL STAYED WITH YOU. This was especially true for me at the Fire Academy, because every day I'd have to take men into the training building to show them how to deal with smoke. I'd be in there with them.

Some of the exercises were designed to give trainees the confidence to wear a gas mask. We had a model house made of brick and concrete, so we could set it on fire over and over. I wanted to simulate the exact conditions of fighting a fire where a lot of smoke was present. Smoke cut visibility, sometimes completely, but a firefighter still had to work through it. I covered the window openings with tarpaper so it was nearly pitch black inside. I knew the place pretty well, and I could move around with little visibility. I got packing material, excelsior, and put it in the corners of rooms and set it on fire. The house filled with smoke, so I snaked a hose line from outside the building up the steps. The idea of the exercise was to get into the building, "follow the line," and get out again. As the recruits followed the hose line, keeping low and sometimes crawling, they encountered obstacles, such as a barrel, to get around. The exercise separated the men from the boys. Inside their gas masks, and with no light due to the covered windows, some of the recruits found that they were claustrophobic. It was their first encounter with the real world of fire fighting. Their gear weighed 70 pounds. If it was summertime, the heat was intense.

I was always inside the building, and I had to shout instructions to the recruits so they could hear me. That meant I couldn't wear a gas mask.

"Stay down! Move!" To breathe, I had my mask stashed. I'd run to a corner where I had one hidden, suck in some air, and then run back when I heard the next bunch of recruits coming and yell some more. Seeing me standing there without a mask, they thought I was a superman.

Afterward, they wanted to know, "Hey, lieutenant, how can you stand all that smoke? We had gas masks, but where was yours?"

I left them guessing to prove the point that it was a job of nerve and guts.

I was 36 years old, an old man to those guys who were 18 to 20. I remember my own instructor impressing us by doing one-arm push-ups. In the morning, it was *my* job to lead the calisthenics. "Okay, give me 20 push-ups!" I'd be down on the ground pumping them out with the recruits. When they were finished, I'd shout, "On your feet!" But I'd stay down and do a couple of one-arm push-ups. I'd kept the promise to myself to learn to do a one-arm push-up, and I could—two of them! But the recruits thought I'd been doing one-arm push-ups all along while they were doing the two-arm kind.

I'd hear them saying, "You better not mess with the lieutenant. He's tough!"

A six-story-high tower was used to give the recruits practice running up flights of stairs in their heavy gear, carrying hoses. Once on top, they would rappel off the roof—and I was the one up there kicking them off! A trainee started out standing with his back to the open air, then he leaned back and jumped off, keeping his legs bent so he could kick away from the wall as he descended. Gloves were used to guard against rope burn.

Most of the training was intended to teach self-assurance. A firefighter's confidence in himself was a critical tool in a life-threatening situation.

Everyone had to jump into a fire net. They were ridiculous, useless things, those nets. The only time I ever saw one used in action was in the movies. Round like a circus net, they were folded in half and strapped onto the side of the hook-and-ladder trucks. There they dry-rotted, because we never used them, until we removed them from the apparatus. Eventually, the nets stopped being replaced, because people might expect them to be used. But if a person had to jump from above the third floor, nets were useless. Our ladders could reach higher than that.

It was also hard on the firefighters holding the net because of the jolt to the wrist and arms when the jumping person impacted. At the Fire Academy, the trainees were instructed to yell, "Jump, and fall flat!" They could get seriously hurt—and fall spread-eagle—if they didn't land properly. In real life, people would jump feet first. They would bounce off, as if they were on a trampoline, or their knees would come up and crack them in the face. To show how dangerous the nets were, one guy who was 200 pounds jumped incorrectly, and he went right through the net. He could have broken his back.

There was classroom instruction, and we gave some trainees counseling if they felt they had problems with any part of the course. After all, we couldn't have half the class drop out.

There was much to teach about the science of fire fighting. The "bible" we used was a fat one-volume encyclopedia put out by the National Fire Protection Association, the *Fire Protection Handbook*, which contained every fact about *flash point* (the temperature when fumes emitted by an object ignite), *flash over* (the moment gases ignite), and *ignition point* or *flammable point* (the temperature when the object itself burns) of various materials. There was data that might appear on an exam: *Acetylene gas has an explosive range from 2.5 percent to about 81 percent in air at atmospheric pressure, which is a wider range than that of any other gas used in the industry.*

I would instruct the newcomers about the basics: "A building's *fire load* is the sum of everything inside that will burn. It's why a furniture store, with all its wood and upholstery inside, is more combustible than a candy store, with its stock of chocolate and jawbreakers in glass jars. When you're answering an alarm and you already know the type of building you're headed for, you'll have a better idea about the fire load you're up against, and you can prepare for it."

"*Offensive fire fighting* is when we go inside," I'd teach. "*Defensive fire fighting* is when we fight from the outside, usually if the fire is out of control. This is a containment situation."

The recruits took notes, and the sharper ones asked questions, such as: "What does the color of the smoke indicate?"

"Smoke and flame color can tell you a lot," I'd explain. "Knowing what flame colors mean is important to a firefighter. Yellow flames come from a mixture of material. Wood burns orange. Red flames can be anything: wood, paper. Red means a 'normal' fire. Blue flames mean you're dealing with a natural gas leak, so you have to get the utility company to turn off the gas in that area. If a flame is blue, let it burn. It's like a blowtorch on a building. Work around it. It may also be propane gas from a storage tank. You train the water line on the surrounding area and on the propane cylinder, because you may have a serious explosion if it gets too hot. At times like this, where there's a potential for an explosion, any reasonable firefighter will be scared. Any firefighter who says he's not is lying or a damn fool. If you're on guard, you do better. You're always scared of secondary explosions, or the roof falling in.

"Get to know smoke. Brown smoke means you've got a combination of combustibles, and you don't really know what's burning. Black smoke means the fire is going good. It's at the height of its power. Gray smoke happens after we've gotten in there, and the fire is working its way toward the end, getting extinguished. When the smoke turns gray, that's when the fire chief and the top brass who may be there will say, 'See you.' It won't be long before we get white smoke. White smoke means that the fire is almost knocked down.

"It's always the fire ground commander who determines when the fire is out. He gives the word, and you roll up the line. One company remains to do cleanup."

I told them about the dangers—that objects gave out so much toxic gas that going into a burning room was like putting a person in a gas chamber. Every burning object gives off gases, especially plastics, which emit *toxic* gases.

Being a veteran firefighter allowed me to work my own experiences into the teaching. "When we pull up to an automobile accident, the first thing we do is disconnect the battery. I remember we were attempting this once, and before we got the wires off, the car exploded. A spark from the electrical system ignited the gas fumes. Everyone in the car was out, but there was still a danger to the firefighters, and it was lucky that no one got hurt."

I tried to be innovative when I saw a chance to do something new or better. In East Baltimore, there were blocks of vacant houses, so I decided that we could do hands-on training in a vacant dwelling that was going to be torn down anyway. The exercise would give the recruits experience in actual house fires. The Housing Department gave its approval, and I drove the recruits over in a bus.

I set a room on fire, and then a group came in and put it out. I set it on fire again, the next group was brought in, and they also had a chance to train a hose and fight fire for real.

Then I set a house on fire. It was summer, the wood was dry, and the dwelling burned fast. I was the only seasoned firefighter among the trainees. They didn't have enough experience, though, and when the wind came up, the fire got away from us. The flames spread to the next abandoned house.

In a minute, the fire was out of control. The trainees kept their cool and continued to battle the blaze, but I had no choice but to call headquarters and ask them to send a "box alarm," which meant three-engine companies and a truck company.

When the captain arrived, he raised hell. "Whose idea was this?" I couldn't lie, and I told him it was mine. I didn't receive a reprimand, but it was embarrassing.

I had misjudged the conditions that made the exercise dangerous. I was always hard on myself when I showed poor judgment. You have to be self-critical when you do any job, but it's especially important when making decisions in life-and-death situations such as fire fighting.

But there was another incident that made me angry at myself for the way I mishandled one of the few unpleasant incidents involving my recruits.

I wasn't supposed to be their daddy or their friend—I was their instructor, the lieutenant, whose job it was to show these trainees, black and white, how to save lives and property and keep themselves out of harm's way.

The last thing I wanted was to be feared. I wanted respect, because trainees would absorb lessons better from someone they respected. If they hated me, they would fear me, which is not the same as respect. If they resented me, it would make it harder for them to absorb lessons. Any good instructor knows the difference between instilling respect and fear. At the same time, a Fire Academy instructor had to be tough, no-nonsense, because the nature of fire fighting didn't permit fooling around.

One year toward the end of training, we had a field trip. I drove the trainees around in a bus to hospitals, the city morgue— all the important places they'd have to be familiar with in the line of duty. If we were fortunate, sometimes at the morgue the doctors would be performing an autopsy. This would be the recruits' first exposure to dead bodies, another experience that separated the men from the boys.

We had just finished our little trip and were headed back to the academy. The recruits were young guys, full of high spirits and machismo. Some of them started whistling out the window at any skirt they saw. I warned them, "Hey! I don't want anyone shouting or screaming out the window. You understand?"

"Yes, sir!" they answered.

"You're representing the fire department!"

"Yes, sir!"

But there were two white guys who couldn't control themselves. We passed a strip joint where there were some young ladies outside. The two recruits let go with wolf whistles. I didn't say anything.

When we got back, I stood up from the driver's seat and turned to the class. "Everybody off, except you and you." I pointed to the two troublemakers. They looked at each other like they didn't know what was happening. Maybe they didn't, because they hadn't impressed me or the other instructors with their performance or their attitudes. In fact, they'd been smart alecks. One of them outright resented me, I could tell.

I walked down the aisle to where they sat. I took off my cap, and then my lieutenant's badge. "You disrespected me. If those people on the street had known that fire department trainees were carrying on the way you did, we'd all be in trouble, including me."

They sat like two statues, in complete silence, as I put my cap and badge on the seat next to theirs. "So, I don't want to be lieutenant anymore, because I'm going to whip your ass."

Both trainees were bigger than I was, and I was old enough to be their father. No doubt, in a fight they could have beaten me. But they saw what was in my eyes, and they looked back at me, shocked. One started trembling, and he began to cry.

"We're sorry, Lieutenant. We didn't mean anything!" They apologized, and I saw that they really hadn't been thinking.

"Okay, I'll forget it. But if you so much as breathe hard for the next two weeks, I'll be all over you." I took up my cap and badge, and I left them.

I felt bad. I knew I'd gone too far, and I questioned my judgment. I saw that they really did respect me, but they just weren't very bright. I shouldn't have come on so strong. Frightening someone was no way to go. But at the time, I knew I didn't want to put them on report, because that would have terminated them from the program.

That was when I decided that in the future if disciplining was necessary, I'd give out lectures and read them the riot act until they'd swear to themselves never to get in the position again where they had to hear me go on and on!

The last day of instruction, I would line up all the trainees and congratulate them for getting through the course. Then I would smile and say, "I can't let you go without telling you something. I can only do two one-arm push-ups. And when you guys were following the line in that smoking house, I had a gas mask stashed in every corner!"

They would laugh and groan, and give me a little round of applause for seeing them through. Then they would go off to their assigned firehouses. When I'd been a trainee 20 years before, the white recruits had already turned against black firefighters by the end of the course. They'd been initiated into the racist attitudes of the white firefighters they started working with while training at the firehouses. There were no African-American officers around as role models to counter the propaganda. But at the Fire Academy, I could set an example. Being a role model wasn't my purpose for being there, but I knew that I helped some of those guys question the prejudices they were expected to inherit.

THE NEW FIREFIGHTERS WOULD SOON GO into a job where a section of the city's population considered them enemies, not saviors. The respect that people felt for firemen for selflessly risking their lives to save others ended up being a casualty of the conflicts of the 1960s.

The seeds of this unhappy turn of events were sown in the Deep South during the Civil Rights marches. In Baltimore, the assassination of Dr. King brought on the crisis locally.

I strongly supported the civil-rights movement and thought that Dr. King was a good man. There was no such thing as affirmative action before he began his mission. The most prestigious jobs for African Americans in Baltimore at the start of the 1950s were positions with the post office or the Social Security Administration.

The '60s saw the beginnings of Black Power, the raised fist, which really appealed to working-class blacks. There was a defiant attitude that said: "We're free. Uncle Charlie can't tell us anything!" But Black Power didn't translate into *economic* power, and it left some people feeling disillusioned.

Malcolm X was familiar to us in Baltimore. When he started speaking at a local mosque, people of my generation tended to look at him with a jaundiced eye. "Who's this guy, comin' here talking this crazy talk?" We knew he'd been in jail. In those days, he'd talk about the white man as a devil. We'd see Malcolm on the street, and some guys would laugh, while other guys were teed-off: "Go back to where you came from. No one wants to hear about that!" But people started to listen to him.

I remembered Malcolm X from 1951, when I was a musician playing on Pennsylvania Avenue. He would hang out at the clubs, and a lot of musicians joined him. His message was very radical. He often stayed in Baltimore because this was where anybody who played music came through. He opened his mosque off Pennsylvania Avenue because that was where all the clubs were. Before Malcolm turned the place into a temple, the meeting hall was "Daddy Grace's House of Prayer." Daddy Grace was sort of a religious franchise in the African-American community at one time, and he had congregations all over the East Coast and in the South: Atlanta, Mississippi, and down in Carolina.

Dr. King, Malcolm X, Black Power—they all addressed in their own ways the inequities that African Americans faced. But problems for fire departments everywhere started when Bull Conner, the sheriff of Selma, Alabama, had that city's firemen turn high-pressure fire hoses on civil-rights marchers. That was when firefighters became the "enemy" of black folk in many people's eyes.

On TV, I saw the images of marchers getting pummeled by water lines that were designed to put out burning buildings. I vowed I'd never turn hoses on civilians. I'd quit the department before I'd do that.

I told Marjie, "I'd turn the water on the mayor who ordered it!"

But I doubted that the Selma situation would be repeated in Baltimore. Even our racist white firefighters who thought Martin Luther King, Jr., should be hung upside down by his toes were disgusted by the use of fire-fighting apparatus against peaceful marchers. They knew it made all firefighters looks bad, and they also knew what those hoses could do—100 pounds of pressure straight out of a nozzle could break an arm, knock somebody unconscious, or even kill a person. It was lucky that nobody got killed that way.

I was teaching at the Fire Academy in March 1968, and when I heard that Dr. King was assassinated, I was sick to my stomach.

Washington, D.C., about a half hour away, erupted first. Then Baltimore. I was put into emergency service, and I would not see my family for two days.

All the officers at the Fire Academy, from instructors to the captain, were ordered to report to various fire department companies, and the academy was temporarily shut down. Vacations were cancelled throughout the department, and every available man was assigned to reserve companies that worked out of different houses.

We were constantly kept running, putting out fires left and right. Pennsylvania Avenue, right in the heart of the African-American community, was in flames. Clubs, bars, shops, theaters, gas stations, groceries, and apartments I had known for years were set afire. It was sickening, and it was a revelation to everyone, including the rioters, how much rage people felt. When a violent assassin gunned down Dr. King, the apostle of nonviolence, something snapped. It was as if the forces that wanted to oppress black people wouldn't even give peace a chance.

When a fire was reported to us by the police—forget about the fireboxes, they were all vandalized or set off as false alarms by rioters—we would rush to the scene. What greeted us were angry, rock-throwing mobs. The people wanted those fires to burn forever, out of control. And as far as they were concerned, firemen were preventing that from happening. The Baltimore Fire

Department itself was seen as part of the Establishment. For one thing, we worked with the police. Second, the department's racial composition hardly matched the city's. Integration's effects had been marginal. Out of 2,000 firefighters, only 200 of us were African American. And black firefighters were still ineffectual tokens ignored by the union that was supposed to represent us.

So, the people threw rocks—at me, too. They threw anything they could find at us. There were times I wondered if I might get shot for doing my job. I hated the rioting that was going on. I always hated the destruction that fire could do. The rioters who committed arson were like kids playing with matches, setting loose a force they didn't understand. A community was wrecking itself, and it broke my heart to see it.

The by-the-book tactics for fighting fire had to be dispensed with. Normally, we would stay at a fire scene until we were sure the last ember was out. Then there would be cleanup. During the riots, we didn't have that luxury. There were so many fires, and there were the rowdy crowds to contend with.

So we'd pull in, soak the building, and get out. We rode in the apparatus with a police escort. The utilities still worked, so I could phone Marjie out in the suburbs to check in. She was nervous from watching the rioting on TV with the kids, since the stoning of firefighting personnel was reported. I assured her that I was all right, and told her I would check on our relatives in the city.

The water pressure wasn't compromised, and the hydrants still functioned, so the police department really got a workout. They had to protect the firefighters, and at the same time stop the looting.

I thought back to when I was a child, fleeing Harlem during the riots of 1943. I knew exactly how people felt in their anger and frustration, but I didn't like the idea of people burning down their own neighborhoods. As a firefighter, I didn't think they knew what they were doing, or that they understood the destructiveness of fire. The mob saw the flames as exciting; they were swept up by it. But none of them had ever seen or smelled a burnt body.

People had a problem with me being there, a black guy with these white firefighters. There was a lot of looting going on, and our presence interfered with that because the police escorting us put a stop to the stealing.

Ten years before, white guys were shouting angry catcalls when they saw me riding a fire truck in the Fourth of July Parade: *"Hey, nigger, what do you think you're doing up there?"*

And now, my black brothers and sisters, just as angry, were shouting: "Hey, nigger, what are you doing with that hose? Get away from there!"

They called me "Uncle Tom." That hurt. I'd taken a lot of hits from the white public while integrating the streetcars, buses, and the fire department. I knew I wasn't a sellout.

I went to my sister Muriel's house to see how she was doing. Whenever I was close to where relatives lived in the city, I'd drop by. The riots were spreading, going on all over town. We saw the flames from the porch at Muriel's. A liquor store was on the corner, and we watched as a guy pulled up in his car, got out, ran in the store, and kicked in the door. This was so others could get in, I supposed, because he immediately left. We just watched to see who would be the first to enter the store. People came running from around the corner, like they were waiting. They went inside and started helping themselves. I hollered, "Hey, get away from there!" They ignored me. It was a helluva thing, seeing your neighbors looting. They were disrespecting themselves.

After two full days of rioting and setting fires, people got tired. The mayor and city officials sat down with community leaders for some serious talks, and the immediate crisis ended.

But the incident showed the bad state of race relations in the city. The fire department was now seen by many African Americans as the people's enemy. It was a sad reversal of the way people had always thought about firefighters. The department responded with paranoia, and relations between the community and their fire protectors would get worse in the years ahead.

DURING THE TIME I WAS INSTRUCTING at the Fire Academy, my kids were in high school. They were good students, and they all excelled. However, I made the mistake of pushing them too hard. Especially Herman, my firstborn son. He suffered from my insecurity that my kids not repeat the problems I endured or the life I lived. Without realizing it, I was repeating what my own father did to me. I wasn't satisfied with B's or C's; I wanted to see A's. I didn't *hope* for good grades, I *demanded* them, which was wrong. I punished Herman when he brought home B's and C's. I denied him things, and up until junior high school, I would bend him over my knee for not getting A's.

The other kids saw how I treated Herman, and it made an impression. I think they were probably scared of me, particularly when I was in a mood, fretting over something from work. It's a terrible thing to have your children afraid of you when you become a tyrant who demands perfection from them.

(Many years would pass before a doctor suggested that my mood swings might be related to a brain tumor, one that had been growing, unknown to anyone, at the back of my head for decades. A tumor can affect your mood, I was told.)

My father never told me he loved me, and I didn't tell my kids I loved them that much when they were young because I didn't know any better. But in later years, I would tell them every day. I appreciated that they weren't bad kids. They were never involved in crime and didn't ever do drugs, so I didn't have to give them that lecture.

I never influenced my children's choice of friends. When I was growing up, "my boys" and I played rough, and we could be wise guys—but we didn't steal, smoke, or use drugs. But Pops was never satisfied. He never approved of the guys I was running around with. He said they weren't good enough, so he imposed a ridiculously early curfew, thinking that what he was doing was for my own good.

Because we lived in the outer suburbs, my children were limited in their choice of friends. It basically came down to the neighbors and the kids at their school. They were assigned to an all-white school, Andover High, and I was concerned about the racism they might face. But the only alternative was a high school in Annapolis, 27 miles away.

Andover was in an all-white section of the county. The kids were bused there, although it was voluntary and not court-ordered.

All four of my children were outstanding in their individual ways. Marjorie sang and did drama. Clolita was in the honor society and won scholarships. Herman did well academically and was a star on the wrestling team. Montel was president of his class, and like me, he did everything. He was in the band, and played football and other sports. He was very popular.

Their accomplishments taught me that integration opened doors for blacks.

All of the kids had Afros and walked around with giant globes of hair that made their heads look enormous. Montel had one, along with the high-heeled shoes the guys had as the '70s wore on. If they wanted to wear the latest fashions, that was fine by me. Unlike the way my father had been with me, I let them pick out their own clothes. If I'd imposed my own tastes, there would have been civil war in our house!

Around the dinner table, I found that my children shared the strong political views of their generation. Herman expressed what he felt about the Vietnam War—that he didn't think it was right. At their school, the kids had some concerns—for example, there was a controversy about saluting the flag—but there weren't any protests.

The Vietnam War touched many African-American families, ours included. I had a nephew who was in Vietnam whom we called Jimmy, and when he came home, he was very quiet. He'd been an attaché to a colonel, and he'd seen combat. We watched as he started drinking, and it got worse. Then he killed himself. Just before he died, he tried to talk to me about killing women and children over there. That haunted him. When he was going through his drinking problem, he was really crying out for help, and we didn't see it. I would always be troubled by that.

My father never gave me a sex talk, and I didn't have to give one to my children either because it was in their school curriculum. I trusted my kids completely and never questioned whom they dated.

MY FATHER'S LIFE HAD CHANGED, ALSO. He was a proud man who was never permitted to live up to the potential that his college degree and abilities should have earned him. But by the

'70s, he was a member of the country club set. My father broke the color line at the Sparrows Point Country Club, but he had to fight a battle for that privilege as well.

Sparrows Point was a company club, belonging to Bethlehem Steel, where Pops had worked since the 1940s. To be a member, you had to be a white-collar employee. He'd never had much interest in the club's activities—he didn't play golf or tennis. But he joined to make a point. The company made him a supervisor, finally, because he was such a good union representative. He fought and won concessions for the workers, and he never let up. That was why we suspected they made him a company executive—to get him out of the way. But he still fought for workers' safety and benefits.

Pops was 63, two years away from his retirement, and there were four other black supervisors in the company. None of the others cared to join the country club, or perhaps it had been made clear to them that they weren't welcome. But Pops had never been intimidated by anyone in his life. He reminded the company management, "I'm a supervisor, and I want in."

The only thing Pops used the club for was to eat. There was a good dining room at Sparrows Point. Then Bethlehem Steel was hit by a downturn in the steel business, and they started downsizing. Cuts were made in the white-collar workforce, too. The club had difficulties, and they changed their policy so that members could bring in their children. Pops asked me if I wanted to join. I went over, looked around, and thought it would be fun because I didn't know any black guys who belonged to a country club.

I took up golf, bought a set of clubs, and just showed off, taking people to dinner. I did more eating than playing golf, and it was good to see Pops there, at the top of the world at last.

In my own life, there were two things I felt I hadn't accomplished: (1) I'd never gotten a college degree; and (2) I'd never served in the armed forces. I was too young for World War II, and for Korea I was classified 1-A. People around me were drafted left and right, but the army didn't call me because I was married with two children. The G.I. Bill would have paid for a college education.

After joining the fire department, the shift work that rotated from day to night meant that I couldn't go to college because I couldn't schedule classes. But right after I moved into the Fire Academy, the local community colleges, in a combined effort with the fire departments of Maryland, began offering a degree in fire technology. The course was designed for firefighters, and classes were scheduled to fit our changing work shifts. Lessons were given twice daily, day and night. If you had the day shift, you went to the night lecture, which was a repeat of the day class.

I joined immediately, taking up my studies at Catonsville Community College. It took me seven years to get an Associates of Arts degree, finishing in 1975, and those credits could be transferred to a four-year college. I was accepted by the University of Baltimore, and began working toward an undergraduate degree in business management.

I also felt that going to college when I was in my 40s would be an inspiration and motivation for my kids. Here I was, their old man, and I was in the library, studying, showing them the importance of a college education.

And it worked. All of our children went to college.

Marjorie was the first to leave home. She chose Morgan State, which was ironic because that was the school my father had chosen for me, which I never ended up attending. In 1949,

Morgan State was about the only school around that an African American could attend, but my children had a wide choice. Marjorie was followed by Clolita, who went to the Baltimore County campus of the University of Maryland.

AROUND 1970, I HELPED FORM THE VULCAN BLAZERS, an association of African-American firefighters. Charlie Thomas, who had been the president of the Social Association of Firefighters, went up to New York, met with the Vulcan Society of New York, and joined talks about forming an international black firefighters' association.

Vulcan was the Roman god of fire. The Baltimore association that bore his name didn't seek to be a union—the organization was created, for the most part, to fight the union, where the needs of African-American firefighters were neglected. The problem was that when a black firefighter lodged a complaint about discrimination, the person who'd precipitated the complaint was always white and *also* a member of the union, so the union's all-white executive and senior membership wouldn't act on the complaint.

As the 1970s began, there were no African-American captains, battalion chiefs, or deputy chiefs, and of course, there had never been an African-American fire chief.

The Vulcan Blazers were just what black firefighters needed, and they joined up. The organization met with the Fire Board, and they received a very good response to some areas of top concern: (1) racial bias in the selection of duties; (2) racially assigned beds (a practice officially outlawed in 1956 but still practiced in 1970); (3) failure to post announcements about firefighter examinations in African-American communities; and (4) insufficient training of black firefighters in diving, pumping, tillering (operating the rear steering controls of a hook-and-ladder truck) and ambulance service.

The Fire Board was impressed. This was no longer the old obstructionist board. Mayor Thomas D'Alesandro III ("Little Tommy"—the son of Mayor Thomas D'Alesandro, who had integrated the fire department in the '50s) appointed Rev. Marion C. Bascom to become the first African-American commissioner of the Fire Board. Rev. Bascom was highly regarded in the African-American community, and he served with another new commissioner, the liberal lawyer Konstantine Prevas. The Fire Board held hearings into discriminatory practices in the department. They heard an earful about life at the firehouses from African-American firefighters struggling to do their job with dignity, and advance up through the ranks against powerful but invisible hands holding them down.

When the board felt that it had heard enough, the commissioners formally recognized the Vulcan Blazers as an organization that spoke for Baltimore's African-American firefighters. Then the board ordered, "A written or unwritten rule, policy, or practice that may cause discrimination in any form whatsoever will be eliminated immediately."

Some battalion chiefs said, "Forget it!" For their defiance, they were slapped with reprimands.

But to show that times hadn't changed all that much, the firefighters' union lodged a complaint over "the Fire Board's constant focus on race relations." And still, no black firefighters advanced into the higher-echelon positions.

Harper v. Baltimore was a way for the Vulcan Blazers to seek a court remedy for past and present abuses. Four African-American firefighters sued the city for systematic discrimination, and when Judge Joseph Young reached his decision in May of 1973, he agreed. He found that black firefighters were being held back from promotions.

His decision read, "Black firemen were made the brunt of 'house pranks,' were made to sleep in a 'black bed,' and were required to use segregated facilities. Responsibility for each of these instances of discrimination rests squarely with the Fire Board and the city authorities."

The Baltimore Fire Department had staunchly maintained for decades that no discrimination existed in the department, and that lie was blown to bits. The judge ruled that written tests had to be administered fairly, that Baltimore city residents be given preference in hiring—more African Americans in the department would better reflect the city's racial composition—and that promotions for battalion chiefs and other officers would be put on hold until the testing system was reformed.

These were the most significant steps toward making the fire department representative of the community it had served since the department was integrated 20 years before. Much had to be done, and the problem of poor community relations needed to be addressed.

To many African Americans in Baltimore in the early '70s, firefighters were still part of the Establishment, serving interests other than their own. Stones were still thrown at us, and if rioting broke out again, we would again be on the firing line. So something had to be done.

❧ CHAPTER EIGHT ❧

Command Officer

There's probably no more spectacular crash than one involving a fire truck. I came closer to death than at any time in my firefighting years when I was riding in a hook and ladder that went out of control.

I was stationed at Truck Company 18. As a lieutenant, I would be the command officer at a fire scene unless a superior officer arrived and requested to take charge. We were responding to a fire alarm on Clifton Avenue, in Northwest Baltimore.

The driver was going too fast, like a bat out of hell. He had a reputation for fast driving, which was permissible up to a point because you had to get to a fire scene quickly as long as no civilians were endangered along the way. We were racing, siren going, in one of the older-style trucks with the open-air cab. I could see that the driver's speed was unsafe.

"Slow down," I told him, in a normal tone of voice.

But he had just turned onto Clifton Avenue, a tight curve. "Sir, I can't!" he said.

I felt the centrifugal force push us sideways. I saw the danger we were in. I shouted, "What do you mean you can't?! Slow the goddamn thing down now. We're going too fast!"

The driver panicked. He slammed his foot down on the brake and lost control of the rig. The long truck jackknifed, and the rear trailer swung around. We were still traveling forward, but the cab and the trailer both moved sideways in a V-shape, the trailer now pushing the cab. Smoke came up from the tires, and the noise was deafening.

"Straighten this up!" I shouted.

"I can't!" The pin at the bottom of the steering column snapped, and the steering wheel spun around and around. There was a line of seven parked cars by the curb, and we plowed into them one by one. Like in a movie, they seemed to get wrecked in slow motion, metal bodies buckling and windshields exploding with shards of glass.

My fear was that when the truck finally stopped, the trailer would come to a halt on top of the roofless cab, crushing us. And just like in a movie, my whole life flashed before me. I thought, *You've been in this department 20 years, and you're going to die in a vehicle accident!*

I had a death grip on the windshield frame. We wiped out all the parked vehicles, but they slowed down the truck, so we stopped. I still held on, expecting the trailer to jump off "the fifth wheel," as we called the turret connection. The trailer strained against the turret but didn't move. In the silence that followed, I loosened my grip on the window frame. The palms of my hands were covered with blood, and the back of my head was injured. I was wearing a helmet, so maybe my head hit something, but I don't remember.

How many lives does a fireman have, that allow us to escape death again and again? At least nine, I'd say. We're the cats of the human species.

I needed to calm down. At a pay phone, I dropped a dime in the slot and spoke to my wife. "Hey, Marjie, it's me, baby. You won't believe what just happened. . . ." The engine company started hosing down our own truck to dissipate the gasoline.

To add insult to injury, the fire call turned out to be a false alarm. A city tow truck came to take away the wreck, and we went back to Firehouse 18. I was again working in Cherry Hill, the poor, mostly black section of Baltimore. The riots brought me there.

Although it was five years after Dr. King had been assassinated, relations between the fire department and the public continued to sour. Baltimore's African-American community had never recovered from all the burning and looting that followed the assassination. That meant that Baltimore had never recovered. No community is an island; until Pennsylvania Avenue and the people it served thrived again, a vital organ of Baltimore would not be functioning. This could not continue or the city would never be whole.

In the aftermath of the riots, the African-American community deteriorated. A lot of businesses, especially on Pennsylvania Avenue, were black owned. For years after the riots, vacant lots testified to where businesses had once been before they were burned and bulldozed. It was in these sections of the city that resentment of the fire department ran high. It was strange, because some people threw stones at firefighters when we showed up to put out fires, but other people in the community resented us for not doing enough to stop the arson.

The habit of stoning firefighters continued for years. People pulled false alarms just to get firefighters there, and when we arrived, they let us have it. Folks set fires in abandoned buildings so we would show up, which of course we had to do, and then the hail of stones would come down.

It was unfair, since firefighters, least of all, didn't deserve such treatment. Why us? The first reaction among firefighters was to feel hurt and victimized. As community relations worsened, firehouses went into paranoid mode. For the first time, they started locking the front doors. When that happened, it was sad, and symbolic of the schism between firefighters and the public. Captains feared that some loony would come in with a gun and do some damage, maybe steal a fire truck and go on a joyride. But the main accomplishment of the locked doors was to isolate the firehouses from the community. We became what our critics said we were: cut off from the people we served. Every firehouse became a fortress, especially in black neighborhoods. That elicited even more resentment.

Some of the more enlightened top officials at the department saw the isolation of the firehouses and the distrust of the community toward us as a dangerous trend.

One day, I got a call at the Fire Academy from the fire chief's office. I almost stood at attention when I heard the chief's voice.

"We've got to stop the stone throwing down there at Cherry Hill," he said. "I want you to set up a community relations office."

He told me that I was being temporarily assigned out of the Fire Academy. I would work with some other officers to bring about an improvement in attitudes between the people and firefighters, the firehouses and the community. I'd never done anything like this, but neither had the department. I didn't know anything about public relations, but I knew about people.

I told my family about my new posting. My father repeated what he had been telling me all my life, but his voice was now more mellow and reasonable, so the message rang clearer: "Respect yourself, and if you respect other people, they'll respect you."

I'd been at the Fire Academy for six years, and I had to wonder if the new firefighters locked behind the closed doors of their firehouses looked like a bunch of cowards to the community. I couldn't order changes in procedure, or have any influence over the way individual firehouse captains chose to run their operations, but in Cherry Hill, I could ease open the closed doors a crack by venturing outside.

I was assigned to Engine Company 18, and the first thing I did with my team was to go out on foot, walk around, and let people see us. Eventually, I even played basketball and baseball with the kids in the neighborhood.

My message to everyone we met—the homeowners cleaning their storm gutters, the housewives watering plants on their windowsills, the kids on skateboards, and the teenagers idling in parked cars, was this: "Hey, we're firefighters. Stop throwing rocks at us."

I spoke with people, and they talked to us. I wasn't surprised to find that most folks had common sense. They knew they needed their fire department. They didn't want to be unprotected in case there was an emergency. It's just that they'd had some problems with white firefighters employed by the city who came from out of town and who disrespected the city's poorer citizens. I'd seen this myself, but hearing it from the people was important. It was something to be reported—and rectified. The community relations project was to last a year, and we learned a lot about the concerns of the people we served. It was an education for me.

After a while, when we'd earned their trust, people started volunteering information. They told us who was responsible for the stone throwing and arson, and in some cases, the police got involved. But I asked the people if I could talk to the stone-throwers. I wanted them to know that they weren't attacking an enemy, but someone who cared whether their grandma or children got burned to death, and who had the ability to stop that from happening.

I did have some talks with young men, some of them unemployed and angry. I tried to direct their anger away from firefighters, where I thought it didn't belong.

Before I knew it, the year was over, and my involvement with the project ended. It was 1974, and I was assigned back to the Fire Academy because a big class of recruits required additional instructors. But when that class left for their firehouse postings, I wasn't sent back to Company 18, as I wanted. I was surprised by another assignment.

I held the rank of captain now, but once again, the promotion hadn't been easy. I'd been a lieutenant for seven years, and there hadn't been any vacancies for captain in the Fire Academy for some time. I knew I could pass the exam to be a captain at a firehouse, but this would require a move out of the academy and into the department's mainstream rank and file. For some reason, this was opposed, and I felt the invisible hand of discrimination at work once more.

I'd strengthened my political connections by continuing to support candidates and their charity functions over the years. They knew I had limited means, but they appreciated my consistency and my loyalty. None of the politicians who knew me were going to break any rules for me, and I wouldn't ask them to do that. But they listened to what I thought was my legitimate grievance at being held back from another advancement.

On Christmas morning, I got a call from an official at headquarters. The officer was angry. "You got your help!" he snapped. It seemed he got a call to approve my transfer and promotion, and it was made clear that he should give me the news that day, Christmas.

It was a great holiday gift, for which I thanked my Santa Clauses—the "political operatives" of the city who knew which buttons to push to get things done for their supporters.

When I made captain, I wanted a position in the field. One of the Fire Board members, Commissioner Owens, who was the president of the board, asked me if I would become the department's first safety officer. It was a brand-new position in Baltimore, and I would be the first African-American safety officer in the country. The department always had fire inspectors who worked with the Fire Prevention Bureau to check every structure in the city for compliance with fire regulations. But the new job of safety officer was to ensure the safety of firefighters at the scene of an alarm. I was told that the fire chief wanted me on his staff.

The chief of the fire department was Thomas Burke. He was a dedicated and capable man, and a different breed from the dinosaurs that used to run the department—he was one of the first fire chiefs to start modernizing the department. He was still old-fashioned in one way, though: He insisted on responding to four-alarm and greater alarm fires. When he arrived at the scene, he would take charge, and the command officers stepped back to let him call the shots.

When I was officially designated the department's new safety officer, my position gave me undisputed power at fire scenes, analogous to a doctor aboard a navy vessel who could order the captain to leave the bridge and go to the infirmary for medical reasons. During a fire, if I said a building was unsafe for a firefighter to enter, my word was final. With that decision, I outranked all the other superior officers—the command officer in charge of the fire scene, and even the fire chief.

The department was serious about cutting the number of firefighter casualties. It was my responsibility to monitor conditions that might put the men in harm's way.

Burning buildings became unsafe when they were "fully engulfed," when they became infernos of flame beyond salvation, too dangerous to enter. I would issue an order that we had to just let them burn, and tell everyone to stay out.

"Get those guys off the roof!" I'd tell the command officer. "Move the apparatus back away from the building."

"You're the safety officer!" the officer-in-charge would say. He was getting used to the new authority at the fire scene, and there was no resentment. Command officers appreciated someone who could restrain overeager firefighters and provide a safety perspective to the hectic business of fighting fire.

We still poured water on the structure, but at a safe distance.

At the time, in 1974 and 1975, we were called to alarms almost daily at Baltimore's Inner Harbor. The area closest to the water from downtown was lined with old, decrepit warehouses. It was a waste of valuable real estate that had the potential for recreational use. There were plans to completely renovate Inner Harbor and turn it into a center for entertainment and tourism attractions.

Lo and behold, those old brick-and-wood warehouses mysteriously caught fire, one after another, so Baltimore went through an instant urban renewal. The way the warehouses were fully engulfed, there was little to salvage, and as safety officer, I had to pull back the men and let the structures burn. The fires certainly saved someone a lot of demolition time.

Fire fighting is by its very nature a dangerous job. We fought one of nature's fiercest elements. But danger is the furthest thing from a firefighter's mind when they go out on an emergency call. Particularly if the message is that people are trapped in a building, it's at that point that the officer-in-charge has the job of calming down firefighters, who want to rush in. It doesn't matter whether the trapped people are black or white to a firefighter, you want to break the door down. But the commander knows that if a victim is trapped, the conditions exist where a firefighter could become trapped. He has to tell his group, "We'll get them, but everybody be cool."

No emergency job was possible without the medics. They were a fairly selfless group, who did their job because it was something they wanted to do. I saw that they liked what they did. They were out all hours of the day and night, and they could administer drugs, give IVs, and provide all manner of lifesaving skills. The Baltimore Fire Department had under its Medical Bureau, 22 ambulances, two people per ambulance, with medics (the title became "firefighter/paramedic" in 1997) working four shifts. That was about 175 personnel, to which you'd have to add a few reserves employed during the regulars' days off.

All medics had to be trained as firefighters, and this was true even in the '50s. They took a 12-week course at the Fire Academy, and while there, some chose to become full firefighters. The other medics worked in the department assisting with the endless variety of daily crises, from a near drowning in the bay to elevator rescues.

Elevators got stuck, but only in the movies did they drop to the ground; safety brakes held them in place. The door was opened by a key located in a wall box nearby, and the building owner was required to give a key to the rescue squad. If the elevator was stuck between floors, the squad would hand-crank the cable down, using a mechanism on the roof. The real challenge was controlling panic. In newer buildings, if the power went out, the elevators automatically descended to the first floor. Elevators were never used during a fire or rescue. There was danger of the power going off, and heat-activated sensor buttons could send the elevator directly to the fire floor.

We watched such a thing occur in a movie called *The Towering Inferno,* which came out my first year as safety officer. Mostly, we shook our heads at the inaccuracies. What irritated me most was the way that fire leaps around in Hollywood movies. A chair burns in one corner, and the drapes burn on the opposite wall. In real life, fire flows, like lava, or it bursts like an explosion. In *The Towering Inferno,* the fire consuming the world's tallest skyscraper (built in San Francisco over an earthquake fault!) had a mind of its own. The fire skipped floors it didn't like, and preferred floors where the film's stars could be put in danger. And when Steve McQueen lost his grip on the firefighter he was holding, the guy fell and was saved by an old-fashioned net. The audience cheered. Marjie wanted to know why I was groaning.

That scene was almost as goofy as the firefighter in *Backdraft* a few years later who decided to get it on with his girlfriend on top of a fire truck, inside the garage of a firehouse, a place about as private as a baseball dugout during a playoff game. And no one noticed, even when they drove off to answer an alarm!

Another thing you see in the movies about firehouses are dogs, those spotted dalmatians. I never knew where they got that, because animals haven't been permitted in firehouses since the horses that once pulled the fire wagons were put out to pasture. But we did have what we called "house cats." These were civilian guys who were fire enthusiasts. They were like strays. They'd hang around the house because they found the life exciting. Some of them wanted to be firefighters but couldn't make the grade. The others took it like a hobby. They liked to hang around and listen to calls. They were the ones who closed the doors after the trucks went out on runs.

There was another innovation around the time I moved from the field to headquarters. The Manual of Procedure (MOP) was started in 1973. Updated regularly, the MOP showed how things were done "by the book." This *was* the book, and when a firefighter didn't adhere to it, he could face disciplinary charges.

There was a procedure, a little ceremony, which was enacted when a firefighter was suspended for committing a serious infraction. He was required to stand at attention at the fire station's ground-level assembly point and hand over to his commander his copy of the MOP, his keys, and his hose strap. The hose strap was a short rope used to tie a hose to the side of a ladder so it would stay in place while fighting a fire.

The MOP contained everything:

"Beds assigned according to rank: Captains, Lieutenants, First Acting Lieut., Pump Operator, Emergency Vehicle Operator (Tillerman), Paramedics. Beds shall not be used between the hours of 1700 and 2100.

"The United States flag will be displayed at the peak on flagstaffs of all FD buildings from sunrise to sunset.

"Fire boats shall be operated in accordance with the United States Coast Guard Regulations."

There were two main fireboats, both 100 feet long and named after former Baltimore mayors. The Mayor Thomas D'Alesandro was commissioned in 1956, and The Mayor J. Harold Grady came into service in 1960. Both were built in Camden, New Jersey, with steel hulls, diesel-powered engines, and a top speed of 14 knots per hour. We kept them berthed at Curtis Bay.

The life span of the water apparatus was put at 20 years, but like much of the department's equipment, the boats were well maintained and lasted years longer. They were used in the outer harbor, where warehouses, industry, and shipping were concentrated. The ship's "turret pipes," like water guns mounted atop turrets on the bows, were so powerful that they could damage the new shops, restaurants, and museums going up at Inner Harbor, and they only showed up there to shoot streams of water into the air as part of civic celebrations.

I was safety officer for three years. During my watch, not a single firefighter lost his life.

MY FAMILY'S LIFE IN OUR GLEN BURNIE HOME was coming to an end. I hated to see us leave that house, which I'd built with my own hands. But the rules were changing in the fire department, and for good reason. Officers above a certain grade were required to reside in the city.

My nephew James was married in that house, and in 1970, I built a swimming pool, which made the kids even more popular. But by 1977, their rooms up in the dormers were mostly quiet. Our last-born, Montel, went into the Marine Corps straight out of high school. He finished basic training and went into the Naval Academy prep school for one year at Newport, Rhode Island. He was serving his country the way I had once hoped to, living out his old man's dream. And he did it with honors. Montel received a presidential appointment to the Naval Academy; he studied hard, distinguished himself, and graduated in 1980.

Montel's older brother and sisters had long since gone away to college, but their schools were in the vicinity, so they came home often. When Marjorie, Clolita, and Herman found jobs, these were also close by. Marjie and I had the satisfaction of having raised four wonderful kids, each one accomplished in his or her own way, and we were justifiably proud.

I was a Catholic now; I converted in the early '70s. For a long time before then, the Church had been a source of comfort and guidance for me, and I prayed for the firefighters whose safety I was responsible for. It was a moving moment for me when I stood, a man almost middle-aged, at the baptismal font, and was sprinkled with the water of the Holy Spirit. Marjie stood beside me, beaming like a madonna. But now she and I would have to join another congregation—and find a new set of surroundings back in the city.

The need to move came after I took the examination to become battalion chief. A key part was the oral exam, and after all the years lecturing recruits at the Fire Academy, I talked the ears off the examination board, so they had to give me the job to shut me up! For once, there were no tricks pulled to rob me of a promotion. And this was a major promotion. Battalion chief was a big-time job in the fire department. A battalion chief was in charge of several firehouses, and he drove around in a special red car with a red light whirling on top. Out of 35 battalion chiefs in the fire department, only three were minorities. I saw the job as a way of giving me a greater platform to be a role model.

I couldn't wait to get back out in the field. I even suspended my studies at the University of Baltimore, where I was working toward an undergraduate degree in business. When I was promoted to battalion chief, I felt that I'd pretty much accomplished what I wanted in life, and I knew that my job would require me to be on call every minute of the day and night.

Marjie and I bought a block of apartments in Northeast Baltimore on Loch Raven Boulevard. With the money we got for selling the Glen Burnie house, I remodeled the row of red brick townhouses, which were eight attached units. We moved into the end apartment that had been occupied by a doctor's office.

The rule requiring me, as a senior officer, to live in Baltimore was instituted because the city had changed. With the advent of "white flight," many fire department officers were living in the suburbs. Some white firefighters drove clear out of state when they went home, to places as far away as Pennsylvania and Virginia. They had little stake in Baltimore, other than as a place to go to work. This was reflected in their attitudes, and their apathy toward creating and maintaining friendly relations with the community. The new regulations commanded all officers to come back home to the city.

But it was hard on Marjie to have to give up our "American Dream" house, which she helped design, and which she'd made into a home for a husband and four kids. I knew that it was hard on her because of the sixth sense you develop after close to 30 years of marriage. If not for that, I wouldn't have known, because she didn't complain. I never heard her say anything critical about me in all our years together, and she could have said plenty! Marjie was always calm. It must have been her upbringing—

all her sisters were pleasant, too. I've never seen such easygoing people. But it was like Pops said about respect: If you respect someone, they'll respect you back; if you love your spouse with all your heart, she'll love you back in the same way.

I was ready to go into the community. I wanted to respond to fires and let people see me with the white cap on my head, in my red battalion chief's car. What's the use of being a role model if nobody can see you?

But Chief Burke had different plans for me. He wasn't ready to let me leave his staff, and he convinced me that I should stay.

He sat me down in his office, and said, "Herman, I want you to remain here at headquarters. I need you to head the Fire Prevention Bureau."

"That's fine, Chief, and thank you, " I said. "That's a big responsibility, and I appreciate that you think I can do it. But I want to go out in the field."

The offer did give me pause, though. Running the Fire Prevention Bureau, or FPB, was a prestigious job. The chief looked at me, and without a smile to hint that he was joking, but with an expression that showed me he was serious, he said, "Herman, you know that all fire department chiefs once headed the FPB."

I sort of guffawed, and answered, "Why are you telling me that? I'll never be fire chief."

"You never know, Herman. I think you have what it takes."

I stared at him. Fire chief? He must be crazy. It didn't seem so long ago that members of the public were shouting racial slurs at me for daring to be in a fireman's uniform. How would they react if I were to ever run the department?

Chief Burke said, "You know, down in Richmond, Virginia, they've got a black fire chief."

I laughed, "Oh, Richmond's a dinky little burg."

"I still want you to run the FPB. I need you."

"Okay, Chief, if you put it that way." A part of me was intrigued, no matter how farfetched the idea of one day becoming fire chief seemed. No one had ever suggested that possibility to me. Personally, I just wanted to be battalion chief, and I figured that the next and final step would be deputy chief, the end of the line in the department as far as I was concerned, by which time I would be close to retirement.

In July of 1977, I took charge of the Fire Prevention Bureau. It was no cosmetic "Fire Prevention Week" job. I would determine the fate of many city businesses and industries because I had the power to close down operations if they were in violation of the fire code. It was a considerable amount of power, and there was some irony attached to it. Establishments where African Americans had recently been barred in the name of racial segregation, and some which still discriminated in the late 1970s, were now beholden to an African American to keep their doors opened. But I wasn't going to make it payback time. I knew that if I wasn't fair and didn't go by the book, it would prove that I was no better than the racist bullies. Also, I'd probably lose my job, because every business in Baltimore had its patron in the political machinery.

My music career with The Pyramids also came to an end. We'd been playing in places where there were clear fire-code violations, so when I became chief of the FPB, it was time to quit, or risk a scandal. I was ready to leave anyway, since I no longer needed the money. The kids were gone, and the weekend gigs had gotten to be a bore. It got so I didn't want to see Friday come!

I took the job heading the FPB because the chief thought it was the best thing for me to do. He was right—I met a lot of movers and shakers. Nothing could be built without approval from the FPB. I was familiar with blueprints from the years I spent building houses, and I inspected the plans of all proposed construction. I toured the sites and inspected existing buildings. The day-to-day inspections were carried out by a staff of 12 fire inspectors. They issued warnings for violations that might range from faulty fire extinguishers and sprinklers to blocked exits and bad wiring. The building owner had 30 days to comply, depending on the infraction, and some problems had to be taken care of immediately. A restaurant that had a faulty extinguisher system had to remedy the problem before reopening to customers. Any improper fire extinguishers had to be fixed immediately.

The job wielded a lot of power. Sometimes a building owner felt that one of my fire inspectors was overzealous or unfair, and he'd call me to complain. My reply would almost always be, "Calm down, sir, I'll meet with you."

I would, on occasion, overturn an inspector's order if he was wrong. Word of that got around, and Baltimore's property owners gave me a reputation for being fair.

School inspections, hospitals, nursing homes—the rounds required to make dwellings and businesses safe never stopped. The fire department gave the FPB the responsibility of conducting public lectures on fire safety, and I delegated these to my staff when they weren't conducting inspections. I wanted the lectures to be well done, and really impress the listeners. I felt that public education was important—and not only because an ounce of prevention was worth a pound of cure. Having firefighters appear at schools, churches, and community halls was a way of getting us back out with the people, and making a good impression to help tear down the separation between the department and the community.

Of course there were challenges along the way, because even when it came to safety, some matters weren't always simple. There was one school that was located in a bad part of town. The principal would chain-lock all the doors to keep out gangs and undesirables, but before she decided to do that, kids would open the doors to let drug pushers in.

I understood why the principal felt that she had to lock the doors, but it was a clear violation of the fire code, and dangerous for the children. I couldn't allow that. I sent someone to inspect, and ordered them to cut the chains. The inspectors would return the next week, find the chains back in place, and cut them again.

This went on for a while, until I thought I'd better go on down and have a talk with the principal. She was a feisty woman, and she told me off. "This is my school! I'm protecting the children."

"I understand what you're trying to keep out, but you're putting the kids at risk if a fire should break out."

She stood firm. "I'm going to continue to do this."

I said, "I'll continue to cut the chains."

Eventually, I won. Maybe the school ran out of money for new locks and chains, but I insisted on personally speaking to the students at that school's assembly about fire safety. Student patrols were formed to identify troublemakers who didn't belong at that school, and they kept them out.

I spoke at other high schools, and I found that I had a platform, after all, to present myself as a role model. The kids saw me up there in my bright shiny uniform, and I enjoyed going to elementary schools, where I would read to the little kids. I brought along the turnout gear I used in fire fighting, and I let the kids put it on. They stepped into the big boots and tried on the helmet that would nearly come down to their noses.

"Mr. Fireman?" the little kids would ask, giggling, "Why does a fireman wear red suspenders?"

"I thought you'd never ask!" I'd say. "You see how heavy these pants are? If you don't have suspenders to keep them up, your little bottom is going to get roasted!"

They all responded with that delightful sound of little kids' laughter.

Political pressure was sometimes applied to get the rules bent in favor of an establishment that was in violation of the fire code. I couldn't allow that to happen, but I knew the art of compromise. The same ends were accomplished, safety needs were met, and everyone's interests were served.

There was one restaurant that wanted to open on Mother's Day, a big day in the restaurant business. The place was located in Baltimore's Polish neighborhood, but advertisements were run all over the city.

One of my fire inspectors reported to me, "They still haven't put in an extinguisher system, and no exit lights, like I told them last month." He said that the restaurant couldn't open, which is what he told the owner, who was furious, pulling his hair out. He called the city councilman of his area to complain. The city councilman called the mayor, the mayor called the chief of the fire department, and the chief called me.

I stood by my inspector. I had a good team, and they knew their jobs. "Chief, that place is unsafe."

"I'll leave that to you to handle," he said.

I also got a call from the city councilman, who was as agitated as could be. "That place has got to open!"

I went to the restaurant for a personal inspection. The owner was impressed with himself for being able to get the top guy down there. He probably thought that someone had chewed me out. Sure enough, I found some serious problems.

"There's a ramp blocking the kitchen exit," I told the owner. "It's got to go."

I confirmed my inspector's other findings. "The only way you can open on Sunday is if you put in an extinguisher system."

"No way! In two days?!"

I calmed him down by suggesting a way for him to open as advertised. He jumped at it. Within 20 minutes, he had a gang at the kitchen door with a jackhammer, tearing up the ramp. On Sunday, with lots of fanfare, the restaurant opened, but without an operating sprinkler system. In its place, I agreed to let him employ a squad of fire watchers. These were off-duty firefighters who stood at every exit with fire extinguishers. He had to pay the city of Baltimore a lot for them, because the guys put in overtime. But he was happy to open on schedule after he saw I wasn't going to bend the rules. His city councilman, seated with his party at a table, was happy. The mayor was happy. And the fire chief, who didn't want to get involved, was happy with the resolution.

The owner could have gotten everything done a month earlier when the fire inspector first issued the warning. I used the story as an example of compromise, but also as an illustration of people not taking fire safety seriously, and concentrating instead on other things.

I loved the FPB job; I liked to make things happen. But the job lasted only two years, and suddenly I was out of the fire department.

For once, politics swung against me. The decision to leave the fire department for a job in another city bureau was mine, but it was a case of either me voluntarily jumping, or being involuntarily pushed out.

FIRE CHIEF BURKE'S PREDICTION that I might one day take over the top post was actually taken seriously by the authorities in the fire department and city government, as well as political bigwigs who pulled the strings behind the scenes.

Their decision was that in 1979, Baltimore was not ready for an African-American fire chief.

If I simply remained in place at the job I was in, then they had no worries. But I had decided to take the civil service exam to try my luck at being deputy chief.

The department had five deputy chiefs, and from these, a fire chief was chosen. After I took the test, I got a call tipping me off that I'd come in first. So I was a little suspicious when the results were posted, and I came in fourth. I knew some of the other guys listed ahead of me, and it seemed unlikely that they did better on the test. I thought the test results had been manipulated. It wouldn't have been the first time.

According to the rules of the civil service, the person with the highest score was appointed to the post. If I were to become deputy chief, I would be in line for fire chief. African Americans now made up the majority of the city's residents. The black community was pressing for more city jobs and more high-level administrative posts. There was talk that it was high time for a black fire chief.

The powers that be were faced with a dilemma. If I became deputy chief, they knew that the most likely candidate to make history as the first African-American head of a major city's fire department would be me. So, they had to get rid of me. They knew me, and didn't dislike me—it was nothing personal.

How did I know all this? It might seem strange, but I was told how things were by people I knew and for the most part respected: the city's movers and shakers, the great "politicos," including some of my mentors. We had a meeting, and there were no threats or intimidation. They appealed to me by "telling it like it is." These were the political big shots I'd given campaign contributions to. It was like a scene out of the movie *On the Waterfront,* where the Rod Steiger character tells his brother (the boxer played by Marlon Brando), "Kid, it's not your night."

It didn't matter that I was capable, or even deserving. The politicos simply said no. They wanted to help advance my career, but in another city department where I wouldn't be stalled. So I listened to them. It wasn't like I was a candidate for the job. There was a fire chief in place who had no intention of retiring, and he wasn't in any danger of being let go. But the political operatives were looking ahead, and they wanted to hedge their bets. There were reasons why a black fire chief would be a problem, they said, like the unions. Also, it would disrupt a delicate balancing act that distributed jobs to different groups.

I said to my wife, "Marjie, you can't fight city hall."

I wasn't disappointed for two reasons. One was that the job of fire chief wasn't open, so I hadn't thought about it, and I wasn't disappointed at losing something I wasn't going after. But even if I had wanted that job, I knew the politics of the city, so I knew what I was up against if I didn't cooperate.

Finally, although this struck me more forcefully in later years when I would look back at that time, I wasn't ready to be fire chief. In 1979, I would have been the worst chief Baltimore had ever had. I needed more executive experience. The men who spoke with me also mentioned this. They told me where I could be posted to get that experience, but it would be outside the department.

They left it open. "In the future, who knows? You might come back."

But the truth was, when I left the fire department, I wasn't sure I would ever return.

A lot of people in the fire department were shocked by my departure. They knew that fire fighting was in my bones—I'd been doing it for 26 years. "Telegram/telephone/tell-a-fireman." The word of my leaving spread fast, but the message always ended with, "Herman will be back."

Time would pass, and I would run into somebody on the street. "Hey, Herman, I can't wait until you come back!"

Around town, I'd see the guys I worked with at the firehouses, and they'd ask, "When are you coming back?"

And I'd always vaguely answer, "I'll be back sometime."

But I said this to humor them. As the years went on, I forgot about the fire department—consciously, that is.

I willed myself to forget, but in my heart, I never really did.

❡ CHAPTER NINE ❡

The Commish

Baltimore's Department of Public Works handled all manner of city construction, and that meant contracts and jobs. Politicians, unions, city workers, private companies—everyone wanted consideration. I didn't know if I would ever return to the fire department, but just in case that day ever came, I was preparing myself by accumulating executive experience and building administrative skills. But Public Works wasn't a lesser city service than the fire department. Try having a city without a sewer system or road network. There wouldn't be any need for a fire department because nobody could live there.

I was soon dealing with every special interest group a city official had to be in contact with. You couldn't buy that kind of experience. But if you took a wrong step, you could fall down hard. In hindsight, though, I saw how lucky I was to get into the rough-and-tumble of Public Works. If you could survive there, you could make it anywhere.

After taking the civil service exam, I was offered the position of chief of administrative services to fill a vacancy for a guy who was retiring. I would be in charge of the hiring, firing, promotion, and training of 5,000 city employees. It was January 1980, and the city was busy with the Inner Harbor redevelopment; as well as the usual street and road infrastructure, and government building maintenance; and some new highway projects.

I knew nothing about my new department, and I wondered if I was put there so I might fail, thus eliminating me as a candidate for future executive positions. I'd go back to being a good old firefighter.

Francis Kuchta, the director of Public Works, felt that once he made me chief of administrative services, his decision shouldn't be questioned. We worked out of a nine-story building downtown, the Municipal Building, an old turn-of-the-century structure. There were some people on the sixth floor where the executive officers were located who clearly felt I had no business being in my new position. To them, it was so obvious that I was unqualified that they assumed that even the director must have known I was some kind of racial figurehead to be humored while they did the real work. The first day on the job, my secretary, whom I'll call Jane, made clear that this was her view.

Her way of saying "Hello" was to place on my desk what she said were the "important manuals."

"Everything you need to know about Public Works is in those books," she said in a tone that showed she was being condescending, not helpful. I thought that here was a person who didn't want to work with me. But the choice was hers. I told her, "What I want you to do is take these off my desk. Anything I need to know, you'll tell me."

"Jane" went straight to the office of the director. A few minutes later, I got a call from his secretary saying that he wanted to see me.

I went to his office, and my secretary was seated there. I didn't know what she'd told him, or what type of history she and the director had, but her expression was haughty as she looked at me, like she had arranged a tongue-lashing for me. Well, it was my first day, and I needed to know where I stood, even if it resulted in a very short career at the department.

"Sit down, Herman," Kuchta said. He turned to the secretary. "Jane, you came to see me, and you asked me what you're supposed to do with Mr. Williams."

She smiled at him, "Yes, sir."

"What you're supposed to do is anything Mr. Williams tells you."

I had my vote of confidence. The secretary's face dropped. That wasn't what she expected at all. Kuchta told her, "I think you may have a problem. Let me leave you two alone and see if you can come to a determination, or, Jane, we'll try to find you something else."

He left us sitting there, and Jane started to cry, "I didn't mean anything, Mr. Williams."

I said, "Jane, you don't have to worry. If you can't work with me because of my skin color, I'll speak with the director of personnel, and they'll assign you somewhere else."

Her attitude changed completely. "I'm sorry, sir! I want to work with you!" What she wanted was to work on the sixth floor, the director's floor, which was the prestige location.

The director had no time to be bothered with my problems either—not when he felt that I should handle matters myself.

I ended up completely revamping the department as far as personnel was concerned, but that meant run-ins with some entrenched interests.

One of the first guys I confronted was an Italian highway supervisor. In those days, almost all highway crews were Italian. I had no problem with Italians or any other group, and I always enjoyed Baltimore's ethnic diversity. The Italians did a lot to build the city, and I'd gotten hooked on the restaurants at Little Italy, not far from Inner Harbor, which were some of the best on the East Coast. But when it came to hiring, it was a matter of fairness that everyone was given a chance.

That highway supervisor must have seen *The Godfather* one too many times. He would only hire Italians, and he saw himself as a "don." He sounded tough on the phone, and his language was crude and filled with racial slurs.

After hearing me out about the need to diversify hiring, he let me know where I stood. "Listen to me, and listen good. I'm going to hire anyone I like. If I don't want a nigger, I'm not going to hire a nigger."

He hung up. I went to the director and complained that the supervisor was undermining me. Kuchta also made it clear where I stood. "If I have to tell you how to do your job, I don't need you at Public Works."

It was his way of telling me to handle things as I saw fit. After that, it was butt-kicking time as far as I was concerned. I went to the supervisor's office, and the moment I came though the door, he started with the racist language. He had a big jeweled ring on one finger, and I wondered if people entering that office were expected to kiss it.

He was saying, "One thing the niggers who want all the jobs better wise up to . . ."

I cut him off, "That's the last time you call someone a nigger."

He was so surprised that his eyes about popped. "What do you mean—"

"If I ever hear you call someone a nigger, I'll not only fire you, I'll probably knock you out."

Then I laid down the hiring plan I expected him to follow, using his own crude language so he'd understand, "For every wop we hire, we're hiring a nigger."

He was speechless, and as I got up to leave, I told him, "One last thing. No more racial slurs on city time."

I saw the irony that while I pressed for affirmative action, I was accused of only caring about minorities by people who wanted the jobs to go to people of their own kind. But they didn't see the humor.

Everyone wanted a city job for a son, niece, nephew, cousin, brother, sister, or constituent. I got a lot of calls from politicians inquiring about jobs for people.

"I'll be happy to set up an MQ," I always replied. It wasn't the answer they wanted, but they understood where I stood. An MQ test, or Minimum Qualification test, set the requirements that all aspiring city workers had to meet. A certain skill or license might be needed, depending on the job. I didn't do any favors. I was fair all around. After a while, word got around the Municipal Building that "Mr. Williams is a little rough, but he's fair."

I believed strongly in training employees. Because of my background at the Fire Academy, instruction and training was something I was a stickler for. The Public Works' training officer wasn't doing a damn thing; he was just going through the motions, so I made him step up the program. A majority of the department's workers were laborers. They

were the ones who collected trash, fixed roads, filled up pot-
holes in alleys, cut grass, and did everything that went into
keeping a city clean and functioning. I had all the workers
take training the very first thing, including becoming familiar with safety and operating equipment.

City drivers were retrained if they had a bad record. I started
a safety program and also set up a safety review board. The drivers had a poor overall record, but now if they were involved in
an accident that was severe, they could be terminated. One guy
had a mishap, but instead of firing him, I made him an offer.
He was driving a dump truck, spreading salt over the icy roads
in winter. The hydraulic lift had fully raised the truck bed, and
he was driving along like that with the truck bed up in the air.
When he came to a bridge, half the vehicle tore away. I made
him pay for part of the damage. It set an example, and the other
guys paid attention. But those who didn't get the message helped
give me a reputation for firing people.

If I did fire people, and always with cause, I hired many
more. I set up the department's first apprenticeship program. I
felt a need for women and minorities in some areas, such as
chemists in the water department. The program was a way to
bring in a greater diversity of workers. People were hired at a
lesser salary and trained for two years on the job. When they
finished, they had a job waiting. I worked closely on the con-
cept with Local 44 of the Municipal Employees' Union. The
union chiefs loved the idea, and they cooperated.

In those days, I could talk the white off rice, but I was a no-
nonsense person. "This is what we're going to do . . . ," I would
start off. And almost always, I'd hear from the vested interests,
the old-timers in the department or the people who benefited from
patronage and nepotism to get jobs: "You can't do that."

"The hell I can't. The days of discrimination are over. You'd better get on board."

People knew I had the approval of the director. Not once in my eight years with Kuchta did he send back a letter I wrote for him. I began advising him on policy.

It wasn't long before I started cooking for people at the office, something I would do from then on wherever I worked. I would make my "famous" Cajun blackened chicken, and bring enough for everyone on the sixth floor. They lined up for that, as well as my equally renowned meatloaf.

I wore a different suit every day, a three-piece. I made it a point to be well groomed—my father's influence, again. As I settled into my job, I grew more confident and more good-natured. But every so often, I'd have to remind someone, especially the labor guys, that the three-piece suit and the smile weren't signs of weakness.

I got word that another highway supervisor was being discriminatory and abusive to his black employees. He put them to work on the worst jobs, and he wouldn't allow African Americans to operate machinery, such as the road graters or backhoe tractors. He had them cutting grass and digging ditches. All workers were expected to do those jobs, but this supervisor wasn't fair when it came to doling out better assignments.

I had an open-door policy, and I let everyone know about it. Some workers would come to me with their complaints or their suggestions, and I was happy to hear them out. Or, I would ride out to various yards, such as the highway yards where equipment was kept and men gathered in the morning to get assignments. I'd make it my business to speak with the guys. I spoke their language. Also, I enjoyed getting out of the office, and this added to my good nature when we talked. The guys knew that "Mr. Williams is The Man, but you can talk to him."

That was how I heard the story about this one supervisor, and how he was a racist bully. They told me he had a punching bag in his office. He would call black guys into his office, and to intimidate them, he'd put on a show. When they arrived, they'd find him with his shirt off. He'd be punching the bag, showing what a tough guy he was, and he'd keep flailing away at the bag as he chewed them out in the worst racist language. "Listen, nigger (punch!), get this into that woolly head of yours (punch!). I'm not going to take any more of this crap from you, and when I tell you to do something, you do it, and you like it (punch!). Got that, nigger (punch! punch!)?

"I'll put a stop to that," I said when they told me the story.

I went to see him, but he wasn't in. I told his secretary, "Call him."

I waited in his office. I knew the kind of guy I was dealing with, and I knew the approach I had to take. The minute he came in, before he could close the door, I grabbed him by the collar, pushed him across the room, and slammed him against the wall, twice. He bounced off, and I pulled back my fist, cocked and ready to hit him. I made sure the door was open so people could hear.

"The next time you call someone a nigger, or punch on that goddamn bag, you're punching me."

I left him. That was the end of that. No more complaints from the guys about unfair work assignments.

Now that I was in the position of hiring, firing, and promoting, and also influencing employment policy, I had to examine the logic of affirmative action programs. I believed that they were necessary, but I didn't care for President Johnson's Great Society approach that suggested that racial quotas were the answer. My fear was that once you met a 10 percent quota or the quota that was set, you were stuck. I preferred the more informal approach under an overall design to let the public workforce mirror the racial composition of the population at large.

I also had to deal with the attitudes of African-American workers. Some were angered by real discrimination they faced on the job, but I had to talk others out of using discrimination as an excuse to keep them from being overly aggressive in their careers. For example, there were two African-American engineers in the department, and one of them complained to me, "I can only go so far as a city employee. They'll never make me director of Public Works because I'm black."

I had a crude, one-word answer for him: "Bullshit."

He would one day become director of Public Works.

IN 1984, THE EXECUTIVE ASSISTANT to the director of Public Works retired, and I was the logical replacement. I wanted the job, but not as it was then constituted. The retiring assistant director was a high-paid "gofer." He spent most of his time at the state general assembly lobbying for legislation that affected the department. He was the number-three man in the department, but he had less work and responsibility than my job as chief of administrative services further down the line.

I went to see the mayor and told him that if he would consider me, I wanted the executive assistant's post that was opening, but I also wanted to retain my current responsibilities. I said I would do both jobs. I sold the idea as a way to save money. I still wanted to be in charge of hiring, firing, safety, and training. The mayor agreed.

All I had to do was look around Public Works to see where improvement was needed. All of the African-American women were low-level clerks. There were more than 100 of them in the Municipal Building. The first thing I did as assistant director was get the names of all of the black female employees (I collaborated with the civil service director). I went to her and told her I had a problem.

"What do you want me to do?" she asked. "There are only so many promotions coming up, and you're talking about massive retraining." She said that she agreed with my goal, and that it was ridiculous that all the African-American women in the department were stuck in secretarial jobs, but she said that the restructuring I had in mind took time.

I had an idea. "Can't we change their work titles, and that way at least give them more money?" The civil service director agreed, and we changed the title of Secretary to Office Assistant I or II, depending on the employee's seniority. In one swoop, all the women got promotions, and a little more inducement in their pay envelopes.

But you can't please everyone. There was one African-American woman in the department who told everyone she was suspicious about my motives. "What's in this for him? What's he looking for?" She was insinuating that I was trying to ingratiate myself with African-American women employees as a way to get sexual favors. My feelings were very hurt by that. I knew it was only office gossip, but it was painful when good intentions were turned on their head. One thing that the Baltimore City Attorney's office never had to bother about was having my name attached to a sexual harassment suit or complaint.

Giving the women some extra money and a better-sounding title wasn't the same thing as promoting them up the ranks. They had to take the civil-service exam like everyone else for promotion. But I encouraged them to do so, and spread the word that the effort would be worth their while—they would be taken seriously. So, people started sitting for the exams. When the list of promotions came up, if there were two openings, I would look at the deserving candidates and make sure that one at least would be a minority: an Asian, a woman, a Native American, or an African American.

We also had an effective work-release program to give inmates employment, and a break from the confines of prison life. The prisoners were put to work on road gangs. This wasn't affirmative action, because all races were involved, although a majority of the prisoners were black. They didn't join one of those old-fashioned chain gangs with the leg irons and the boss man's dogs growling at them. By the Reagan era, Baltimore would have an African-American mayor and a gleaming new Inner Harbor. This was a changed Southern city, and changed for the better in spite of some poor neighborhoods and a new drug epidemic that would keep these areas below the poverty level.

There was a need to clean the city: to scrub and landscape, so I took advantage of that. Low-end criminals (not murderers or rapists), who were at the end of their sentences and who were able to leave the prison on their own recognizance, worked under supervision. The city paid the jail, and the jail paid the prisoners.

Some of the guys had never had jobs before, so they could now be released with some work experience. In some cases, they stayed on as city workers. The Public Works Department was glad to keep them on, because they knew the job. Most highway workforces were made up of guys without high school educations.

The mayor was mindful of the innovations I introduced at Public Works. He said he watched the way I handled unions, the politicians, the workforce, and other city officials. If he had ever asked me where I got my management style, I would have told him from Uncle Buddy and my brother-in-law.

Uncle Buddy, a low-level employee for the Pennsylvania Railroad all his life, had a forceful and honest personality, and his approach to life was so straight and unafraid that I wanted to model myself after him. He showed me how to look any man in the eye so he would look back at you with respect. Also, he had a sense of fun at work. He would take his co-workers out to lunch. When I started running departments, I would do the same. Or I would make one of my special meals to take in, like my turkey loaf. It was the Uncle Buddy in me doing that.

I learned how to be an administrator by emulating my wife's brother-in-law, George Russell. He was a lawyer, one of the best and most respected in Baltimore, and he opened doors for others. He became Baltimore's first African-American judge, and our first African-American city solicitor.

He worked every day, and when I was a fireman, I used to go to his office on Saturdays. I just liked George, and his success made me want to emulate him. I noticed the way he operated, like the crisp and professional way he answered the phone: "George Russell here." He had style. George set himself apart from the pack without setting himself above anyone. Over the years, too many successful African Americans in Baltimore learned to act elitist from their white masters. The pride my father and his generation had was instilled in them by their fathers, whose own fathers had survived slavery with a knowledge of their ancestry and the discipline of the hierarchy of African society. They retained their pride in being descended from such a society. Indirectly, without ever discussing our African ancestry, my father managed to instill some of that pride in me.

THE FIRST TWO OF MY SEVEN GRANDCHILDREN, Rene and Michelle, were coming to visit Marjie and me at our townhouses on 33rd Street, and I saw it as my future duty to make them feel proud about themselves. The grandkids had a name for me: Pop Pop.

Marjie did a lot to make our eight-unit apartment block a community. One January, a blizzard closed down the city, so Marjie organized the neighbors on the block. The women made food, and the men shoveled snow to clear the streets and sidewalks. Two of the disabled vehicles on the street were buses, snowed in right in front of our apartment, and the drivers had to stay with their vehicles. So Marjie made sure they were supplied with coffee, fried chicken, and cake. Typically, emergencies like that brought neighbors together by reminding folks how much we needed one another.

Our youngest son, Montel, had graduated from the Naval Academy, and for some years, he served on a submarine. Then he went into covert operations.

"I can't tell you what I'm doing or where they're sending me, Pop," he said. "I'll give you a call when I get back."

We'd hear from him after a month or so. When he came by the house, his mother and I were surprised to see his head shaved as bald as a billiard ball. At that time, young black men were wearing their hair long, and curling it up with lots of shiny activator. The only person I knew who shaved his head was the actor Lou Gossett, Jr. I had no problem with it, and thought Montel looked good. I saw it as a military thing. Montel hinted that he had to go bald for a covert operation, and I deduced that he'd been sent to Libya or some such place. The look became his trademark. Montel was starting to speak at high schools to tell the young guys about life in the armed forces, and he said that his appearance got the kids' attention.

Before long, Montel started speaking to other groups, and he became successful as a motivational speaker. A father wonders what he passes on to his offspring, and in Montel's case, it might have been my gift of gab.

Herman, my eldest son, was finding success as a sculptor, something that none of us saw coming, which made it all the more impressive. Without any formal training as an artist, but going on pure instinct and talent, he started sculpting. The first work he created was a remarkably realistic bronze statue of a muscular weight lifter squatting with a heavy bar over his shoulders. The detail of the anatomy was amazing. It looked like a Rodin, and the family said that Herman must have been thinking of his old man when he did it, because I would lift weights to keep in shape.

Herman's work started appearing in shows up and down the East Coast. He became adept at sculpting with wire, and he worked that wire until his fingers bled. He did a wire portrait of Marjie that became one of our most cherished possessions.

Herman got a commission to do a bust of the vice president of the United States, George Bush. Mr. Bush's son Jeb saw Herman's work at a show in Florida and hired him to do the sculpture of his father.

Marjorie and Clolita pursued successful careers nearer to home. Marjorie did computer programming with the Social Security Administration, and Clolita became a vice president at the University of Maryland, and later an attorney. We saw a lot of them, and our grandchildren, even though Clolita, who spoke fluent French, liked to go to Paris for weekend trips. I was envious of her. One thing I hadn't done a lot was travel. I liked Baltimore, but there was a whole world out there to explore.

In 1988, I was thinking of retiring, looking for another job, and doing some traveling with Marjie, which I'd always wanted to do but had put off for so long.

But Baltimore's recently elected African-American mayor, Kurt Schmoke, had other ideas for me. I'd known the new mayor for a long time, and I'd contributed to his campaigns over the years as he worked his way up through city government.

One Saturday morning, I picked up the phone and it was his office calling. I could tell by the mayor's tone of voice that this was no weekend social call. I expected to hear about some emergency.

I stood in the hall, and Marjie asked who was calling. I cupped my hand over the receiver and told her, "It's the mayor!"

Into the phone, I asked good-naturedly, "Hello, Mayor, what did I do? Something wrong?"

"No, no," he said. "I'm sure you read in the papers about this problem with the Department of Transportation."

I'd read the stories, and working for the city, I'd heard even more about the bad blood between the acting commissioner of transportation and the City Council. The tension between them was making it hard for the mayor, and he was faced with a political embarrassment. The mayor appointed people to posts such as transportation commissioner, but the City Council had to approve them. The mayor had to formally submit the acting commissioner's name Monday morning, and he knew that his appointment would be rejected. If the City Council voted down a mayoral appointment, they would be casting a vote of no confidence for the mayor.

"Sure, I've been following that."

"I'm calling to ask you a favor . . ." I could see what was coming. I was so surprised that my knees suddenly grew weak, and leaning against the wall, I started sliding down ". . . I'd like you to take this position."

I was so overwhelmed that I was literally floored, sitting on the hallway floor. "Mayor, I don't know anything about what goes on at Transportation."

"I understand you're a good administrator. That's what I need. I won't have a problem getting you through City Council."

I suddenly remembered, "Mr. Mayor, didn't you once say you wanted to make me fire chief?" It was as if the unexpected offer to run the transportation department had jolted me into realizing where I really wanted to be.

"I still have that intention. But I can't do that now."

They all knew me, the City Council and the movers and shakers, the political operators and the unions. We'd been working together for so long, and I'd been told that the consensus about me was, "Herman, he's a good guy. We don't have to twist his arm to buy tickets to our political affairs. He's tough, but fair, and you can't put anything past him." I asked the mayor, "When do you have to know?" He said immediately.

Marjie came by, and she looked at me wide-eyed: "What are you doing on the floor?"

I covered the mouthpiece. "The mayor, he wants me to be commissioner of transportation!"

In her calm voice—but when had Marjie's voice ever been anything but calm?—she asked, "What do you want to do, hon?"

I didn't hesitate, and said into the phone, "Mr. Mayor, I'll do it."

He thanked me, and his very next call must have been to *The Baltimore Sun* and the other newspapers, because the Sunday headline was: "MAYOR APPOINTS HERMAN WILLIAMS AS COMMISSIONER OF TRANSPORTATION."

The next day, Monday, my name was submitted to the City Council for a vote. All 19 councilors approved the mayor's choice.

The dissenters were in the Department of Transportation, the guys I would have to work with. Unfortunately, race was again a factor. All the department directors and head engineers were white, and I got word that instead of devoting themselves to working under me, they were going to do a little sabotage. Some of the gossip I got wind of was frightening, like construction projects would be messed with so structural failure would result. If that happened, the commissioner would be blamed for approving the project. But worse, people could be injured and lives could be lost. I knew I'd have to do something, because I would have no choice but to depend on the directors and engineers when they said a project was sound.

To the department, I knew, I would have to earn the right to be thought of as "the Commish."

My very first day on the job, I felt I had to make a point. Word reached me again that some of the managers said they were going to fix me.

I called a meeting. All the top people, the chiefs of departments—from highway, emergency, construction—more than two dozen of them gathered in the boardroom, along with the department engineers and architects. I was the only African American there. The department had some lower-level minority engineers, but no directors.

I pulled out a pen and paper, and I drew a picture of a dog. I put its tail on its forehead. I passed the picture around. "What does that mean?"

Everyone looked at it and said they didn't know what it meant. I smiled, and said, "This picture means the tail doesn't wag the dog. I hear that some of you are grumbling. You're saying, 'This guy Williams isn't an engineer. He doesn't know anything about highways.' Well, you're right. I'm not an engineer. I don't know how to build a bridge. But you do."

My voice was calm but no-nonsense. "This is what's going to happen. You're going to bring contracts in for me to sign. But before I do, you're going to sign them yourselves. What I'm going to do is okay your approval."

Some of the directors' faces turned beet red, and I knew that the rumors I'd heard were true. They were thinking of trying to get me to approve faulty plans. But they knew I had them now. Before they brought me something, they'd have to go over the plans until they had the confidence to put their own names on them, because if someone were to go to jail when a bridge collapsed, it would be them.

"No, gentlemen," I said, "the tail does not wag the dog."

That meeting ruffled a lot of feathers, but I left the boardroom feeling like I was the commissioner.

The way I jumped into that job, you might have thought I'd been preparing for it all my life. But from building my own houses and the Public Works projects, I could read a blueprint. There were 2,000 employees at Transportation, but I was used to running a big department at Public Works.

I looked into the personnel. I was in a position to make things happen—and make things better. I remembered Kuchta, the director of Public Works, who was Polish. He was always candid with me, and in our talks, he'd say, "Herman, you have to look after your own. The Polish look after the Polish. The blacks look after the blacks. The Jews look after the Jews. God knows the Italians and the Irish look after themselves. You shouldn't be unfair with the others, but if you don't look after your own, who will?"

Keith Scroggins was the department's EEO, or Equal Employment Officer. When I took over, I found him to be a very frustrated young man, because he couldn't get anything done. He saw everything in black and white, with no gray areas, and people he had trouble with he thought were villains, so he'd get upset.

I pulled him aside for a talk. "Keith, you get more of what you want with honey than vinegar. You're allowing yourself to get all angry. Never let people know you're angry."

He changed after that, and we worked together to raise the profile of women and minorities in the department.

The city's bus and trolley drivers were employed by a private company, but I found a way to establish more jobs, particularly for women, by setting up a corps of traffic officers. Baltimore needed more police, and I sold the mayor on the idea of freeing police from their traffic-control duties by allowing my department to hire people to do it. I convinced him that it would save the city money.

There were critics. Some people said, "No, you can't do that. Civilians can't direct traffic and write tickets." But we got approval, and it worked. A large proportion of traffic-control officers were women. They wore the same type of uniform as police, including badges and white caps. Later, they started writing up traffic citations.

The department was expanding. Two years before I took over, the Department of Transit and Traffic became the Department of Transportation. The maintenance of traffic lights, parking policy, and parking tickets was the traditional responsibility of the department. In most cities, a transportation department was just involved in moving traffic. In Baltimore, I was in charge of snow removal; and the maintenance of alleyways, footways, and construction projects such as bridges and highways, which in other cities would be under Public Works.

The mayor put highways and water under my department. The sewer lines ran under the streets, and to fix a leak, we'd have to dig up a street, so these were also separated from Public Works and given to us. (Public Works continued to handle water purification and sewage.)

I ended up supervising the same guys whom I'd previously hired and fired at Public Works. Just when they thought they were rid of me, I was again their boss. We'd joke about it, and I'd say, "You can't get away from me!"

I gave people opportunity to challenge me and to express themselves. I always allotted time to discuss important issues, but once a decision was made, I didn't look back, and I wouldn't allow others to second-guess themselves, because by then it was too late. I had to do that because everywhere I went I had to make a lot of changes, and I needed everyone on board to effect them. The directors, engineers, and workers had to buy into every innovation or they'd never get off the ground. I had meetings so that different people could give their input, and I would just listen. I might not always agree, but I always let people have their say.

I knew how to say thanks, too. I always praised people. I had season tickets to football and baseball games, the Colts and the Orioles, but I rarely used them. They'd go to someone in the department whom I'd buttonhole with the question, "Hey, you want to go to the game?" Showing appreciation wasn't something I learned in school. I simply knew that you treat people the way you want to be treated.

I looked back to when I was a young firefighter, and I remembered that I didn't get praise—in fact, I only got discouragement. People began to question me about those early days when we integrated the fire department, wondering, "Weren't you bitter?"

"No, I'd get emotional," I'd answer. "But I was never downtrodden."

Experience also taught me that you had to choose your battles; otherwise, you might be using up your energy fighting all the time. On the other hand, you had to stand up for yourself and your principles. It was a matter of judgment.

For instance, one Fourth of July holiday, I was driving with Marjie to the Inner Harbor to see the fireworks in an official car. I wanted to park, but the cop on duty was pretty arrogant when he said, "You can't come in here."

"I'm the commissioner of transportation."

"I don't give a damn who you are!"

What irritated me was that he saw me with my wife, and he was rude anyway. It may have been a racial thing, but he was wrong to deny parking to an official who determined parking policy. In any case, his attitude was a matter I didn't want to pursue.

But, on the following Fourth of July, I had to have a highway supervisor fired. It was a case of the one final goof-up resulting from too many cases of negligence. A lot of people were headed for the restaurants and attractions of Inner Harbor that holiday. By the late '80s, the harbor, with its new museums and freshly scrubbed brick warehouses, which had been turned into trendy new stores, was a big tourist attraction. I drove there to find that the median grass on the roads was ten inches high. I didn't need the mayor or other dignitaries to see how the streets were being neglected.

In my position, I would never stand for dirty streets. I had a radio in the car, and I called up a supervisor when I spotted a problem. I might see that a traffic light wasn't functioning properly, so I'd make a call: "I want this light fixed in 15 minutes!" Then I'd wait to see that it was done. The crew would show up, and assure me, "Don't worry, Commish, we'll have this light fixed!"

They knew I was the "Commish" because I dressed the part, in three-piece suits from Joseph A. Bank Clothiers, one of the better men's stores in town. I ordered wrinkleproof material because there would be times I'd be sitting at a desk all day.

Transportation, like Public Works, could be a candy store for corruption if the people in charge were inclined to accept bribes and kickbacks. There were so many big-ticket projects going on, but Baltimore had a bidding system the officials respected, and the law gave the job of repairing a street, building, or overpass to the lowest bidder. The sealed bids were looked over by the Board of Estimates, consisting of the mayor, the president of the City Council, the city comptroller, the director of Public Works, and the city solicitor. The Maryland Interstate System within city limits was handled by a division of the transportation department, and financed by state money under my control. Another bidding system was in place for those jobs. In the past, there was a "good ol' boy" system at work, where all of those involved were friends and associates of someone. I was a straight shooter and made sure all contracts were announced in the newspapers.

I was commissioner when Camden Yards, Baltimore's new baseball stadium, was built. The entire roadway around the stadium was my responsibility. Some civic groups didn't want the stadium, which I thought was ridiculous, because Baltimore needed this attraction. I went to various community groups and assured them that on opening day there would be no traffic problems. "Commish," some people in city government told me, "you're committing suicide with that promise."

But I had confidence in my people, and the result was like a Cinderella story. More than 40,000 people showed up for the opening pitch, and most of them drove there. (Trivia question: What's a "Baltimore Chop," invented by the Orioles? It's when the batter hits a ball into the infield that usually bounces too high for the infielder to have time to catch it and make a putout at first base.) When the game let out, everyone went their way without clogging the streets. If something had gone wrong, there was only one direction the fingers would have pointed: my office. I told Marjie, "Transportation is my name, so I'd get the blame."

I liked the job of "Commish." The good thing was you could go out on site and see the projects come together. It felt very fulfilling to point to something while driving around the city, and say, "I did this." For example, I built a traffic bridge over St. Paul Street at the Pennsylvania Train Station depot. The Hilton Parkway, a curving downtown street, was a menace because every time it rained, there were accidents; people were getting killed. I had it straightened out, and the improvement cut down on traffic deaths. I also oversaw the construction of Baltimore's Light Rail System. Like the old streetcars, the sleek new modern cars were run by electric power from lines above. (Okay, the system proved an underutilized white elephant and was put together under great political pressure before my time, but you play the hand you're dealt, and my job was to see that construction was done effectively and with minimal disruption to surrounding traffic.)

It made me feel good to see women driving the big trucks and operating machinery, whereas when I started, there were no women supervisors—in fact, no women doing anything. I was also glad to help out good causes. Every year, I gave money to the city to pay salaries to underprivileged kids so they could have summer jobs doing city work.

But four years into the job, I felt the urge to move on. I wanted to retire from the public payroll and see what else was out there.

But once again, the mayor had other ideas.

I shouldn't have been surprised. No one else was surprised by what happened next. They knew how I'd always felt about the fire department. You don't put up with as much frustration and b.s. as I did while integrating the fire department unless you truly loved the place.

I would drive by a business, dwelling, or warehouse and recognize the scene from an alarm of long ago, and I'd feel a terrible sadness. Marjie might be in the car, and I'd say to her, "I remember when we fought a fire there. Some of the guys died there."

It seemed that I had a lot of unfinished business at the fire department. I had enjoyed a successful career at Public Works and Transportation, and I could have retired with dignity from public service.

But first, it seemed, I had to go "home." They could call me Commish, but in my heart I was a Smoke Eater.

❧ CHAPTER TEN ☙

Fire Chief

Another surprise call came from the mayor's office. Mayor Schmoke asked me, "Herman, what are your plans?"

"I'm thinking of retiring, Mayor."

"Why don't you retire as chief of the fire department?"

"You've got to be kidding," I laughed. "When?"

"Right now."

He told me that my time had come—and the time had also come for a major U.S. city to have an African American in charge of its fire department!

Baltimore's fire department had a sensible policy of promoting its officers from within, and not hiring anyone from the outside. With my background as a firefighter and officer, my time away at Public Works and as commissioner of transportation didn't seem to bother anybody. But by 1992, I'd forgotten about ever becoming fire chief. Mayor Schmoke promised to steer the job my way back when he was elected in 1988, but I wasn't sure that I even wanted the post because I understood that the department was in bad shape. Apparatus and firehouses were run-down, and morale had deteriorated in the previous years. I would never publicly criticize earlier fire chiefs, so when we ran into each other, we'd have a drink and discuss anything other than department business, but if I were to take the job, I would inherit a mess in desperate need of reorganization and new thinking.

That was what the mayor wanted to have happen—and done by someone who still knew the department from the ground up.

What the Fire Board wanted was what all the previous boards wanted: a fire chief they could control, who would let them run the show. They had their own candidate, and they were in no mood to compromise.

So, the mayor fired the entire Fire Board and appointed another one.

Times had certainly changed.

On April 16, 1992, I walked into my office, and the welcome I received was like a homecoming. The prodigal son had returned. But I did bring someone with me from those years away: my loyal secretary, Mary Wolf, who had been with me for 12 years, from my days at Public Works. Mary happened to be of Polish descent, and she had a sweet temperament. But her loyalty to me was such that people referred to her as my "pit bull." At the fire department, she continued to be one of my most invaluable staffers.

I was introduced to the rest of the staff, and then I entered the boardroom that would be the scene of so many meetings and press conferences. There was so much to be done, so many reforms that had to be made, that my thought that first day as I looked at the department emblem on the wall was, "I'm not here to rock the boat; I'm here to sink the boat!"

The Baltimore Fire Department was floundering badly when I took over, and it might have sunk all on its own. But there had been some notable improvements in my absence. Women had been allowed in as firefighters in 1981, although there were only a handful. Firefighting technology had improved, so we could retire the hose towers where the old-style hoses had to be hung to dry. And the street-corner fireboxes were replaced by a 911 emergency phone system.

But when I took over the department, the firefighting companies, which had five men per truck when I joined the fire department in 1954, were down to three men. In an engine company, the lead-off man would be at the hydrant, the pump operator would be at the truck, and that left one lone guy hosing down the fire all by himself.

"This is ridiculous," I told the mayor. "It's unsafe for the public, and it's unsafe for firefighters. I'll find ways to save the city money, but not this way."

I got more manpower, and for the moment, the unions were delighted with the new fire chief. But resistance to any change was fierce. For an organization that almost had to run along military lines, such reluctance came close to mutiny.

Some of the officers might have hoped that the first African-American fire chief would just be window dressing, and that after the headlines and TV profiles, things would return to normal. But I'd worked outside the department for 12 years. I was more than a firefighter—I was an experienced administrator who knew how to clear away dead wood and run a city department like a business. And I gave myself the mandate to create an efficient organization. The mayor had no agenda in mind when he appointed me.

When I arrived, there were eight deputy chiefs and a chief deputy, and none of them had anything to do but sit around waiting for a fire. They didn't even know what a budget looked like. They called themselves administrators, but I saw that they were firefighters.

I had a problem with that. I met with the top echelon and announced that I was eliminating the night shift. Some of the deputy chiefs were already at retirement age, but I allowed the eight chiefs 60 days to decide who would stay on. If no consensus was reached, I would have to make a decision. But by the end of that time, four deputy chiefs had decided to retire. The four remaining were appointed to a new post.

"Gentlemen, I'm creating a new position: assistant chief." I told them they would come in by day, do administration, and everyone had better be prepared to hit the ground running. My first day on the job was halfway through April, and the city's fiscal budget began on July 1. We had to make policy quickly, or wait until July of the following year to get the money.

It was a wonder somebody didn't kill me, the way some of the department brass felt about this change at the top. But I had other things to worry about: training four assistants—fast. The assistant chief of operations was put in charge of all apparatus, procuring new equipment and repairing the old. Equipment had been allowed to get run-down, and its rehabilitation was a priority. This assistant also looked after the department's 2,000 firefighters.

To the new assistant chief of administration, I said, "You handle the budget."

I told the new assistant chief of research and development, "New ideas in fire fighting, gas masks, helmets, and a new communications system I've got in mind—that's all yours."

To the new assistant chief of fire prevention, I said, "You handle safety and investigation." This last post wasn't entirely necessary, and I could have done without it, but I felt it would have been too radical to go from eight deputy chiefs to three assistant chiefs.

None of them knew about administration, so I introduced them to the budget and how it operated, with the simple truth, "Money is the backbone of the department." Sometimes it seemed like school when I'd give my assistants assignments. "This is what you do; if you have problems, come back to me."

After six months, I rotated them. They didn't like this because they didn't like change. But in my view, I was there to make change. After a short time, one of the assistant chiefs came knocking on my door and told me: "Chief, this isn't for me. I'm not cut out to be an administrator. When I was deputy chief, I could fight fires. I don't like sitting at a desk." So he took his pension and left. I liked him, and I was sad to see him go. But pragmatically, I was down to three assistant chiefs, the number I had wanted all along

Actually, I wanted only two assistant chiefs for administration and operations, with everything flowing up through them to me. But that wouldn't happen until just prior to my retirement.

Marjie was as proud as she could be about my appointment as fire chief. I could tell she was, but to other people, she wasn't the boastful type. My kids were all excited, too, and they asked me why if I was top dog at the fire department did I trade in the last of the new BMW cars I started buying for myself when I became an administrator at Public Works (after a lifetime of clunky used cars).

I told them, "I'm making a lot of cuts in the department, and it would look bad to the public if the chief went around in a luxury car." So I used the department car assigned to the fire chief. Ironically, the car was a black chief—a black Jeep Cherokee Chief, that is—which had a radio to keep me patched into the city's emergency communications system.

Difficult decisions had to be made about personnel cutbacks and firehouses that had to be closed. When I entered the fire department in 1954, Baltimore had a million people. The suburbs had drained the population down to 650,000 when I became fire chief, and there were blocks of vacant buildings. When I was a new fireman, I entered a force of 54 engine companies and 28 truck companies. As chief, I inherited 45 engine companies and 22 truck companies. As the city downsized its population, there was logic to also downsizing city services, with the exception of the police resources required for the war on drugs.

I got feedback from the rank and file, and I heard through the grapevine that a lot of them thought I was crazy. They couldn't understand what was going on in the first real shakeup the department had known in 40 years. Everyone had wanted me to come back to the fire department, but some people thought I was a traitor because I'd returned and upset the apple cart. Over the years, I'd gotten a reputation as a nice, easygoing guy who knew his job, wasn't afraid of the work, and would do what it took to get everyone on board when it came to policy. This was another reason why they were surprised by the changes I made that turned things upside down. I was still a good guy, but I knew I had to push forward those needed changes because there wasn't a lot of time to reverse the damage.

Just about every day, I would hear, "We've been doing it this way for 15 years, and you come along and change it."

"Look, pal, change is inevitable."

Even the driver assigned to me complained, "Well, Chief, we didn't always do this—"

I cut him off, "Look, this is the last time I want to hear you say that. It's a new day."

Not all the officers were happy that an African American was in charge, but what upset them more was change. When orders came down regarding uniforms, for instance, one shift commander gave the order to the firefighters at lineup by saying, "Look, I don't like this any more than you do, but the FC wants it."

He would do that every time, trying to instill an "us versus the chief" mentality. I heard about it and removed him. Such insubordination would be unheard of in private business or the military. Why should it be allowed in the fire department?

One contentious point was appointments. Up until I became chief, every position required a written test, and the first person on the list had to be selected. When I abolished half of the deputy chief positions, and then made shift commander and assistant chiefs appointed positions, the rank and file became angry because I cut off their way to advance through testing to battalion chief level, as far as civil service was concerned. I was accused of politicizing the top positions. I knew that there was no danger of that, because I knew I would never play that game. I just wanted to put the most competent people in top positions, and I knew that a test didn't necessarily determine the best man or woman. How could 100 questions tell if a person knew the job, or even the contents of the encyclopedia-size building code and fire code books, or most important, how the person performed in the field? From then on, we conducted candidate interviews and scrutinized the candidates' performance records.

In order to effect change—and not get shot!—I hired a consultant. I told the mayor that the department was top-heavy, and I wanted to cut it, while the number of firefighters manning companies had to increase from three to at least four, even though the overall number of firefighters was excessive because there were too many firehouses. The consultant compiled a report that confirmed my suspicions that the department was overloaded. He wanted six months to do the job, and I gave him six days. I'd used consultants when I'd been the Commish, and I knew what I could expect. I referred to his report, which was a good one, to justify my policies.

I found that by closing firehouses, I could downsize the rank and file without firing anybody. But there were political risks involved. Residents of every neighborhood thought they owned their local station, and they would fight to retain them. But some firehouses were simply redundant. I could remember when Baltimore had a firehouse every three or four blocks. That made sense in the era of horse-drawn fire apparatus. But with the 911 system, fast trucks, and new technology, firefighters could arrive at the scene in three minutes, which was once considered an amazingly swift response time. The quality of the city's fire coverage had to be judged by response time, not by the number of firehouses. We had a scale model of the city at headquarters, and we plotted response times, trying to keep them within a three-to four-minute period, although five minutes was acceptable. If I found an area adequately covered by several firehouses, one would be a candidate for closure.

So, I scaled down personnel through attrition. If we had 50 vacancies in the department, and a firehouse that was closed had 23 people, I'd knock 23 off the number of vacancies, and reassign 23 guys to fill those assignments.

The unions weren't satisfied. If they had their way, there would be 2,500 firefighters. Implied in every communication to me from the union was, "We want to keep things the way they are."

An executive has to know how to deal with rumors, which for the most part are based on people's fears that arise when they don't have sufficient or correct information. I wanted to personally explain the reasons for my policies to the firefighters and officers. I went on firehouse "inspections," and visited as many as I could so I could get to know the personnel and they could get to know me. When I entered a firehouse, procedure was followed, and the watchman would throw the gong. The firemen (and I was happy to see a few firewomen now), lined up. We shook hands, and I enjoyed meeting with them. They'd be standing at attention, and then I'd tell the captain, "Okay, you can let them go."

We'd go to the kitchen, somebody would bring me a cup of coffee, and we'd get down to business in an informal, friendly way. "What's going on?" I'd ask. "What's the latest rumor? Anybody have any problems?"

"Hey, Chief, is it true you're going to shut our house?" They'd hear the news straight from the horse's mouth. They saw I wasn't crazy, and I had the firefighters' best interests at heart. When I took over the department, morale was low, and as anyone in a work situation knows, morale is largely a matter of pay. I explained that to get more money for salaries, the department had to become an efficient business.

I don't think I ever left a firehouse without an invitation to come back for a home-cooked meal they wanted to prepare for me.

The firefighters were even looking like firefighters again. When I became chief, physical appearances had been allowed to deteriorate, and a lot of firemen looked like dirtbags. I couldn't help but feel that their slovenly, informal dress was reflected in low morale, in a lessening of pride that they felt about their work and themselves.

A uniform is a symbol. Before I left the fire department, all officers and firefighters wore dress uniforms at all times, unless it was someone's day off. But while I was away, the white firefighters convinced the fire chief that uniforms were like a bull's-eye. They complained, "We have to go into these black neighborhoods, and uniforms make us targets." The white firefighters were scared; they feared getting stoned. It was the time when the firehouse doors started getting locked as protection against the community.

Racism and paranoia go hand-in-hand. If you assume that a bunch of people are out to get you, and you lock yourself away from those people, your fears will worsen. The thing to do is go out and face your fears, and find out that they have no basis.

The fire chief of the time was happy to do away with uniforms because the city was paying for them. He saw it as a way to save money. But the firefighters, both white and black, had a hidden agenda for not going to and from firehouses in uniform. A lot of firefighters moonlighted—they had second jobs. They complained that they weren't making enough money as firefighters. A dress uniform slowed them down because they couldn't show up at their second job advertising their primary job. By saying that they feared they would be attacked by unknown assailants from Baltimore's African-American community if they dared wear their uniforms outside the firehouse, and getting the administration to believe it, these firemen were saving themselves time by not having to go home and change clothes. They blew the "threat" out of proportion to achieve their ends

The result was a motley-looking corps of firefighters. It got so bad at funerals that some firemen looked like bums. Guys showed up at work in shorts.

The psychology of wearing uniforms was to show that you were always ready for the responsibility of fire fighting. If you have to go to night shift work in uniform, you won't hang around in bars all day.

The first thing I did when I became chief was to go down to a store that specialized in uniforms and order one for myself. The manager was surprised and happy to see me. The two previous chiefs had never been outfitted. They wore suits instead of uniforms. I felt good about my uniform, and I wore it every day . . . and everywhere.

Marjie smiled when she saw me come through the door, "Oh, my!" Wearing that uniform really made me feel like the chief. I knew that if I felt that way, the firefighters would feel the same pride when they were outfitted. While I was at the uniforms company, I ordered a new design for the department. I put out word that all firefighters had to get a uniform, and wear them like in the earlier days. I copied the style used by the Los Angeles Fire Department: dark blue shirt and pants as the on-job uniform (no dungarees like my first years as a firefighter), and the dress uniform was dark blue serge jacket and pants.

The young guys grumbled, but the older guys thanked me for "bringing pride back to the department." But all the guys looked sharp. In a year, every fire department in the state of Maryland put their people in the same type of uniform.

I had to look into everything, including grooming. The problem was the gas masks. Beards and long mustaches could interfere with the seals, cause leakage, and endanger the firefighter. I don't know what it is about us firefighters, but believe me, if a firefighter can find a way to get injured, he will. I came in, and guys were wearing earrings. I thought, *Oh, no!* At the risk of ruining my popularity with the young guys, I outlawed earrings, which could have been a danger if they got caught in something. Body tattoos I left alone, and some of the firefighters were covered with some real beauties.

Now that they looked good in their new uniforms, I wanted the firefighters to show themselves off. I put out an order that in every city parade, no matter how small, firefighting apparatus would participate. I created the post of public information officer, whom people could contact about fire department news, and he coordinated parades. I saw this as a way to instill pride and raise the department's profile with the public. People loved fire engines. After all those years, *I* loved fire engines, and I liked climbing up on an old vintage wagon and waving at the crowds as their fire chief.

But some of the firemen resented the duty, and this went back to them not being part of the community. Almost 55 percent, more than half of the firefighters, lived outside Baltimore in the suburbs, some of them out of state. They'd come in, put in their shifts, and go back to where they lived and paid taxes. So when they appeared in city parades, I'd see them looking stone-faced and unenthusiastic. I actually ran beside the fire apparatus shouting instructions up to the guys: "Wave! Smile! Have a good time! You're representing the fire department!"

The apparatus they rode on even looked like real fire engines, after years of color experiments. In the '70s, all apparatus was repainted to something called "Omaha orange." A lot of cities were experimenting with colors other than red. At the time, I thought the shade of orange they chose was the nastiest color.

Being a traditionalist, I thought fire trucks should be red, and fire-engine red at that. A sort of madness came over fire departments, and apparatus became white, yellow, and one department even had lime green. Civilian drivers were confused, and they wouldn't pull over when they saw one of those things in their rearview mirror. They thought it was another city vehicle.

I changed the color back to what it should be, fire-engine red. That was a big morale booster for the men. Every new piece of apparatus was to come in red. When old equipment went to the repair shop for maintenance, they'd repaint it.

Not all changes to apparatus were bad. When I entered the department, a majority of the aerial ladders on trucks were wood, and they were so heavy that it took four men to raise one: two men to butt it, and two to lift it. New 30-foot aluminum ladders could be raised by two men.

I also revived Memorial Day, the church service where the department remembered our fallen comrades of the previous year. I didn't make attendance mandatory, like in the old days, and at first we'd be lucky if a dozen firefighters showed up. But as the years went on, it got better. Firefighters were feeling greater pride in themselves, and relations with the community were improving.

For one thing, the firehouses were opening up again. I put out the word: No more fortresses. Unlock those doors and let some sunshine in. Let the people see those gleaming machines they're paying for. Relax—no one's going to shoot you.

There would come a time, I knew, when some of the older firehouses would have to be replaced, and I sat down with my assistant of operations with a goal of designing a new, open, community-friendly firehouse, an interactive house that would draw in the neighbors like a social center.

Racism was alive and well at the Baltimore Fire Department when I took over, resulting, I felt, in African Americans being under-represented among firefighters and officers. I knew I could make a difference reconstituting the workforce, but could I change attitudes? I was determined to try. I knew that what I would need more than anything else was patience.

A defensive person might have flown off the handle when the regulations called for all firefighters to salute the chief, and one guy gave me an improper left-handed salute, which could have been construed as an insult. Instead of getting angry, I laughed, "What's that?"

"Sorry, sir!" He corrected himself and saluted me with his right hand. I could see from his inexperience in saluting that his battalion chief wasn't lining up the firefighters for drills. I'd go to another firehouse, and no one would salute me. They all had their hands in their pockets. I laughed, "What's the matter with you? Your hands broke?"

"Sorry, Chief." They saluted like it was a new experience.

"Guys, you got to understand," I explained. "In respecting my title, you're respecting the organization, and respecting yourselves."

Changing bad habits took time. I showed up at one station, and the gong was pulled to alert the house that the fire chief was in attendance. The firefighters ran in to line up, all but one black firefighter who ambled down the stairs in no particular hurry.

"What's the matter with you?" I said.

He just about yawned his answer, "Well, I was upstairs—"

"I don't give a shit. When that gong is pulled, the chief is in the house! You line up, fast!"

I called the department heads together, along with the battalion chiefs and assistant chiefs. "You teach the firefighters that when each one of you comes into a house, the gong is thrown, they line up on the apparatus floor, stand at attention, and give you a salute until you let it go."

I asked around, and found that the previous chief had done away with saluting when the new firefighters complained about the formality. The dropping of that routine so clearly reflected the general sloth and lack of discipline that had taken hold in the department that I brought it back. The older firefighters in their 40s and 50s understood, and they were happy. They knew that saluting instilled discipline and pride. There's a relationship between ceremony and pride, and between discipline and doing things right. They told that to the younger guys.

I'd be tested by the firefighters to see how far they could go with me. But some of the guys were so clumsy I caught them laughing at me behind my back because they thought they'd gotten away with disrespecting me, like "forgetting" to salute. And even though it was the end of the 20th century, there were still guys who hated to salute me because I was black. I could tell they were only doing it to avoid disciplinary measures.

One early test for me came at a staff meeting of senior officers. It was the custom when the fire chief entered the boardroom for everybody to stand up. One battalion chief, who also wasn't wearing his dress uniform of shirt, tie, and jacket, remained in his chair.

I told everyone, "Be seated." I turned to the one out of uniform, but chose not to ask why he didn't stand up. "Where's your jacket?"

"I left it at home."

It was as if we were in a grade-school classroom, and he was a surly student. "Aren't you aware that whenever you come to a meeting, you have to be in uniform?"

He grumbled something, and I told him, "You're out of the meeting." The other guys were embarrassed. "I told him, Chief," one officer said. "He said he left his jacket at home, and I offered him mine."

Well, Dr. Freud could have told that battalion chief that he left his jacket at home so we could have our little confrontation, but I didn't understand what he was after. What was he trying to prove? Why would he risk his next promotion?

Not to mention: Was he willing to give up my turkey loaf? Because the first thing I did was start cooking for the people in our offices in the red brick fire department headquarters building on 414 North Calvert Street. My secretary, Mary, would slice up the loaf to make sure everyone got some, careful about seconds because it was so popular.

I'd come into the office, with a smile for everyone, and shout my greeting, "Wazuuupp!" A few years later, that same phrase in the same tone of voice, would show up in a TV commercial. Everyone in the department had a good laugh. "What's the chief doing on TV?"

There was already a Williams on TV by then. Montel had found success as a motivational speaker, and this led to a syndicated television show. He didn't do a typical talk show, though. He had real people on sharing their real problems, talking about how they overcame obstacles. Other guests tried to defend their less honorable actions against Montel's probing, because the host was armed with some fundamental values that his grandfather and I had tried to instill in our kids, particularly the need for everyone to take responsibility for his or her actions. Montel coined a phrase, "Mountain, get out of my way." It was a good attitude to take in life. I would borrow it for some of my speeches as fire chief. Lots of the guests on Montel's show had moved their own mountains.

Marjie and I were delighted when Montel became a star. What parent wouldn't be proud? His clean-shaven head and muscular good looks made him stand out, and after all the Montel bald jokes died down and Michael Jordan adopted the look, shaved heads became the thing for young African-American men—almost a symbol of identity.

With Marjorie and Clolita busy with their careers in Maryland, Herman expanding his art, and Marjie involved in a variety of civic and charitable organizations, nobody had time to begrudge the youngest sibling his fame, which you sometimes found in a family where one member became a celebrity. When the kids and grandkids came home for visits, nothing had changed. There were still the same pranks and jokes, debates over current events, and plenty of food consumption, particularly by Pop Pop.

Home was no longer the apartment block on 33rd Street. Back when I was recovering from a gallbladder operation in 1985, I decided to sell that property, thinking, *Who needs this?* Marjie and I moved into a large apartment complex in the Jewish section of Baltimore, and we surrounded ourselves with lovely neighbors who were well-off (winter would find them vacationing in Boca), and who didn't mind the fire chief departing at all hours of the night to tend to an alarm.

I didn't sound the siren on my fire chief's car. In fact, one of the first instructions I gave as chief was that no fire engine sirens be sounded in the middle of a city block, where they served no purpose and just disturbed people. Sirens would be sounded only on approach to an intersection to alert traffic. Incidentally, there are two distinct sirens on modern fire trucks. The first is the high-pitched "screaming banshee" siren, and the second is the low "growling monster" sound to draw attention from both ends of the audio spectrum.

When I first became chief, I saw so many dumb things that I acted like an old-time fire chief: I YELLED! I was frustrated when firefighters didn't realize that their job was unlike any other job. A slipup didn't result in lost productivity or profits, but injury and death. Discipline and pride were tools as important as hoses and ladders. But once when I caught myself losing my temper, I decided I didn't want to be like that. I remembered Uncle Buddy's example: that to get respect you had to recognize the other person's dignity, and get along with everyone. I stopped issuing verbal orders entirely, and phrased my "orders" as suggestions after that.

"Don't you think you should put that line over there?" I'd say to a captain about a place on the apparatus floor where his men should line up. I needed information and input to do my job, and making suggestions instead of issuing orders allowed people to respond. With an order, they could only obey. With a suggestion, they could offer a counterproposal that could be better than the one I had in mind.

But doggone it if, even as fire chief and the top dog in the department, some of the white guys still had a problem with my drinking out of their coffee mugs! I was offered a cup of coffee at one firehouse, and instead of grabbing any mug, I saw the guy going through them all to find one he wasn't going to use! I kept quiet about it. I had bigger fish to fry.

One priority: bringing more women and minorities into the department. I noticed that all the people in the Fire Prevention Bureau, which I used to head under Chief Burke, were either lieutenants or captains, and very few women and minorities were there, because in the department, not enough women or minorities had achieved those ranks. There were no vacancies to allow new-comers to enter the Fire Prevention Bureau.

I created the position of fire inspector, ranking above fire-fighter but below lieutenant, to provide some inducement, and I made it an appointed position. For the 12 new jobs, all union positions, I appointed 11 male firefighters—6 white and 5 African Americans—and one African-American female fire-fighter. It was the first time in department history that a person at that level didn't have to take a test for a promotion. Every person selected sat down with a panel and had an interview.

There was grumbling, of course. I was appointing my friends, they said. Never mind that none of the candidates knew me, and I didn't know them. I could not have been more fair than apportioning the positions 50 percent white and 50 per-cent black. But I starting hearing that I wasn't doing enough for "my own kind."

To my surprise and disappointment, my old colleagues in the Vulcan Blazers, the African-American firefighters' organi-zation I helped found, started criticizing me in the commu-nity and with the NAACP. Some of the anger came from unre-alistic expectations, because there were some black guys who really expected me to do some "ethnic cleansing" in the depart-ment, throw out the whites, and appoint only blacks. I could brush that off as just nonsense. No city official in Baltimore history had done more for black empowerment in city gov-ernment than I had at Public Works, Transportation, and now the fire department, where frankly just about every day I was playing footloose with the regulations to get what I wanted. This was why the disagreement with the Vulcan Blazers was a discouraging distraction I felt I didn't need or deserve. The organization was upset with me because I could not—not would not, but could not—entirely end the testing system for job promotions.

The unions had originally made testing mandatory to free city jobs from the patronage system. But the Blazers felt that the tests were culturally skewed against African Americans. I disagreed on that point, because the questions were technical and based on information in the department manuals.

"When you say black firefighters are kept down because of those tests, you're talking to a person who rose to the top by taking those same tests, and beating the other guys at their own game," I said. As a city department that had to run by the same civil-service rules as all the other departments, we were stuck with the tests unless the Blazers could prove to a court that they were discriminatory. I urged the Blazers to file a court suit, similar to the successful discrimination suit against the department in the '70s.

But I learned that some people found it easier to criticize and cast blame than to commit themselves to positive action.

On an individual one-on-one basis with some of the African-American firefighters of the department, I became a father figure. My door was open to anyone. If they didn't come to me, I went to them. We had a big job, protecting Baltimore with the resources we had, while trying to modernize.

The Baltimore Fire Department had always been known for its innovation. Other fire department officials came to the city to see how we did things, and I was invited around the country to lecture to other city outfits and trade information.

Some of the innovations under my watch were symbolic, but I thought they were necessary, and some were imperative to save lives.

I started a diving team, made up of a half-dozen firefighters who volunteered *without pay* to learn to use scuba equipment and handle emergencies at the Inner Harbor, the Baltimore attraction that was now more widely visited than Disney World. Sometimes people fell into the water, or objects had to be retrieved. I thought about my own experience saving the crane driver in the creek, and I wished the department had had divers then.

I created the position of fire marshal, too. Being the former Fire Prevention Bureau (FPB) head, I thought that fire inspectors had a big responsibility, and I wanted the head of the bureau to be compensated a little above battalion chief. The change also allowed me to appoint the person I wanted to the position.

At the same time, I gave firehouses the responsibility of increasing fire-prevention awareness in their neighborhoods. I made the firefighters go to schools to give lectures to the children and give demonstrations at community functions. One day a week, each company went out and did inspections in order to get to know the buildings in their area that they might have to enter during an alarm. Safety violations were also uncovered. Again, as the former head of the FPB and former fire safety officer, this was one area I was really keen on.

I started a cadet program for high school kids, juniors in the 11th grade who might want to become firefighters. They would elect to be in the program, and take either firefighting subjects or learn to be paramedics. I had nine slots per year. These were filled by both boys and girls, and when the students finished high school, I hired them into the department with the title of fire cadet at an annual starting salary of $15,000. That was good money for a young person right out of high school. A two-year training program followed, and the fire cadets would be stationed at different firehouses, administrative offices, the

Fire Prevention Bureau, and the information office, so they could get an overall view of what the fire department was about. When they finished, they'd go into the Fire Academy.

This was a jobs program, not an affirmative action program, and white and minorities participated side-by-side. The union didn't like it because they thought it was a black program, a poverty-alleviation program. But I insisted. I received the support of the Vulcan Blazers on this one.

At the same time, we were failing to recruit new firefighters, and the union suggested an apprenticeship program. Because there weren't enough firefighters, I had a big overtime deficit on my hands. We paid out so much overtime to firefighters doing extra shifts that we went way over budget. I also bought into the union's idea as a means to get minorities and women into the department. A trainee took a three-year course, and when finished, he or she was given the title of firefighter/paramedic.

The apprentices were 18 years old, and to select them, we used the list of candidates applying to the Fire Academy. Usually more than 500 names were on the application list, and not all could be accepted into the academy. A court ruling said we had to recruit from city residents, and the apprenticeship program allowed me to do just that. This brought in a fair number of minorities and women, because a majority of city residents were minorities.

The fire department these young people entered was a more demanding place than ever. The days of firefighters sitting around playing cards were over. Shifts were set up so that if firefighters weren't out on a run, they would do inspections or community work, while keeping up the tradition of cleaning and chores, the first thing they did on shifts. Night-shift people would go out to community meetings to inform the neighbors about department safety and fire-awareness programs.

Just as I didn't want my children to have to face the difficulties I'd known, I wanted life to be better for these firefighters. I thought back on my early years, and the worst part of the job was going into buildings and pulling out dead bodies. If the body belonged to a child, it especially affected me. I had small children myself. Seeing death like that affected you; you didn't know the people, but they were human beings. Firefighters of my generation pushed those traumas out of our minds. We didn't speak about it, so we didn't deal with it. We went back to the firehouse, pretended to forget, made something to eat, and cracked some jokes. To carry around emotions like that with no outlet led to alcohol abuse, and I suspected that it was leading to drug abuse that was taking its toll among firefighters in the 1990s.

As a solution, I instituted stress teams. Volunteers at the firehouses were trained in stress management. The stress teams were counselors, people to talk to. They could recommend professional help if this was needed, and such assistance was covered under the firefighter's medical plan.

As for the public at large, I felt that the best way to safeguard lives was with a vastly expanded smoke-detector program. I championed a law that made it mandatory to have at least one working smoke detector in every room of a high-rise building. We had difficulty mandating anything for private homes, but I found a way around that by offering smoke detectors free to homeowners. Firefighters came to a house and installed them. Starting in 1992, we gave away more than 70,000 smoke detectors. The beauty of this was they were all donated to the fire department by a national chain of hardware stores, and a different national chain of electronics stores, with a supportive publicity push by Baltimore TV station WMAR.

We had some bad fires the first year I was chief, which resulted in the loss of multiple family members, up to seven at a time. None of the homes had smoke detectors that could have alerted the people to a fire. The loss of lives during my watch took its toll on me. At one point, it seemed that we were losing people left and right.

I made use of the willingness of the TV stations to put me on the news to announce fire department innovations. At fire scenes, I showed up not to run the operation—I had faith in the ground commanders at the scene—but to show concern for the victims and moral support for the firefighters. At the site of one fire tragedy that resulted in the loss of lives, it was winter, and as the TV camera was on me, I kept wiping my running eyes because it was so cold. The TV anchorperson back at the studio, seeing me cry, commented, "The chief certainly is a compassionate person."

But I was concerned, so much so that I was almost afraid to go to bed at night. When a call came over the radio that there was a dwelling fire, I held my breath. I visited the site of every fatality and looked at the body. I had to see firsthand the condition of the person, how he or she died, because I knew the media people would expect a report from the chief. I was also there to make sure the firefighters didn't blame themselves, as we all did at times, for not doing enough or not being fast enough, to save a life. I'd ask the guys, "Are you okay? Is everyone okay?"

"Yeah, we're okay, Chief. Thanks."

On the other hand, as head of a major fire department with thousands of personnel and a multimillion-dollar budget, I had no sympathy for cats stuck up in trees. My experience was that it was a waste of firehouse resources to go after a kitten who nine times out of ten would jump to safety as soon as we got near her. I put an end to that, and told my firefighters, "If Kitty gets herself up there, she can get herself down."

And for all the people who locked themselves out of their homes and called the fire department so they could climb up one of our ladders and get back in through an upstairs window, I put out the word, "Tell them to call a locksmith, and please leave us free to fight fires."

Having issued that directive, I was out driving one evening when I saw a woman stuck by the roadside. She had a kid in the car with her, and the car had a flat tire. I drove to a nearby firehouse and asked, "Can I have a volunteer?" It was near the end of the shift, and everyone volunteered. I drove back, and there were two of our guys changing her tire.

I felt good about that. It was the way I wanted things to be: firefighters out there helping people in need.

And then it all came crashing down around my head like a roof collapsing. The catalyst was a major fire, a tragedy at a place called Clipper Mill. Before that ordeal was over, my hair would go from black with a little white at the temples to completely gray, and I would learn as fire chief the true meaning of the expression, "The Buck Stops Here."

❧ CHAPTER ELEVEN ☙

"Passing the Time of Day"

On the wall of the boardroom down the hall from my office was a ten-foot-long painting showing the Great Baltimore Fire of 1904 at the height of its destruction. I saw the mural from where I sat conducting staff meetings, and from where I stood giving press conferences: a constant reminder of the devastation fire can bring to a city. It was also a reminder of my responsibility as the city's chief fire safety officer.

An insurance company donated the mural under my watch. In the painting, it's nighttime, and Inner Harbor is in the foreground looking down from Federal Hill. The warehouses at the water's edge, and the downtown buildings behind, are engulfed in flames, and smoke blots out the stars. That fire started one bitterly cold Sunday morning in February, and it raged for 30 hours. Hose spray froze, and the rubble of 2,500 businesses that were lost was covered with ten-foot icicles. More than 35,000 workers lost their jobs, but at least casualties were kept low because the disaster occurred on a weekend in the financial district, which almost entirely disappeared in the flames.

Every fire chief worries about a major disaster. I oversaw mock disasters for training exercises, and we staged plane crashes, a gas attack on a high school by imaginary terrorists, and other simulations that tested the preparedness of our emergency services. Other crises were beyond our control. As city fire chief, I attended meetings of the State Emergency Management Services and saw the plans to evacuate Baltimore in case of a nuclear attack. All I could do was shake my head at the futility.

"If they drop that kind of bomb on D.C., there's going to be no more Maryland. Hell, if Russia lobbed one of those bombs at Baltimore, all you can do is pray, and hope you're all right with God."

The other emergency-service directors laughed, and one official said, "But Chief Williams, you have to have a plan. Plans make people feel better."

Baltimore is a city that covers 92 square miles: 79 square miles of land and 13 square miles of water. As fire chief, I was mindful that there was a population of three quarters of a million people living there, and I always thought of the tourists passing through, the real estate, the infrastructure. Everything needed protection. I took each fire death as a priority to be investigated. I dreaded them. From an average of 50 fire-related deaths per year when I took over the department, the number had dropped to 19 at the time of my departure. The credit went to the extensive fire-prevention programs we put in place—from the home smoke-detector campaign, to an advertising blitz that saw the sides of buses and public spaces plastered with posters of me flanked by a white and African-American firefighter, as well as a female firefighter—all of us wearing our firefighting helmets and turnout gear. We were pointing at the camera, and our message was, "Don't make us come and get you." We looked like Uncle Sam in an army-recruiting poster pointing like that, but the message was the opposite: We do NOT want you. We didn't want to drag you out of a preventable fire injured or dead.

I was devastated by the news of firefighters' deaths. I knew how easy it was for something to go wrong while fighting a fire. I remembered the burning room I was trapped in once when I was a lieutenant with some experience. Truck 18 arrived at a double rowhouse up in the northwest section of the city. We had five people on that truck: myself as the officer, the driver, a tillerman, a fireman on the left step, and a fireman on the right step. Everyone had his job. We arrived to see flames in the house windows. The tillerman got off and assisted the driver in raising the ladder, and I raised the aerial ladder, or Big Stick. The left-step man took the ceiling hook; the right man took the ax.

I had one guy come with me, but I entered the house too fast. The engine company hadn't gotten the water moving yet. These operations had to be coordinated. But there I was already on the second floor, in the fire room, without any water. I was alone. The other guy behind me didn't follow too closely and stayed out. Where was the engine company? All I could do was go to the window and open it. When I did, I provided a source of oxygen for the flames, and created a path for the fire to follow, directly at me. I didn't know what I was going to do. I stuck my head out the window and took a deep breath. I could have been cooked. Fortunately, the engine company came in with a hose, and another line was trained in through the window. I jumped aside, never so happy to be sprayed with water.

Dangerous situations could turn deadly very quickly, and the duty of the fire chief was to devise techniques to minimize risks. Communication and publicity were important tools. In the modern media age, the fire chief became a public figure everyone knew because I was on the news at least once a week. I wanted people to understand fire fighting. How often had we been trying to save a house, and a homeowner would come up to me and shout, "Why are you tearing the shingles off my house? Why are you wrecking my roof?!"

"Sir, we took off a four-by-four section of roof, and sure enough we found some embers smoldering there. If we hadn't done that, in two hours we'd be back here trying to save your house again."

That was the ultimate no-no, when a company had to come back a second time to a fire scene because the blaze hadn't been properly extinguished. This was what I told the woman who burst into the living room of her burning house because she saw a firefighter ventilating with a ceiling hook. "Why are you tearing down my ceiling? The fire's not there!"

"First of all, you shouldn't be in here," I said. But I explained that we had to see if the fire was hiding up there.

I was concerned with property, especially since most of the fires were in low-income black neighborhoods. I issued a directive to firefighters to avoid breaking windows, or if they had to do so, to avoid breaking the frame.

There were 1.8 million fires in the U.S. during the year 2000, causing $10 billion in damage. That was something every fire chief had to think about. With precautions, almost every fire was preventable. That $10 billion was money wasted.

The city had a few spectacular fires under my watch, broadcast live on local television. A fully occupied 30-story high-rise apartment building in the heart of downtown turned into a classic towering inferno when a 15th-floor unit caught fire. The boys got in and knocked it down, but not before a lot of drama ensued. I called the mayor and some other city officials to come down to the scene to give the public confidence that the emergency was the concern of the highest authorities. We called for state helicopters, belonging to the Maryland State Police, and if necessary, we could have requested backup from surrounding counties as part of the Mutual Aid program. In any high-rise building fire, the only way to get equipment up was to walk. Elevators couldn't be used. The firefighters carried their equipment up 15 stories.

An elderly lady climbing the stairs had a heart attack, and most people fled to the roof. I ordered a helicopter to drop two firefighters up there to calm people and to carry out a rescue by bringing them down through the building once we determined a safe exit. It was a textbook operation, and no firefighters were injured. The cause was smoking. Someone in a 15th-floor unit had fallen asleep with a cigarette burning.

"Maryland and Virginia have a lot to answer for, for introducing tobacco to the world," I told the mayor. He was happy with our handling of the spectacular blaze, and the department received some good press.

But just how quickly the media and old political allies could turn was a shock I discovered halfway through my watch.

Statistically, Baltimore seemed safer, with fire-related fatalities and the number of fires going down even as we were shutting redundant firehouses. When I was a firefighter, I would experience huge blazes of 10, 11, and 12 alarms. The higher the alarm, the more trucks that were called to the scene by the ground commander making his determination of the situation. But as fire chief, I never had a fire above six or seven alarms.

In my position, I was on call 24 hours. It was my duty to respond to four alarms and over. That was what I did the night of September 16, 1995. Responding, I knew I was headed for a big fire, but I couldn't have known that this was a blaze that would fundamentally change things for me. For the first time, a fire chief would be held personally responsible for the death of a firefighter who was a casualty in a conflagration.

I was headed for an old factory called Clipper Mill, which had been gentrified with upscale shops into an office and artists' loft complex. But in a way, I wouldn't leave there for a year. This would be a time that would be filled with tragedy, scandal, and betrayal.

I'D SEEN A LOT OF FIRES IN THE 41 YEARS since I'd joined the department, and this one was huge. For more than 140 years, the Clipper Mill textile factory on Clipper Road in the Woodbury section of northwest Baltimore had managed to avoid a major fire. Erected in 1851 to house the Poole Engineering and Machine Company, it was listed on the National Register of Historic Places by 1995.

The old mill had been rehabilitated, and it was completely occupied by new tenants. This reuse of classic structures was revitalizing the city. Several artists had their lofts at Clipper Mill, a gym used the tall interior space and old rock walls for a simulated mountain face for people to climb, and a furniture refinisher was there. But the mill's new life was to be cut short, as I saw when I arrived around 10 P.M. to find the main building, connected to other structures, completely engulfed in flames.

I could see that the building was gone. Temperatures in the attic were reaching at least 2,000 degrees, turning the place into an inferno. Engine Company 13 was training their lines on the front of the large structure, which was so big I couldn't see the safety officer because he was on the other side, but their water wasn't hitting anything. Altogether, 185 personnel were at the scene. The light from the fire could be seen for miles.

Truck 13 had gained access to the building by using a chainsaw to cut open a section of a roll-up metal door. They created an opening large enough for a man to go through. I entered the building along with the battalion chief who was commanding the men at that spot. I ventured inside about ten feet, far enough to feel the furnacelike heat, see sparks flying out of wires overhead, and hear explosions that were rocking the building. I turned right around and got out.

"Get the men the hell out of there, now!" I told the battalion chief. I ordered him to notify communications that I was assuming incident command.

I was only out of the building a few seconds when the roof was torn apart by a massive explosion, and portions gave way. Firefighters inside later reported that beams started falling, and they were headed for the opening cut in the metal door when disaster struck. A rumbling shook the ground beneath my feet, and I swung around to find the source of the noise. A pair of firefighters had stumbled coming out of the opening, and other men had turned back to help them. The peaked roof continued to fall, and brought with it the wall above the door. The top of the massive stone wall, two feet thick and made of granite rock, fell inward, while the wall from the outside appeared to bulge like an expanding balloon—a horrifying, roaring thing that seemed to reach out at the firefighters trapped at the opening before it collapsed right on top of them.

I was 20 feet away, the ground shook like an earthquake, and hot debris rained down. I had to get to those trapped firefighters. Dust cut visibility, but I ran back and started lifting stones. They were heavy and smoking hot. We threw ourselves into freeing the trapped firefighters. Some of the men were crushed.

Ten firefighters were injured, some so seriously that they'd never work as firemen again. The path of the falling wall outward saved the men immediately inside, who were about to emerge. But then a shout went up. I saw the body of firefighter Eric Schaefer of Rescue Company 1.

He was wearing one of the new type fire helmets, a Cairnes 1000 model. Built to withstand great blows, it had been mangled by a boulder-size stone. Schaefer died of head injuries. His death when the wall collapsed had been taped by a local TV station, and it was on the air within the hour.

There was a price to pay for such instant communication. The tragic death of a firefighter caused concern among the public that didn't exist a few years before, when five or seven firefighters could die in a blaze people later read about in the paper but not actually see happen in front of their eyes. Legitimate concern about a horrible incident quickly turned into finger-pointing, and what seemed to be a need to affix blame for a firefighter's death.

I had no time for that; I had to assume the terrible responsibility of presiding over the funeral of a fallen firefighter. It was the saddest task that came with the position of fire chief.

When a firefighter died, every firehouse in the city was draped for 30 days with black bunting. At firefighters' funerals, it was not uncommon for the governor, the mayor, members of the City Council, and other city dignitaries to attend. Firefighters came from near and far, along with officials from other fire departments—even from out of state.

At firefighter Schaefer's funeral, tradition was kept up when a bagpiper wearing a kilt played "Amazing Grace." I gave a brief eulogy and described Schaefer as a hero, which he was. An American flag was draped over his casket, and this was folded up and given to his wife.

Such funerals weren't rare. More firefighters died on duty than policemen, but Baltimore was spared the multiple fire-fighter deaths that would occur in New York, Philadelphia, and D.C. It wasn't a matter of preparedness, but luck. Those other cities observed the same safety standards that we did.

I was confident that the department's safety record would be exonerated in the investigation that immediately followed. What resulted instead was a scandal that nearly led to my resignation.

One of my fire investigators at the scene, who was work-ing with the police department arson squad, called me at home. He said they wanted to call a federal agency, the Bureau of Alcohol, Tobacco and Firearms, or ATF, to look into the tragedy at Clipper Mill. "This is getting big, Chief," he told me. "We're thinking of calling in the ATF." I listened to the suggestion, and said that before he called them, I wanted to be informed. The involvement of federal investigators would certainly raise ques-tions, and I wanted to prepare the mayor and the news media with an explanation of why the feds were being called in.

But I'd been lied to. Calling in the feds wasn't something the investigators were thinking of doing. They'd already done it. I found this out when ATF agents from Washington phoned me to say, "We're here."

I called the mayor and asked if he'd called in federal agents. The mayor said he knew nothing about it.

I got back to the ATF guys. "Before you go to the fire scene, everybody come to my office."

I got the whole bunch of them into the boardroom. "What's going on? Why wasn't I informed?" The ATF didn't know; they were just called in. The police and my people just looked at each other and said nothing, so I was faced with a problem. The Baltimore Fire Department was known throughout the country as a premier organization, and for 20 years, chiefs had come from as far away as China and Europe to see how Baltimore did things. On a good day, my investigators could solve a fire case with their eyes closed. I felt we had the finest fire investigation bureau in the country, and we didn't need the feds to take over. Had I allowed them to do that, it might have caused morale problems in my department. Baltimore was the best, so why did I have an outside agency in my boardroom to do what we'd been doing for 100 years?

After all, who taught the ATF about firefighting investigation? We did. There was an ongoing training program between us and the agency. When the ATF got new people in the Baltimore area, they would come to us for training in "fire ground," or on-site, investigation. The department and the ATF always had a good working relationship. When the Coast Guard and other Maryland fire departments needed training, we'd do it. We had the best fire-protection record in the United States. NFPA, the National Fire Protection Association, would consistently recognize Baltimore as being number one. I'd go to conventions of fire chiefs, and I always drew attention—"What's Baltimore doing?" I was asked to conduct workshops to tell the other chiefs what to do and what not to do.

All of this was running through my head as I looked at the feds, wondering what had possessed my staff and the police to put them in charge. I asked the head ATF man, "Where is your investigative team coming from?"

"From New York."

"By plane?"

"No, I-95."

"I'll tell you what you do. You go to the city line, meet those guys, and turn them around, because they're not coming in here without my permission, because I'm not giving it. I have faith in my investigators."

I ended the meeting, called the mayor, said I didn't invite the ATF boys, so I sent them packing. He said that was okay.

But it wasn't okay. I'd made a major blunder. In nearly 50 years with the fire department, I could, at the end, still single out this one decision as the worst mistake I ever made. I would have myself to blame for much of what happened next—and plenty happened. In hindsight, I should have chewed someone out but allowed the ATF to stay, assisting rather than controlling the investigation, and then hurried to assure my department that the presence of the feds wasn't a vote of no confidence in their abilities.

I'm sure the mayor heard from the ATF, but he didn't say anything to me. The police commander wrote a letter to the mayor complaining that he wasn't receiving cooperation from the fire department. I saw the letter after it was leaked to the media.

Suddenly, the press was crying cover-up because the ATF was excluded from the department's investigation into the Clipper Mill fire. There was talk of a conspiracy. The story went out that the mayor and I were battling over the fire, which we weren't.

Reporters questioned my competency at a press conference with the mayor, and in response, he made a statement that hurt me. Instead of coming out with words of support for the fire department, he said he couldn't tolerate bickering between city departments.

"I'll have to evaluate the chief's position," he told the press. In other words, if there was a problem, it was with the fire chief, not with the police commissioner or anyone else.

A sort of hysteria took hold. Newspaper stories began to slant their coverage of Clipper Mill to hint that something was wrong with this fire, and the fire chief was covering up what really happened. A local TV station aired a computerized simulation showing how the fire had started, which was at odds with the facts as we knew them, and the report implied that no deaths or injuries would have occurred if only the right decisions had been made at the fire scene.

People who shouldn't have gotten involved in the situation didn't let that stop them from entering the controversy. The state attorney came out with her own theory—that the fire started in an electrical box in a transformer room on the second floor, which led to an explosion. Had this actually occurred, it would have meant that the fire had to travel down the building's floors. *The state attorney's job is to prosecute, so why is she involving herself?* I wondered. *Did she intend to prosecute, and if so, who?* I heard the suggestion that her target was me.

My situation was not unique among African-American fire chiefs, and once again, a whiff of racism was in the air long after I had hoped to extinguish that nuisance.

Clipper Mill was the first time a Baltimore fire chief was held responsible for the death of a firefighter. The fire chief in question happened to be African American, and some black firefighters came to the conclusion that something was going on. Never had a white fire chief been blamed for firefighter casualties, even when they were weekly occurrences. And for the first time, the feds were called in to investigate a fire in the city without the chief's knowledge.

At that same time, there was a bad fire in Seattle, and several firefighters lost their lives. There was a move in Seattle to place the blame on the African-American fire chief, and he eventually retired. "The hell with it," he told me. In Philadelphia, it was the same thing: a bad fire, several firefighters dead, a black fire chief, and pressure put on him. Up to that point, in the mid-1990s, no one had ever blamed a fire chief when men died. It was as if the rules of the job were changed in response to the advent of African-American fire chiefs, to provide proof that we were incapable. In Washington, D.C., they ran the black fire chief out of town after some firefighter casualties. The media attacks on him took the theme, "The chief wasn't properly training firefighters."

My communications officer, Hector Torres, was charming, handsome, and a real asset to the department. He looked good on TV, and he also made the department look good. I was really feeling the heat of the Clipper Mill controversy, and the weight of all the accusations and rumors. He said to me, "You know what's on your side, Chief?"

I couldn't hide my depression. "Tell me."

"Your popularity."

"My popularity?" I laughed. "They hate me!"

"Nobody hates you, Chief. They love you for reading books on fire safety to their kids at schools, and giving them smoke detectors. They've seen you do that for years."

At home, Marjie was a rock of support, as usual. She reminded me that there were always people who abandon you in a crisis and who wanted to believe the worst. But she said that most people in Baltimore were good, and too smart to believe rumors.

On the TV news that night, the parents of the firefighter who had been killed were interviewed. They complained bitterly about me, and they wanted to know why I was covering up what really went on at Clipper Mill. The TV reporter concluded that it was a legitimate question, and repeated what was being said in the newspaper editorial columns and radio phone-in shows all over Baltimore: Did Chief Williams send away federal investigators because they might have uncovered the truth about mistakes he might have made that resulted in the death of a white firefighter?

I was bolstered by words of encouragement from Torres and Marjie, and the next day I went to the home of the parents, Mr. and Mrs. Schaefer. The father answered the door, and he led me into the room where his wife was watching TV. Ironically, I caught them in the middle of the *Montel* show.

"I want to assure you that things are getting done. We're not sitting on the investigation," I told them. The father was receptive, but his wife wouldn't look at me. She continued to stare at Montel on the screen. I knew she was listening to me, because she had a hurt frown on her face. When I stood up to leave, she turned to me, looked me in the face, and her expression was filled with such hatred that it was as if I had killed her son.

I was speechless. I left that house in such a state of confusion that I almost felt like I was her son's killer.

My confusion worsened, and I actually started doubting myself. *Did I start that fire?* I looked haggard. During those weeks in the pressure cooker, my hair turned gray. I couldn't sleep, and I was physically exhausted. I always deeply felt the death of any civilian in a fire. But the death of a firefighter was like a stab in the heart. And those deaths had occurred without any accusations of wrongdoing on my part. That woman honestly felt that I'd killed her son, as if I had personally put a match to Clipper Mill to kill some firemen. How many other people felt that way? I wondered.

The time had come. I felt that my position was untenable. I had thought of resigning when the mayor failed to back me up at his press conference. Now, finally sure, I prepared everything for my departure. I wrote and signed my resignation letter. I confided in Hector Torres, the communications officer. He played it cool, but if I had been less distracted, I would have seen his mind working.

"Have you told the mayor?" he asked me.

"I'll send him the resignation letter," I replied.

Hector saw he had some time. He left me and went straight to City Hall. Mayor Schmoke was holding a closed-door meeting and couldn't be disturbed. Torres brushed aside his aides and crashed it.

"Mayor, it's important that I speak with you now."

The mayor went outside with him and heard the news from Torres: "The chief is leaving."

"What? When?"

"Now."

In minutes, I got a call from the mayor. "You know that fire at Clipper Mill, I'm sure that's going to work itself out."

"Nothing works itself out by itself," I replied.

"What do you suggest?"

"I want an independent investigation. Not a government agency, but someone outside, someone credible."

"We'll do it," the mayor agreed. "Chief, don't leave us."

I DECIDED NOT TO RESIGN while I was under a cloud. I knew I was innocent of wrongdoing.

Early in 1996, Dr. James Lamb, a structural engineer at the John Hopkins University Applied Physics Laboratory, issued his report on the Clipper Mill fire. I asked the university to do its investigation completely independent of the fire department. Dr. Lamb examined the ruins, analyzed the building's prefire construction, developed theories about how the wall collapsed causing the fatality and injuries, and then performed structural analyses to test these theories using state-of-the-art computer simulations. As a structural engineer, Dr. Lamb examined schematics of the building's truss system and performed metallurgical analyses.

Faulty wiring was determined to be the cause of the fire. The Hopkins University report coincided with the findings of a Board of Inquiry into Eric Schaefer's death, conducted by veteran fire department officials.

The board's conclusion about the danger faced at the start of the Clipper Mill fire:

> "The potential existed for the complete loss of the complex, as well as many of the surrounding homes. More than half the complex was saved. None of the surrounding homes received major damage. The fact that this was accomplished simultaneously with a protracted rescue and recovery operation of injured fire personnel is the highest testament to the dedication and commitment of the members of the Baltimore Fire Department. Their exceptional efforts, under the worst conditions imaginable, were exemplary."

I sent a copy of the reports to the mayor and called a press conference. I felt relieved and exonerated. The questions that had been raised about the tragedy were now answered, the mystery solved. But I learned something about the media. To the press, conflict was more interesting than resolution. I wondered if the reporters even read the findings of the report, because it was ignored in the newspapers. The editorial writers felt no need to congratulate me for putting their suspicions about conspiracy and cover-up to rest. This raised suspicions of my own, that the real issue all along had never been the fire. Once it was determined by way of an independent investigation that I was not to blame, the other facts, such as what really happened, were considered uninteresting. There would be no pat on the back.

However, there was an important reform that resulted from the Clipper Miller fire. To avoid confusion in further investigations, a new working relationship was forged between the fire department, the Baltimore police, the ATF, and the state's attorney's office.

Actually, I did get that pat on the back—from Marjie—who gave me a big hug at the end of the ordeal.

I told her, "I've got to resign for real so we can do some traveling."

"Anytime you say, hon."

FROM TIME TO TIME DURING MY REMAINING YEARS at the helm of the fire department, I would be asked when I was thinking of retiring, and I would reply that I would have left a long time before, but I wanted to finish building a firehouse first.

"I'm not leaving until it's done, until my name is on the plaque out front along with the mayor and the director of Public Works."

It would be the only firehouse to be built under my watch, although I closed many other firehouses. Whenever that happened, I'd feel the heat in the press and from the City Council. Then Mayor Martin O'Malley came aboard in 1999, and he and I collaborated on a plan to shut down more unneeded houses. He made the announcement himself, and he took responsibility for the decision. I backed him up, but at least this time the unions weren't just blasting the fire chief alone.

There were other items remaining on my list of things to do. Women and minorities were still underrepresented. Union officials got tired of the apprenticeship program, which had been their idea, after some of their kids had successfully gone through it. They condemned it as an affirmative action plan, although the main purpose was clearly to bring in more firefighters no matter what their ethnicity at a time of dwindling recruitment numbers.

I pressed on anyway, because here was one program that demonstratively served its purpose. In one year, 1998, the program increased the number of female firefighters by 14, from only 1 in the whole department to 15. In the 1980s, only three women had joined the force as firefighters.

I felt that I had an obligation to help other people advance. I had risen on the shoulders of a lot of people, and I could never have become fire chief if others hadn't reached down and given me a helping hand. I got angry when blacks who had positions didn't help blacks who needed assistance.

When I was chief of administrative services at Public Works, I once got so upset with one arrogant guy that I might have hit him if he had been my size or bigger. He was chief of highway engineering, an African American, and his department had a couple of open posts. I felt that he should have promoted a black candidate, a young guy who was going to John Hopkins and getting his engineering degree. I called the chief, "You've got this position, and you don't have any black engineers at that level, so why don't you promote him?"

"Fuck that. I don't go for that. I pulled myself up by myself." He absolutely would not promote the guy. I had to find another way myself.

I saw this time and time again. During President Johnson's time, blacks were put in charge of model city programs in Baltimore. Some of them wouldn't go out into the community. All they were interested in was holding on to their positions. That upset me. In hindsight, I wish I had spoken to my kids about all this. I wish I had taught them about their history, the struggles of their race, so they would know that every single African American's achievement was built on the earlier sacrifices of other African Americans. I should have told them about what I was doing and what I was up against, so they might have understood my moods. Fortunately, my kids came to understand, and when I was in the position to do so, I quietly pursued a policy that was never anti-white, but pro-black. There was never any publicity when I promoted people, and I don't think that the black community ever learned about it, but I could count the job successes every year.

I had an obligation, because of what had been done for me. Ron Lewis was the first African-American fire chief of Richmond, Virginia. We were all so proud when he was made chief that I drove down with some others to his swearing-in. He was a real gentleman. When I was studying for deputy chief, I asked him for assistance. He was catching hell from the

Richmond version of the Vulcan Blazers for not firing all the whites from the department. He could have become bitter. But when I phoned him one week before the test and asked his advice about what material to study, he said, "Oh, I've got something you can use."

I got in my raggedy old Dodge station wagon and drove 150 miles through a snowstorm without stopping. I got to his house, and he gave me the material. "I think you should study this." He gave me copies of the fire ground commander manuals and other documents. It was helpful. I headed back to Baltimore, and by then, the snowstorm was a blizzard. The windshield wipers gave up. On I-95, I was driving with one hand out the window, wiping away the snow, but I was happy because of the generosity Lewis had shown me.

Of the three female firefighters who had entered the department starting in the early '80s, two were elevated to positions traditionally held by men, and one assumed my old job as pump operator. The other woman firefighter I promoted to fire inspector. Unfortunately, the third was "terminated for cause," to use the sad official jargon.

Also, unfortunately, quite a few firefighters were suspended under me because of drugs. I terminated 20 people or more because I had to address the problem quickly. When I took over as chief in 1992, I discovered that the fire department was affected by the city's drug problem in two ways.

First, because the department mirrored the community, some firefighters were users. Baltimore had no organized crime, but the drug racket was widespread. When the police cleaned up one area, the pushers just shifted operations to another neighborhood. Clean up East Baltimore, they went to the West Side, so gang wars broke out over territory, and murders were rampant as rivals moved in. The African-American community was stigmatized because of this—a half-million people given a bad rap because of 2,000 drug pushers. In fact, the neighborhood kids were too poor to purchase drugs. Approximately 80 percent of the buyers were whites from out of town.

With the union's blessing, I instituted mandatory drug testing. From the fire chief on down, we all went to Mercy Hospital for a urine test. Several firefighters were caught, for all types of drugs. A drug user was immediately suspended for 30 days and put in rehab during that time, without pay. If he or she refused treatment, they were terminated. When they came back to work, they signed a contract that stipulated that if they were caught again using drugs within a two-year period, they'd be let go.

My personal policy was that if a second-time drug offender had been in the department for more than 20 years, I'd let the person retire. It was sad, these old guys, 20-plus-year veterans getting caught a second time with drugs.

The second way the fire department was affected by drugs was seen in the amount of time we now spent responding to incidents related to drug use. Almost 75 percent of medic calls dealt with drugs. Drug users also started fires. They would be freebasing cocaine and burn down vacant dwellings. They'd tear off some kindling—a staircase railing, a post, or a door panel—and start a fire right on the floor, a wooden floor! Baltimore had more addicts than any major city in the country, and that was a matter of public record. For a city of its size, Baltimore had more poor, more elderly, and more drug users. Mayor O'Malley was elected on a crime platform, and he was doing a good job when I left the department.

There were gay firefighters, but the department policy was like the military: Don't ask, don't tell. Considering how much firefighters gossiped, it was usually about department matters, and they didn't get involved in others firefighters' personal lives.

I would get an earful of gossip when I passed the time of day at the firehouses. Baltimore's TV watchers might have thought it was a publicity stunt when Hector Torres arranged for me to be filmed cooking for some firefighters, and then us all eating together. Sure, there was an element of P.R., but I would do that for real. Or I'd get a call from a firehouse: "We're sending out for pizza; come on by." (I wonder if they did that because they knew the chief would insist on paying?) Or they'd have a special dinner and request, "Please, Chief, if you've got time, come by."

The firefighters liked to invite me for a meal to hear the latest news. They'd pass it on "telegram/telephone/tell-a-fireman" style, and the person listening would say, "How'd you hear that b.s.?" "I'm telling you, man, the chief was over for dinner!"

I'd mess with them. I'd go into one firehouse near Inner Harbor and say what a great theme restaurant the place could be. "We could serve belly busters and four-alarm chili, and pump beer out of a hose nozzle."

When I accepted an invitation, I'd check things out. The chain of command was followed so I wouldn't do nuts-and-bolts inspections, but if I saw something wrong, I'd call the chief of operations and ask him to take care of it. At one firehouse, a big black drop of oil fell on my head. I looked up, and oil was dripping from the ceiling. The walls were dirty, all sooty from exhaust from the apparatus. Every time they started the diesel engines, small particles rose to the ceiling, where they collected and dripped down.

I got concerned, since men lived, ate, and slept there. So I had the assistant chief in charge of research and development look into it. We had every firehouse in the city install an automatic exhaust system, so when the gong was thrown, the system started. A hose connected to the wall ran to a truck's exhaust pipe and popped off when the truck drove away.

One thing was certain: I found that firefighters' diets hadn't changed over the years. The belly-buster burgers were still baseball size. The guys would bring out the biggest pork chops I'd ever seen, an inch thick, center cut. Vegetables were always mashed potatoes, carrots, and peas.

"Don't go yet, Chief, we've got dessert!" They'd bring out a gallon of ice cream.

I'd rib them, "Why don't you guys get a healthy diet?"

"We'll worry about that later."

Afterward, it would be question time. "Give us the scoop, Chief."

"What do you want to know?"

"Hey, Chief, you retiring?"

"Forget about it. I'm not getting out until that station we're building is finished and my name's on it." They'd roll their eyes, because they knew they'd have me around another year or so.

"Hey, Chief, we getting a new pumper?" Maybe their engine was 10 or 15 years old. If there was new equipment coming, I'd say, "A new pumper is coming in August, and your name's on it. I'm assigning it here to Engine Company 20." They'd be so happy that they'd cheer.

The next day, I'd go to the office and say to the assistant chief of operations, "We're getting new apparatus in August, aren't we?"

"Yes."

"For Company 20?"

"Eventually, but not before a couple of other companies."

"See that Engine 20 gets it."

He'd look at me cockeyed, because I was messing with his plans. "Did you have dinner at Engine 20 last night?"

My management style with department officials was a little different. I needed to jar these old, conservative, tough-ass firefighters into thinking in new ways. They were a stubborn bunch, and there was nothing more deadly than when men of action had to sit around a meeting table. I had to do a little playacting. My secretary was now Mary Lester, an enthusiastic and dedicated woman who took over when Mary Wolf retired, and she said I could be frightening, but she admitted it was effective.

When things went wrong, I called all the department heads. I came in, and they all rose. I sat down and looked very serious. I remained silent while they looked at me, getting nervous. Finally, I said, "I'm not in a happy mood. I am not in a happy mood. I'm trying my level best with you guys. But I'm not getting through. Maybe I'm asking too much from you. Or maybe it's me, I'm the one who's failing. But I'll tell you what. I'm in such a bad mood that I'm going to go around the table, and you'd better tell me something that will make me happy."

Each department head would mull over what he thought might be wrong in the department. They thought of all sorts of things, now that they were pushed into it, and that was good. But I wasn't on a fishing expedition. I had a real problem in mind, and at the end I told them what it was. Their faces lit up, they were so relieved, because I said the problem was manageable if we discussed ideas.

After all my "acting," I'd smile. "Okay, let's find a way to solve this." We'd brainstorm and come to an understanding. "So, everybody is signed on? Good!"

"You were scary," Mary said when it was over. "But you got those guys to think!"

I INSTITUTED A MEDALS DAY for the Baltimore Fire Department that was held in late spring every year. I did it to boost morale, and soon all the surrounding counties' fire departments took up the idea. Before, if a firefighter had done something to warrant a medal, the battalion chief would find out when the guy was on duty and go down to the firehouse to give it to him. I thought the presentation should be more structured so that everybody could know about it and look on. So we had a catered affair at the War Memorial meeting hall. The mayor and City Council attended. If the weather was good, we'd do it outside. The response from firefighters was gratifying, and I was again glad I'd put everyone back in uniform, because they never looked better than at such occasions.

Box 414 was there. This was a fire buff group, civilian volunteers who responded to alarms. They had a van with a coffee urn, hot plate, and cooler. They showed up at fires in winter with coffee for the men and women, and soft drinks in summer. This was thoughtful, because fighting a big fire made for a long night, and they'd be there with coffee and doughnuts. On Medals Day, they opened their wagon and gave out sodas. To show the department's appreciation, I presented them with an abandoned firehouse. They used the second floor for their meetings, and the first floor for a little museum.

One Medals Day, I said to Marjie, "I think this may be the last one of these I preside over."

"You thinking of packing it in?" She would be happy if I did, but she would be accepting if I continued with the job. That was Marjie, a wonderful person who never grumbled about anything. When illness caused her to lose sight in her left eye, the children and I never heard her complain. The secret to a long marriage is respect between a husband and wife. I never left the house without a kiss. I could go out of the house ten times a day, and Marjie would want that kiss. And we never went to bed without saying our goodnights.

I told her, "I've been thinking about it, and now that the new station is finished, I don't have an excuse not to leave."

The new firehouse, in East Baltimore on 25th Street and Kirk Avenue, was completed, and I had the pleasure of opening it as fire chief. We put in a community room so the Cub Scouts and Girl Scouts could have a place to hold meetings, the old ladies could play cards, and the League of Women Voters could have their functions. The symbolic reopening of the fire department to the community was complete: We had not only unlocked the doors, we had the neighbors come in and use the place for their activities.

When I told the mayor of my plans to retire, at first he didn't believe me. Nobody did. The mayor was so used to calling headquarters at 9 A.M. and finding me there. When I convinced him that I was sincere, he said the city would name the new station The Herman Williams, Jr. Fire House. I felt proud about that.

I would leave hoping that there would be no backsliding in my efforts to get more women and minorities into the department. I would see to the continuing endowment of the

Herman Williams, Jr. Humanitarian Award, which was given every year at Medals Day to the firefighter who did something outstanding for the community. It was also for acts of bravery. I started the award by giving a plaque and a check for $250 to the recipient.

In the future, fires will be fought by robots. Tracking machines on treads to get over debris are already available, and I once watched a demonstration as they roamed a room and sent out TV pictures. Those are the types of expensive gadgets we looked into, but there was never enough money, nor were there funds for thermal-imaging machines that would allow firefighters to take x-ray-like pictures of a burning building to identify the hot spots inside. That piece of equipment cost $20,000, but dropped down to $8,000 as more fire departments purchased them. The United States has 10,000 fire departments, including volunteer forces, and with that many customers funded by a public that demands safety, the equipment companies are motivated to bring out innovations to combat the fire menace.

As word got out that I was retiring in 2001, tributes began to flow in, and while I was grateful and humbled, it got to be a bit much. Some testimonials meant a lot to me, though. At their annual dinner, the Vulcan Blazers gave me a Longevity Award and a Humanitarian Award. One was inscribed, "For showing good leadership and service to the rank of black professional firefighters. You are a true role model."

As the date of the retirement dinner held at the Hyatt Regency Baltimore approached, civic groups, companies that did business with the department, and charities all called me to their functions to award me plaques. These started piling up in boxes, but I was touched by the outpouring.

It was inevitable that I look back over the years. I was asked about the past for newspaper profiles. I thought of everything that the other African-American firefighters and I had gone through. When the firehouse was dedicated in my name, the union picketed the ceremony because the mayor was closing firehouses, which was also the reason union officials later boycotted my retirement dinner. It made me think that if there wasn't some kind of conflict always happening, I don't think I'd recognize my life.

As I prepared the good-bye speech I would have to deliver, I thought about the city, the people who had helped me get where I was, the kids, grandkids, and then the city again. Montel was a big celebrity, but he learned that his Old Man was Mr. Baltimore. He was in town, and he called me up. "I want to take you to dinner. What's the best restaurant in the city?"

Baltimore had a number of fine restaurants competing for that title of "best," but we settled on The Prime Rib. Montel called the restaurant and was told he couldn't get a reservation. He phoned me back at the office, and I told him, "I'll handle it." So I called them.

The maître d' was most obliging, "Oh, yes, Chief Williams. How many will be in your party?"

I called Montel back, and he was astonished. "What happened?" In Hollywood, he was used to receiving the red-carpet treatment. I laughed. "Hey, you got to remember, this is my town."

Baltimore was my home. I had been there most of my life. Other than Fort McHenry, Baltimore didn't have many landmarks compared to D.C. It was seen by outsiders as a pass-through place while they were going somewhere else. A quiet, laid-back city with nothing to do.

But for me, Baltimore was a special place. I've been a part of its growth, from the 1940s to the present, during a transformation that put Baltimore on the map. For years, the town had just been a place on Route 1 that went from north to south, and we suffered from proximity to Philadelphia, D.C., and Annapolis, the state capital. A small-time big town. But it was a friendly place, even though it had its problems, like its racial segregation.

Baltimore was a unique place for music in the '40s and '50s. You could hear good jazz. The concert hall was the Lyric, where operas were held, and the Baltimore Symphony Orchestra played at the Meyerhoff Symphony Hall when it was built in the early '70s. In the '80s, officials from other cities came to copy what we did at Inner Harbor to revitalize their own downtowns. With the new millennium, our new football team, the Ravens, brought home a Super Bowl championship.

Many of the people who lived through those years and contributed to the city's growth came to my retirement party. There were 700 guests, and Mayor O'Malley couldn't pull himself away, he was so busy networking. "How do you know so many people?"

The highlight of the evening was when I spoke about all the people who had influenced and helped me, and whom I loved, with special thanks to Marjie, Marjorie, Clolita, Herman, Montel, Marjie's parents, George Russell, Uncle George, Uncle Buddy, Mom, Pop . . .

It was an emotional moment.

I cleared out my desk the next day and said good-bye to the staff. Another emotional moment. It was February 14, but my retirement had nothing to do with Valentine's Day. That was the end of the pay period!

In the boardroom was the long painting of the Great Fire of 1904. With satisfaction and some relief, I thought, *The city never burned down under my watch. I kept her safe.*

I WAS AT A CAR WASH, and an old guy came up to me. "You look familiar," he said.

"I'm Herman Williams."

"Oh, you're Herman Williams's son? You know, your father was a little guy. Some people didn't like him, and some people liked him. But everybody respected him. He'd come in to work wearing a tie, even though he was just a common laborer. At the end of his shift, he'd take his shower, get himself cleaned up, and put that tie back on."

"Yes," I said, "he was quite a guy."

My father would have been at that car wash a few months before. Toward the end of his life, he drove a Cadillac. He sure liked his cars.

Dad was 88 when he died. The x-rays showed asbestosis, but it was a heart attack that got him. He was sitting at the table in the living room of his assisted-living residence, a big house where he paid rent and got his meals, like a boardinghouse in the old days. The lady who ran the place said, "Mr. Williams, you need a haircut. I'm going to give you one."

He thanked her, got up, and was going up the stairs when he had a heart attack on the way to his room.

With my father's death just a few months before, I was wondering if I'd live to see his ripe old age when a brain tumor was found in the back of my head a month after I left the fire department.

For my "retirement," I'd plunged into consulting work. While fire chief, I would receive offers regularly from other cities to run their fire departments, but I wanted to stay in Baltimore. I also kept busy as a board member of the Municipal Employees Credit Union (MECU), a $515 million operation with 68,000 credit union members. They named one of the two MECU bank branches after me, which was an unexpected honor.

At lunchtime at the credit union's general meeting, I was standing, introducing members of the board. I suddenly broke into a heavy sweat. It was like someone was pouring a bucket of water over my head. I felt faint, and I couldn't remember names, people I'd known for 20 years. No sooner had the episode come, then it went away, and I sat down.

That night, I tested my blood pressure with one of those little contraptions we old folks keep around the house, and it was very high. I told Marjie about the sweating incident and wondered if I'd had a heart attack. She urged me to call the doctor, and he told me to take a blood-pressure pill. I did, and the blood pressure went down, but I was afraid to fall asleep that night.

The next morning at Good Samaritan Hospital, they wired me up to a treadmill for a stress test. There was nothing wrong with my heart, and the arteries were clear. There was nothing wrong with my lungs either.

"You were a firefighter?" a doctor asked me. I told him I was.

"You fought fires?"

"Almost 50 years."

"You'd never know it from the x-rays. Your lungs are clear."

But when the MRI pictures came back, there it was, as big as day, a large tumor that had been growing for years, maybe decades. I was shocked. The doctor told me, "This has got to come out as soon as possible. You could go blind. It's grown so big that there's no more room to grow, and it's starting to exert pressure."

"The Bible only promises three score and ten," I told the doctors. "Well, I'll be three score and ten this year."

For once, Marjie's calmness nearly cracked when I broke the news to her. I emphasized that the tumor appeared benign. There were surgeons in Baltimore to remove it, but when I called up Montel ("Hey, man, I got a tumor in my head!"), he insisted that I fly out to Los Angeles to be operated on by an African-American surgeon he knew, Dr. Keith Black, who worked out of Cedars-Sinai Medical Center.

Clolita came out with us and stayed for the "first shift" of the two weeks when I was operated on and recovering, and then Marjorie came out for the second week. Dr. Black was as good as Montel said. On the day of the surgery, he came in rubbing his hands together like he couldn't wait to get at the tumor. He said there would be no problem as long as the tumor hadn't wrapped around an artery.

The trouble was, it had. During the seven hours I was on the operating table, I lost three units of blood because the tumor interfered with a vein. But I was in good hands. Two days after surgery, I was walking around Beverly Hills with one daughter at my side, and putting in a mile a few days later with the other daughter.

I was passing the time of day with my girls, and it felt good.

The medical emergency, even more than my leaving the fire department, made me take pause and think back. It had been nearly 50 years since I'd joined the fire department, about 60 years since the Harlem riots, 70 years that I'd been alive. That was a lot of history! I asked myself, *What was it all about?*

Perseverance was one thing that came to mind. If we African Americans had not persisted in our struggle for dignity and equal rights, we would still be doing low-end jobs in a segregated society. We earned the respect that all men and women are due.

And judgment. I had gotten far by knowing when to shut up and turn the other cheek, and when to press for what I believed was right.

Let's not forget fairness. You can't improve on the Golden Rule. To treat people fairly, to treat people with consideration, just about guarantees that you will get respect in return. Helping people—for me, especially fellow African Americans—was a duty, and something I felt fortunate that I was in a position to do.

Of course, there's also faith. I believe in the philosophy of Jesus, but faith comes in many forms. You must have faith in yourself. You can't do anything without it.

I've always had my own little "pop philosophy": I don't trouble trouble until trouble troubles me. Life is too short. When I turned 70, I was astonished. Where had the years gone? Wasn't it just yesterday that I was hollering with the A-rab street vendors, "Watermelons! Get your good-time watermelons!" And cranking up the Chevy to make it go? And courting Marjie? Fighting with Pops? Crooning "Mona Lisa" to the starry-eyed girls at The Swallows shows? Dodging building blocks and insults as a streetcar driver and a young fireman?

It was all ancient history, but it also seemed like something that should not be forgotten. Others might learn from it.

"Why do you always have a smile?" people asked me. Something inside made me do it. "Why don't you get upset?" Oh, I could tell them, I've spent a lifetime being upset. But one piece of timeless wisdom is that you accomplish more with honey than vinegar. I learned this from observing the people I grew to admire and love.

Okay, I was lucky. I lived in a great city. I found a wonderful woman to share my life. We have four great kids, and now seven wonderful grandchildren. Visionaries in the African-American community were opening doors just as I was ready to enter them, and if a few doors thereafter seemed stuck, I was able to kick them ajar.

And I would be very lucky indeed if the lessons of my life can inspire some other people who are up against big odds.

One word to you good young men and women, wherever you are:

Whatever you do, have faith in yourself, always.

And may God bless you.

— Herman Williams, Jr.
Baltimore, Maryland, August 2001

About Herman Williams, Jr.

Born in 1931, in Harlem, New York, **Herman Williams, Jr.,** rose through the ranks to become the first African-American fire chief of a major U.S. city. During a time of deep-rooted racism, he managed to struggle through the hardships to become highly decorated and respected. Before his days at the department, he traveled around the U.S. as a jazz musician, meeting and playing with an impressive list of jazz heroes.

Herman married his high school sweetheart, Marjie, 53 years ago. Together they raised their four children: Clolita, Marjorie, Herman III, and Montel. Herman is now enjoying his retirement and still resides in Baltimore, Maryland.

We hope you enjoyed
this Mountain Movers Press/Hay House book.
If you would like to receive additional information,
please contact:

c/o Hay House, Inc.
P.O. Box 5100
Carlsbad, CA 92018-5100

(760) 431-7695 or **(800) 654-5126**
(760) 431-6948 (fax) or **(800) 650-5115 (fax)**

Hay House Austrailia Pty Ltd
P.O. Box 515
Brighton-Le-Sands, NSW 2216
phone: 1800 023 516
e-mail: info@hayhouse.com.au

Please visit the Hay House Website at: **hayhouse.com**